D1196312

MEMOIRS OF CHAPLAIN LIFE

REV. WILLIAM CORBY, C.S.C., CHAPLAIN, 88TH NEW YORK VOLUN-
TEER INFANTRY, IN 1863. (UNIVERSITY OF NOTRE DAME ARCHIVES,
NOTRE DAME, INDIANA)

MEMOIRS OF CHAPLAIN LIFE

*Three Years with the Irish Brigade
in the Army of the Potomac*

by

WILLIAM CORBY, C.S.C.

Edited by

LAWRENCE FREDERICK KOHL

FORDHAM UNIVERSITY PRESS
New York
1992

Copyright © 1992 by FORDHAM UNIVERSITY PRESS
All rights reserved
LC 89–84565
ISBN 0–8232–1251–3
ISSN 1044–5315
Irish in the Civil War, No. 2

Library of Congress Cataloging-in-Publication Data

Corby, William, 1833–1897.
Memoirs of chaplain life : three years with the Irish Brigade in the
Army of the Potomac / by William Corby ; edited by Lawrence Frederick
Kohl.
    p. cm.—(Irish in the Civil War ; 2)
    ISBN 0-8232-1251-3
    1. Corby, William, 1833–1897. 2. United States. Army of the
Potomac. Irish Brigade. 3. United States—History—Civil War, 1861–
1865—Personal narratives. 4. Chaplains, Military—United States—
Biography. 5. United States—History—Civil War, 1861–1865—
Participation, Irish American. 6. Irish Americans—History—19th
century. I. Kohl, Lawrence Frederick. II. Title. III. Series.
E493.5.I683 1992
973.7′78′092—dc20   89-84565
                                                               CIP

Printed in the United States of America

CONTENTS

Illustrations following page xxv.

ACKNOWLEDGMENTS

Even on a small editorial project such as this, one can incur a great number of debts to those who have offered their assistance. For help with research on Corby's life and in obtaining illustrations for this volume I would like to thank Rev. James T. Connelly, C.S.C. and Brother Andrew Corsini, C.S.C. of the Province Archives Center, Priests of Holy Cross: Indiana Province, Notre Dame, Indiana; Pat Gillen of South Bend, Indiana; Albert Kuhn of Hanover, Pennsylvania; Charles Lamb and Peter Lysy of the University of Notre Dame Archives, Notre Dame, Indiana; the Library of Congress, Washington, D.C.; A. Collin MacDonald of Leesburg, Virginia; the National Archives, Washington, D.C.; Robert H. Prosperi of Gettysburg National Military Park, Gettysburg, Pennsylvania; Robert Smoger of the Snite Museum of Art, University of Notre Dame, Notre Dame, Indiana; and Steven Wright of the Civil War Library and Museum, Philadelphia, Pennsylvania. I would also like to thank Johanna Shields of the University of Alabama–Huntsville and my colleague in Tuscaloosa, Rich Megraw, for some excellent criticism of earlier drafts of my introduction. Finally, I must gratefully acknowledge the financial assistance for this project provided by the National Endowment for the Humanities and the Research Grants Committee of the University of Alabama.

Introduction

LAWRENCE FREDERICK KOHL

IN THE SUMMER of 1863 the Irish Brigade was no longer the impressive force it had once been. Nearly two years of war had worn its thousands down to a small band of seasoned veterans. Because of their fighting reputation they had always been where the action was hottest: at Fair Oaks, Gaines Mill, and Savage Station on the Peninsula; in the Bloody Lane at Antietam; before the Stone Wall at Fredericksburg. Now, late in the afternoon of July 2nd, they were once again poised to launch themselves against the Confederates, this time in a wheatfield just south of the small crossroads town of Gettysburg, Pennsylvania. The men stood at order arms, nervously awaiting Colonel Patrick Kelly's order to advance.[1]

Suddenly, Father William Corby, their chaplain, turned to the colonel and asked for permission to address the men. Receiving it, he hurriedly reached into his pocket and pulled out a purple stole which he placed around his neck. Then he climbed up on a large boulder so the troops might see him. As he gazed out over the dense columns his first concern was for the souls of these men, men who at that moment stood so close to eternity. There was no time for private confession, so he told the brigade that he would pronounce a general absolution of sins for those who were sincerely contrite and who would resolve to make a confession at their first opportunity. But as he reminded the soldiers of their duty to God, he did not forget their duty to country. He also reminded them of the noble cause for which they fought and declared that the Church would turn its back on those who deserted their flag.

[1]On the general history of the Irish Brigade, see David P. Conyngham, *The Irish Brigade and Its Campaigns* (New York: William McSorley, 1867).

Finally, he stretched his right hand into the air and began to recite the Latin words of the absolution.[2]

As he did so, every man in the brigade, Catholic and non-Catholic alike, fell to his knees. Though the battle raged around them—off to the left by Devil's Den and the Round Tops, over to the right in the Peach Orchard—for just a moment, on this part of the field time seemed to stand still. The entire Second Corps fell silent as they watched Father Corby pray over the kneeling regiments. Major General Hancock, mounted nearby with his staff officers, was clearly moved himself by the scene; he took off his hat and reverentially bowed his head. Then, just as suddenly as it had begun, this special moment was over. As they rose to their feet the penitants became soldiers once again, the columns were reformed, and the brigade began its advance into the wheatfield.[3]

There was nothing particularly unusual in Father Corby's concern for the men's souls as they went into battle, nor in their sincere response to his pronouncements. Yet the circumstances of the moment—the imminence of danger, the significance of the battle, the respectful reaction of the thousands who looked on—contrived to make it a celebrated event in Civil War history. Many who witnessed it would never forget it, and many who did not would nevertheless celebrate it for its symbolic depiction of the bond between Catholic faith and American patriotism at the nation's supreme moment of crisis. Over the years it would become the subject of poems, sculptures, and an impressive painting.[4]

In this celebration of the larger significance of the event, however, it is easy to overlook the man at the center of it. There

---

[2]St. Clair Mulholland, former colonel of the 116th Pennsylvania Volunteers, wrote the definitive account of Corby's absolution at Gettysburg. Often reprinted elsewhere, it appears in his *The Story of the 116th Regiment Pennsylvania Volunteers in the War of the Rebellion* (Philadelphia: F. McManus, Jr., 1903), pp. 407–8. For additional detail see notes on Paul Wood's painting of the scene in the Paul Wood Collection, University of Notre Dame Archives, South Bend, Indiana (hereafter UNDA). A fictionalized account of the event for children is Grace and Harold Johnson, *A Hand Raised at Gettysburg* (Milwaukee: Bruce Publishing, 1955).

[3]Mulholland, *Story of the 116th Pennsylvania*, pp. 407–8.

[4]For more on the artistic celebrations of the event see appendixes.

was a great deal more to William Corby than this absolution at Gettysburg. For three long years he ministered to the men of the Irish Brigade, enduring their hardships, sharing their dangers, and serving their spiritual needs. For a lifetime he served his religious community and the Roman Catholic Church as priest, professor, and university president. Corby's splendid moment on a boulder in Gettysburg's wheatfield was not distinctive, but representative, in a life of devotion to his faith and to the people he served.

EARLY LIFE

William Corby was born to Daniel and Elizabeth Corby on October 2, 1833 in Detroit, Michigan. His father had been born thirty-five years earlier in Kings County, Ireland and as a young man had emigrated to Canada. In 1824 he married Elizabeth Stapleton in Montreal. The Corbys arrived in Detroit in 1826 where, over the next forty years, Daniel became a prominent real estate dealer and one of the wealthiest landed proprietors in the county. During these years he was also a generous supporter of the Catholic Church and of charities, both in Ireland and in his adopted home. He was instrumental in the founding of many English-speaking parishes in early Detroit, and contributed liberally to aid the construction of numerous churches. The *Michigan Catholic* reported that "there was not a charitable work commenced in his lifetime that he did not aid generously and continuously." But he seldom took credit for his benefactions; most of them were made anonymously. Even his family was unaware of his annual contributions to aid the poor in his native parish in Ireland.[5]

Though little is known of William's boyhood in Detroit, he could not help but have been influenced by the example of his father's dedication to the Church and his generosity toward those in need. For many years, however, there was no evidence that this example was leading him toward a religious life; if anything, he seemed to be following in his father's footsteps in business. William was educated in the common schools until he

[5]*Michigan Catholic*, March 25, 1886.

was sixteen; then he went to work in his father's real estate firm. For four years he obtained valuable experience in the business world, but his father sensed that he was cut out for some higher calling. Learning that William aspired to go to college and study for the priesthood, Daniel Corby sent him and two younger brothers to the fledgling University of Notre Dame in South Bend, Indiana.[6] The school had been founded only ten years earlier by the Congregation of Holy Cross, a religious community first organized in Le Mans, France by a group of priests led by the Abbé Moreau. Dedicated primarily to bringing salvation to the outlying towns of the diocese of Le Mans, this small community soon threw its influence across the Atlantic when one of its members, Father Edward Sorin, was sent to the wilds of Indiana at the request of a local bishop. Arriving near South Bend, Indiana in 1843, Sorin immediately set to work to found what became the Unversity of Notre Dame.[7]

When William Corby arrived at the "university" in 1853, Notre Dame was still little more than a tiny French boarding school for boys of all ages. The primary school and prep school divisions were much larger than the college in the period before the Civil War, and the whole by 1860 comprised only 213 students and 13 priests. Discipline was paramount, as French boarding schools emphasized order, and backwoods parents used Notre Dame as a last resort in the education of rowdy sons. There was little money in such a frontier enterprise, so the struggling school was constantly in financial trouble. Early Notre Dame even conducted a brick-making business to make the little extra money that sometimes made "the difference between eating and not eating."[8]

Apparently Father Sorin took an immediate interest in the young Corby, who within a year of his arrival had decided on a religious life. Under Sorin's tutelage Corby advanced toward the priesthood, entering the novitiate in 1857 and taking his

[6]*Notre Dame Scholastic* 27 (December 2, 1893): 195.

[7]Arthur J. Hope, *Notre Dame: One Hundred Years* (Notre Dame: University Press, 1943), pp. 1–64.

[8]Ibid., pp. 65–68, 74–75, 137; Thomas J. O'Donnell, "Man and the Moment," *Notre Dame Alumnus* (June–July 1963): 6.

final vows three years later. Corby's attachment to Notre Dame would have a great impact on the institution over the years, but even as a young seminarian he helped the school to prosper. In 1855 he gave to Notre Dame a piece of land he owned in Detroit—evidently a gift from his father—which was later sold for six thousand dollars. By 1859 Sorin entrusted Corby with the duties of Prefect of Discipline, the person responsible for maintaining the regimented order that governed life in nineteenth-century Notre Dame. It was probably good background for Corby's later army experience. In addition, by 1861 Corby was also serving as director of the Manual Labor School and as pastor of what was to become St. Patrick's parish in the nearby city of South Bend, Indiana.

Corby's steady progress at Notre Dame was interrupted by the outbreak of the Civil War in the spring of that year. The war would pose difficult problems for the university and turn William Corby's life in a new direction.[9]

IRISH BRIGADE CHAPLAIN

The Roman Catholic Church took no official stand on the war. As persecuted outsiders in Protestant America, Catholics in both sections faced a troubling dilemma. Only a few years earlier they had been the victims of a powerful nativist movement suspicious that their foreign allegiances threatened the republic. For the Church to choose sides in 1861 would be to brand Catholics as traitors in either the Union or the Confederacy. Yet for individual Catholics to attempt to remain neutral would be to raise renewed questions about their loyalty among the staunch supporters of either section.[10]

Father Sorin attempted to have it both ways. His sympathies

[9]*Notre Dame Scholastic* 36 (October 18, 1902): 108; *South-Bend Daily Tribune,* December 29, 1897: "Father Corby at Gettysburg," (Philadelphia: McManus, no date), annotated pamphlet in William Corby Collection (hereafter Corby Collection), UNDA; Hope, *Notre Dame,* p. 109–10, 126–27.

[10]Chester Forrester Dunham, *The Attitude of the Northern Clergy Toward the South, 1860–1865* (Toledo, Ohio: Gray, 1942), pp. 14–18; Ray Allen Billington, *The Protestant Crusade, 1800–1860: A Study of the Origins of American Nativism* (New York: Macmillan, 1938).

lay with the Union, but he wanted to keep Notre Dame from being torn apart by divided allegiances. During the war he sent seven C.S.C. priests to serve as chaplains in Union regiments and more than eighty Sisters of the Holy Cross to nurse the sick and wounded in Union hospitals. Notre Dame students were allowed to leave to take up arms if they wished, but the educational life of the school was to remain above the fray. Both faculty and students were prohibited from discussions favoring one side or the other and disputes that turned violent were rigorously punished. It was a testimony to Sorin's success in maintaining neutrality on campus that during the war many southerners continued to attend Notre Dame alongside those with northern sympathies, including the children of William Tecumseh Sherman.[11]

William Corby was not among the first Notre Dame priests to enter the army in the initial stages of the war. It was not until the fall of 1861 that Corby headed east at the request of Father James Dillon, another C.S.C. priest who had preceded him to the front. Dillon, under Father Sorin's orders, had been sent to Washington that summer to minister to the needs of Catholics in the rapidly expanding Union army. There he had taken up his duties as chaplain of the 63rd New York Volunteer Infantry, one of the three original regiments of Thomas Francis Meagher's famed Irish Brigade. Made up almost exclusively of Irish Catholic soldiers, this unit of nearly three thousand men was too much for Dillon to handle alone, so he asked Father Sorin if he could spare Corby to assist him. Before the end of 1861 Corby had received an appointment as chaplain of the 88th New York Volunteer Infantry in the Irish Brigade and had joined his regiment in camp just outside Alexandria, Virginia.[12]

Civil War chaplains faced a difficult task. The first problem facing the new appointee was to determine what he was expected to do. When Congress created the position of chaplain it never spelled out its duties, nor did it grant chaplains any authority within the command structure. Though they were

[11]Hope, *Notre Dame*, pp. 117–23, 135.
[12]Ibid., p. 125, 127; James Dillon to Provincial Chapter of the Province of Notre Dame, Indiana, August 29, 1862, C.S.C. Priests Miscellaneous Papers, UNDA.

eventually granted the pay and allowances of captains of cavalry, chaplains at first held no rank at all. When, in 1864, Congress finally declared that they held the rank of captain, it specifically noted that it was a rank "without command."[13]

The chaplain's duties had to be worked out on an individual basis, with his authority derived almost completely from whatever respect his actions earned from the men he served. Such respect was not easily achieved. Officers and men often had scant regard for their chaplains and little sense that they were performing valuable services. The chaplain was typically considered a useless "fifth wheel" in a regiment, and soldiers' comments on chaplains were far more often derogatory than favorable. Relatively few chaplains played important and honored roles in their regiments. William Corby, however, was certainly one of these rare men.[14]

For nearly three years Father Corby ministered to the needs of Catholic soldiers within the Army of the Potomac. Though officially chaplain of the 88th New York, his influence spread far beyond his regiment. Many units spent much of the war without a chaplain of their own, since disease and hardship often wore down the fragile health of the men who had been assigned to them, especially those who were advanced in age. Despite the fact that all five of the regiments of the Irish Brigade enjoyed the services of a chaplain at some time during the war, the brigade rarely had more than two actually present for duty. For one period in 1863, Father Corby was not only the lone Catholic priest in the brigade, he was the only priest officially serving any regiment in the entire Army of the Potomac. The camp of the Irish Brigade thus became the spiritual center of Catholicism in the army and Father Corby its most important figure.[15]

Corby's spiritual duties are well described in his memoirs.

[13]Rollin W. Quimby, "The Chaplain's Predicament," *Civil War History* 8 (September 1962): 26–27.

[14]Ibid., pp. 25–37; Bell Irvin Wiley, " 'Holy Joes' of the Sixties: A Study of Civil War Chaplains," *Huntington Library Quarterly* 16 (May 1953): 287–304; David B. Sabine, "The Fifth Wheel: The Troubled Origins of the Chaplaincy," *Civil War Times Illustrated* 19 (May 1980): 14–23.

[15]*Memoirs of Chaplain Life*, pp. 21, 30, 314.

Daily masses, when possible, started the day for many Catholic soldiers. Grand "military masses" were sometimes celebrated to mark special occasions. Hearing confessions and doing spiritual counseling occupied much of Father Corby's time, with soldiers seeking him out from distant parts of the army. Corby was also summoned to help prepare the souls of condemned Catholic soldiers before execution. Such occasions, which seem to have had a deep impact on all Civil War soldiers, were particularly moving to Corby. The memoirs are sprinkled with them, not just because they provide Corby with the opportunity to make his narrative spiritually instructive, but because even decades later they remained among the most indelible memories he carried from the war.

Chaplains, like officers, won the common soldiers' respect with their bravery under fire. In the male preserve of a wartime army, courage is the currency with which men's hearts are purchased. Father Corby's willingness to share the hardships of the men with a light-hearted attitude and his calm heroism in bringing spiritual and physical comfort to men in the thick of the fighting won him the esteem and the friendship of the men he served. Frequently under fire, Corby moved among casualties on the field, giving assistance to the wounded and absolution to the dying. For days after the battles he inhabited the field hospitals to bring comfort to men in pain.

Corby was also an important link between the soldiers and their families back home. He wrote letters for some, answered anxious inquiries from home about others, and served as a conduit for sending money and other valuables from the army to the home front. When Colonel Richard Byrnes of the 28th Massachusetts had a premonition of his impending death, he entrusted Corby with a last letter to his wife and children, and the responsibility of seeing to it that his horse was returned to its proper owner.[16]

It was readily apparent that Corby's personality and character were peculiarly suited to the requirements of a Civil War chaplaincy. James Dillon, who observed first-hand the soldiers' reaction to him, reported that his "gentle and quiet manners

[16]*Memoirs of Chaplain Life*, pp. 237–39.

immediately made him a general favorite." Always a simple, unassuming man, he was devoted to the physical and spiritual well-being of the men he served. Throughout his life, those who knew him best praised his common sense, his humility, his genial good humor, and his kind-hearted concern for others.[17]
For nearly three years the men of the Irish Brigade enjoyed his services. With only a few brief absences for illness, he accompanied them through all their major campaigns, from the Peninsula to the Siege of Petersburg. Finally, in September of 1864, Father Sorin called him home. Urgent business required the presence of all the C.S.C. priests, so Corby resigned his commission and made his way back to Indiana. Yet he could not stay away. In the closing days of the war, with his business at Notre Dame completed, he returned to Virginia to visit one last time with the remnants of the Irish Brigade still in the trenches ringing Petersburg.[18]

BACK TO NOTRE DAME

After the war, William Corby once again turned his attention to the University of Notre Dame. Father Sorin, whose energies were increasingly devoted to higher levels of religious administration, began to turn the reins of the University over to younger men. Rev. Patrick Dillon, brother of Corby's fellow Irish Brigade chaplain, was installed in the presidency in 1865. Almost immediately upon his return from the army, Corby was made vice president of the university. He did not long remain in the second position, however. Father Dillon's untimely death the next year resulted in Corby's election as Notre Dame's third president.[19]
Corby's first term as university president was not distin-

[17]James Dillon to Provincial Chapter of the Province of Notre Dame, Indiana, August 29, 1862, C.S.C. Priests Miscellaneous Papers, UNDA. On the estimates of Corby's character see the many entries in the "Corby Memorial Number" of the *Notre Dame Scholastic* 31 (January 15, 1898): 245–76.
[18]Photocopy of William Corby, Compiled Service Record; Edward Sorin to Corby, September 9, 1864, Corby Collection, UNDA; pp. 269–71.
[19]Hope, *Notre Dame*, pp. 138; *South-Bend Daily Tribune*, December 29, 1897.

guished by any great departures from Father Sorin's early guidance. It hardly could have been, since, although Corby ran the university, Sorin remained his ecclesiastical superior, and, although he was frequently compelled by his position to travel widely, Sorin kept his home base at Notre Dame. The most notable achievements of Corby's administration were the creation of the law school and the founding of the *Notre Dame Scholastic*, a magazine devoted to chronicling events at the school.[20]

In 1872 a new president was named and Corby was sent to Sacred Heart College in Watertown, Wisconsin to help establish the struggling new school. For the next five years he served as its president and as pastor of St. Bernard's parish in Watertown. No doubt the business training he received from his father proved valuable in his new position. By the time he returned to Notre Dame in 1877, his administrative abilities had put Sacred Heart on a sound financial footing and the college was flourishing.[21]

In that year Father Corby was recalled from Wisconsin to serve a second term as the head of the university. There was some irony in Corby's appointment, in that his predecessor was ousted for being too "Irish" for Father Sorin's taste. Though many of the students at Notre Dame in its early years were Irish, its founders were French Catholics who were not always sympathetic to Irish causes and customs. Father Colovin, who preceded Corby, ran afoul of Father Sorin's sense of decorum and his ethnic prejudices when he allowed boisterous celebrations of St. Patrick's day to distract the students from their labors. Shortly, Father Colovin was shipped off to Watertown to take Corby's place at the head of Sacred Heart College, while Corby once again assumed the presidency of Notre Dame.[22]

It may seem odd that Father Corby, chaplain of the Irish Brigade, should have seemed "safer" than his predecessor on

[20]The law school was a modest venture in its early years. In the entire decade of the 1870s it turned out only 21 graduates. Hope, *Notre Dame*, pp. 150–51; The *Notre Dame Scholastic* was called *The Scholastic Year* when it was founded in 1867. Ibid., p. 144.

[21]*South-Bend Daily Tribune*, December 29, 1897.

[22]Hope, *Notre Dame*, pp. 177–79.

the Irish issue to Father Sorin, but two factors made him so. First, Corby was always too close to Notre Dame's founder to incite his displeasure. When Corby had first come to South Bend as a young man, Father Sorin had become his mentor, guiding him to a religious life and installing him in his first positions of trust. Corby had become very nearly his "adopted son." Out of gratitude as well as respect, Corby lived most of his life in the shadow of Sorin's influence. Second, Corby was always more Catholic than he was Irish. Though his popular historical image will always be primarily attached to the Irish Brigade, his first allegiance was to his Church. He had much sympathy and understanding for the Irish soldiers and the Irish students he served, of course, but his own Irish identity was never paramount. His father might have been Irish-born, but neither he nor his mother were. Moreover, his early experience in Detroit as well as his formative years at Notre Dame were shaped by French, not Irish, Catholic influences. Indeed, when many years after the war one of the old veterans of the Irish Brigade learned that Corby had an Irish father, he expressed great surprise. In a letter to Corby he explained that he had always thought Corby was "of pure American parentage."[23]

The choice of Corby as president at this juncture, however ironic, was also propitious for Notre Dame. On April 23, 1879 a terrible fire almost completely destroyed the college. Without Corby at the helm, the institution might have gone out of existence. Almost immediately, he organized a rebuilding effort, pledging that Notre Dame would reopen in the fall. His success in this endeavor won him the title of "Second Founder of Notre Dame." With the University rebuilt and enrollment increasing, Corby turned over the reins to a new president and returned to St. Bernard's parish in Watertown. He left St. Bernard's for good in 1886 when he was elected Provincial General of the Congregation of Holy Cross for the entire United States. As such, he had responsibility for hundreds of

---

[23]*Notre Dame Scholastic* 36 (October 18, 1902): 108; Garrett Roach to Corby, undated letter, Papers of William Corby, Province Archives Center, Priests of Holy Cross: Indiana Province, Notre Dame, Indiana (hereafter Corby Papers, PAC).

C.S.C. priests, brothers, novices, and postulants. Though his headquarters remained at Notre Dame, he was required by the regulations of the order to visit all C.S.C. establishments at least once a year. He thus had occasion to travel widely throughout the United States and Canada.[24]

THE WAR REMEMBERED

A new era in William Corby's life began in 1888, the year when he received a letter inviting him to join other Irish Brigade veterans in a reunion celebrating the twenty-fifth anniversary of the Battle of Gettysburg. The chance to revisit the scene of this battle and see again the men he had served in the war drew Corby, as it did more than fifty thousand other veterans, to southern Pennsylvania that summer. The event had a powerful impact on Corby. He saved the letter of invitation and the program of the festivities to the end of his life. More important, from that day forward, Corby never lost contact with his former Irish Brigade comrades. Though his religious responsibilities continued to expand—he would eventually become Assistant General for the Congregation of Holy Cross throughout the world—many of his activities in his last years would revolve around his war-time experience.[25]

The veterans who tearfully embraced their old chaplain at the Gettysburg reunion were reminded of just how important he had been to them. At a meeting of the brigade's veteran association they endorsed enthusiastically ("with a whoop") a campaign to obtain a Congressional Medal of Honor for Father Corby. This fight was led by Brevet Brigadier General St. Clair Mulholland of the 116th Pennsylvania and Major W. L. D. O'Grady of Corby's old regiment. In his official deposition to the War Department, Mulholland declared that Corby was known as a "Fighting Chap-

[24]Hope, *Notre Dame*, pp. 183–91; *Notre Dame Scholastic* 36 (October 18, 1902): 108; *The Class Day Book of '80* (Notre Dame: University of Notre Dame Press, 1880), p. 17; annotated pamphlet, "Father Corby at Gettysburg," Corby Collection, UNDA; *Notre Dame Scholastic* 27 (December 2, 1893): 196.

[25]W. L. D. O'Grady to Corby, May 24, 1888, Corby Papers, PAC; *Notre Dame Scholastic* 21 (June 30, 1888): 669; pp. 187–200; "Father Corby at Gettysburg," Corby Collection, UNDA.

lain," who always accompanied his men under fire to do his duty. "No spot was too dangerous or too much exposed to the fire of the enemy" for him to abandon them. Despite Corby's constant valor during the war, Mulholland asked that the medal be awarded specifically for his "very gallant and most remarkable act in preaching a most patriotic sermon and administering the religious rite of General Absolution on the battlefield at Gettysburg." Major O'Grady called Corby "a man whose courage was not surpassed by the bravest soldier of our armies, whose unflinching devotion on the march, in camp and under fire, made him eminent, whose magnificent conduct at Gettysburg has become historical, one of the most picturesque and beautiful incidents of that great drama."[26]

The effort came to naught. Despite the persistance of Mulholland, O'Grady, and others, the request for the medal was not granted. It was a great disappointment for Corby, as he was very anxious to obtain the honor. At first glance, his desire for such recognition seems out of character. Father Corby was a humble man who had spent his life serving others and asking little for himself. It is clear, however, that his pursuit of the Congressional Medal of Honor, like all of his efforts to draw attention to his wartime services in the last years of his life, was primarily motivated by a desire to remind Americans of the patriotic service that thousands of Catholics had rendered in the late war.[27]

The most significant of these efforts was the writing of his *Memoirs of Chaplain Life*. The first edition of the work was published in 1893 by the "Scholastic Press" on Notre Dame's campus. The following year Corby obtained bids from other commercial printing establishments to produce one thousand additional copies from the plates created by the Scholastic Press. The business went to the Chicago firm of La Monte, O'Donnell & Co. There was some talk of possible changes in this edition (including the addition of a photograph of Corby himself—a conspicuous omission

[26]James Quinlan to Corby, September 4, 1893, Corby Papers, PAC; William Corby, Medal of Honor File, National Archives, Washington, D.C.
[27]War Department to St. Clair Mulholland, August 12, 1893; St. Clair Mulholland to Corby, August 20, 1893, Corby Papers, PAC; *Notre Dame Scholastic* 44 (June 3, 1911): 546.

in the first printing), but no changes were made, perhaps due to the additional costs that they might have involved.[28]

Since Corby had no extensive diary or letter collection on which to base his reminiscences, he worked almost entirely from memory. In order to gain some control over chronology and the larger pattern of events which surrounded his personal experience, he relied on a few basic works, such as D. P. Conyngham's *Irish Brigade* and James Moore's *Complete History of the Rebellion*. He also decided to include several short pieces written by others that described the labors of some of his fellow Catholic chaplains. Finally, he asked his old friend, St. Clair Mulholland, to contribute a short sketch of the history of the Irish Brigade. The heart of Corby's book, however, is a record of wartime events, both minute and momentous, that became so indelibly etched in his mind that they could be readily recalled after the passage of twenty-five years.[29]

The Irish Brigade fought valiantly in some of the most celebrated battles of the Civil War, but Corby's *Memoirs of Chaplain Life* is not primarily an account of battles and skirmishes. Nor is it merely a religious tract. It is a very human account of life in a Civil War army. Though Corby certainly saw the war through the eyes of a chaplain and wrote his memoirs explicitly "to show the religious feature that existed in the army," few aspects of the soldier's life, tragic or comic, escaped his notice. His work is filled with vivid pictures of heat and dust, rain and mud, vermin and disease—all banes of the soldier's existence. In it also are to be found gruesome descriptions of terrible wounds, of the horrors of the hospitals, and of reckless ambulances, in their desperate rush, running over men still prostrate on the field.

Humor and hope provide some leavening for these fearful scenes. Few have written with more good cheer about the problems of wood ticks, saddle soreness, or petty theft in the army. And

[28]L. W. Reilly to Corby, June 6, 1894; July 30, 1894, Corby Papers, PAC. Inexplicably this 1894 edition carries an 1893 publication date.
[29]On Corby's working from memory, see *Memoirs*, p. 311 and footnote 31 below. For Conyngham citation see note 1 above. James Moore, *Complete History of the Great Rebellion; or The Civil War in the United States, 1861–1865* (New York: Hurst, 1886). The M. F. M. mentioned in the Preface was Mary Frances Murphy, who probably provided some research or secretarial aid to Corby in the writing of the memoirs. See Mary Frances Murphy to Corby, June 4, 1893, Corby Papers, PAC.

Corby describes the boisterous fun of the St. Patrick's Day celebrations in the Irish Brigade. Most important to Father Corby, however, was his ministering to the bodies and the souls of men who lived with constant hardship, and who frequently faced the prospect of their own deaths with an immediacy seldom experienced by those in civilian life. In his graphic but unpretentious way, Corby narrates not only his own story, but also the stories of several fellow chaplains who served with other Catholic regiments in the Union army. The memoirs reveal the important role these chaplains played in the war, and they document the way in which, to quote Father Corby, "in the presence of death, religion gives hope and strength." Corby's own faith emanates from his pages and makes more bearable some of the tragic events—such as his attempt to console a young soldier about to be executed for desertion—that his narrative describes.

The memoirs were generally well received in Catholic circles. *Ave Maria* declared that "many chapters of the work could hardly be excelled in variety and readableness." The *Catholic Citizen* called it "timely" and professed its belief that "every lover of liberty and religion should read it." "The interest remains unabated from the first page to the last," asserted the *Catholic Columbian*. Though many were too poor in 1893 to purchase it at its $1.50 retail price, Irish Brigade veterans were just as enthusiastic. Colonel James Quinlan of the 88th New York read it "with fascinating interest" and told Corby that "while it is an absolutely true record, it is so easy in your simple style that it reads like a charming story." Major O'Grady called it a "valuable contribution to history—more valuable as being from a standpoint entirely different from any hitherto occupied by any writer."[30]

For the next several years Father Corby's mail was filled with letters from old soldiers thanking him for helping them to relive the stirring days of their youth. Some wrote to praise the memoirs, "so different from the everyday war literature, blood and thunder." Others wanted to let Corby know how fondly he was remembered by the men of the brigade. James Brady, former adjutant of

---

[30]*Ave Maria* 36 (June 3, 1893): 607–8; publication notice with testimonials on "*Memoirs of Chaplain Life* by Very Rev. W. Corby, C.S.C." in Corby Collection, UNDA; *Notre Dame Scholastic* 26 (June 24, 1893): 661.

the 63rd New York, confided that he often "heard so many of 'our boys' speak of you with tears in their eyes." Another brigade veteran expressed gratitude for Corby's making him a hero in the eyes of his son by including in the memoirs a daring incident that involved him. Many Catholics, whether veterans or not, wrote to praise the book's influence in combatting anti-Catholic prejudice. "It stands out," said one of Corby's correspondents, "a living refutation to the base calumnies of ranting, roaring, noisy, blatherskites, who keep crying 'the country will be crippled by Catholics.' "[31]

The response to the memoirs must have been gratifying to Father Corby. It clearly revealed to him how useful his wartime experiences could be in encouraging patriotic pride in American Catholics and in defending them against their detractors. During the 1890s Corby missed few chances to exploit for religious purposes the opportunities presented to him by his generation's romantic celebrations of their Civil War past. He was appointed chaplain of the Irish Brigade Association and joined the Second Corps Veterans' Association. He obtained a medal presented to all Gettysburg survivors by the state of New York. In 1896 he readily accepted an invitation to join the Military Order of the Loyal Legion of the United States, a prominent veterans' organization for Union officers. Later he founded at Notre Dame a new post, made up entirely of Catholic priests and brothers, of the Grand Army of the Republic (G.A.R.), the largest veterans' organization in the country. He also began to acquire Irish Brigade artifacts, including one of the 63rd New York's green battle flags, for display at Notre Dame. In November of 1897 he began to make plans to dedicate a portion of the university museum to the history of his old unit.[32]

---

[31]John Finn to Corby, March 6, 1896; James D. Brady to Corby, January 16, 1896; Charles Grainger to Corby, February 17, 1895; P. J. Boland to Corby, June 26, 1893, Corby Papers, PAC. The verification many of the letters give of the incidents Corby describes in the memoirs suggests that his memory of these distant events was fairly accurate.

[32]Charles Grainger to Corby, January 9, 1895; John Finn to Corby, February 14, 1896; State of New York to Corby, October 9, 1893; Corby Papers, PAC; *Notre Dame Scholastic* 27 (October 14, 1893): 93; 29 (May 23, 1896): 546; J. D. Hamilton to Corby, January 1, 1894; William A. Olmstead to Corby, November 21, 1894, Corby Papers, PAC; *Notre Dame Scholastic* 31 (October 9,

Unfortunately, William Corby did not live to see this project completed. The next month, after returning from a business trip to Cincinnati and Chicago, he fell ill with a cold. It quickly developed into pneumonia and, only a few days later, on December 28, 1897, he died. The holiday cheer at Notre Dame suddenly turned to gloom and the hushed tones of mourning fell over the campus. As telegrams of condolence poured in from all over Europe and North America, the body lay in state, illuminated feebly by candles, in the University parlor. The roads and trains brought in mourners from the surrounding area.[33]

At ten o'clock in the morning on the last day of the year, the hearse drew up to carry the body to its last resting place in the community cemetery on the shores of St. Mary's Lake. Long and impressive ceremonies in the Church of the Sacred Heart celebrated the life of a man who had done so much for his university and his religious community. But in one important and fitting departure from custom, the casket was not borne to the grave by Holy Cross priests. Aging Civil War veterans from a local G.A.R. post were employed for this task. The coffin, wrapped in the flag of Corby's old regiment, was lowered into the grave as a heavy snow fell. Volleys of rifle fire split the cold December air. Then the last call of the bugle was sounded for this Irish Brigade chaplain, who was, like so many of the soldiers he had served in his youth,

> Answering to the call of roll on high,
> Dropping from the ranks as they make reply
> Filling up the army of the by and by.[34]

1897): 80–85; W. L. D. O'Grady to St. Clair Mulholland, December 2, 1892; W. L. D. O'Grady to Corby, December 2, 1892, James D. Brady to Corby, February 1, 1896; St. Clair Mulholland to Corby, November 11, 1897, Corby Papers, PAC.

[33]*South-Bend Daily Tribune*, December 29, 1897.

[34]*Notre Dame Scholastic* 31 (January 15, 1898): 264–68. The last lines are from a song sung over Corby's grave by the G.A.R. veterans who took part in the ceremonies.

SKETCH OF WILLIAM CORBY BY PAUL WOOD, IN PREPARATION FOR
HIS PAINTING *ABSOLUTON UNDER FIRE.* (UNDA)

STATUE OF FATHER CORBY ON THE BATTLEFIELD AT GETTYSBURG.
(COURTESY ALBERT KUHN, HANOVER, PA.)

STATUE OF FATHER CORBY ON THE CAMPUS OF THE UNIVERSITY OF
NOTRE DAME, INDIANA. (UNDA)

MUSTER-IN ROLL of *William Corby* in the *85th* Regiment, (_____ Brigade,) of *New York State* Volunteers,

commanded by Colonel *Patrick Kelly* called into the service of the United States, by _____ from the

the *Fifteenth* day of *December* 1861, (*date of this muster*,) for the term of _____ unless sooner discharged.

| Number of each grade | NAMES PRESENT AND ABSENT. (Persons in alphabetical order.) | RANK | AGE | JOINED FOR DUTY AND ENROLLED | | | TRAVELLING | | VALUATION IN DOLLARS OF— | | REMARKS |
| | | | | When. | Where. | By whom enrolled | Period | To place of muster or rendezvous. | Horses, Pixtols, &c. | Horses, Pixtols, &c. | |

Notes: 1. Every man whose name is on this roll must be accounted for on the last muster roll. 2. The discharge of men by enlistment, and the undumeral swapping or loaning of horses *after muster are private, are always furloah.*

William Corby — *Chaplain 30 Dec. 1861 New York Gen 12 of Sept 1890* — *Where to date June 15th '61. Is authority from the War Department.*

I CERTIFY, ON HONOR, That this Muster Roll exhibits the true state of _____ for the period herein _____ mentioned; that each man answers to his own proper name in person; and that the enrollment, according to our honest, imperial judgment.

We CERTIFY, ON OATH, That the figures opposite the names on this Roll, for valuation of horses and horse equipments, represent and show the true cash value of the horses and equipments of the men, respectively, at the place of enrollment, according to our honest, imperial judgment.

Appraisers.

Sworn to and subscribed before

Date: _____

Station: _____

_____ Mustering Officer.

I CERTIFY, ON HONOR, That I have carefully examined *the Officer* whose name is borne on this Roll, _____ and have accepted *&c.* into the service of the United States for the term of *three* *from* this *Fifteenth* day of *December* 1861. *Was only once discharged*

Wm Robert F Smith
Asst Comy Muster Div 5th Corps
Mustering Officer.

Date: *October 26 1863*

Station: *Falling Run Va.*

DIRECTIONS TO MUSTERING OFFICER.

The Mustering Officer will see that four copies of this Roll are made, three of which he will retain; the fourth will be mustered by the Company Commander, or in case of Field and Staff and officers and men registered into service separately on its rolls, by the Senior Officer. He commanded, or the Persons standing first on the list if private or mustered in, is to be handed by him to the person whose muster them to him at his own expense, that the new Muster Rolls may be property made out. The Mustering Officer will dispose of the three copies of this form retained by him as follows: He will send one to the Paymaster General of the Army, one to the Adjutant General of the Army, and one to the Permanent General of the Army, to which the troops belong.

(A. G. O. No. 21—First.)

WILLIAM CORBY'S MUSTER-IN ROLL, SIGNED OCTOBER 26, 1863, BACK-DATED TO ORIGINAL MUSTER OF DECEMBER 15, 1861. (UNDA)

The People of the State of New-York

y the grace of God ——— Free and Independent.

To ——— *William Corby* ——— **Greeting:**

We, reposing especial trust and confidence, as well in your patriotism, conduct and loyalty, as in your integrity and readiness to do us good and faithful service, have, by virtue of the power and authority vested in the Governor of our said State by the laws of the United States, and of the State of New York, appointed and constituted, and by these presents do appoint and constitute you, the said *William Corby*

a Chaplain in the Eighty-Eighth Regiment of Infantry

NEW YORK STATE VOLUNTEERS;

raised under the authority of the President and Congress of the United States of America, "to aid in enforcing the laws and protecting public property," with rank from *December 1 1861*. You are, therefore, to observe and follow such orders and directions as you shall from time to time receive from the President of the United States, the Governor of the State of New York, or any other your Superior Officer, according to the Rules and Discipline of War, and hold the said Office in the manner specified in and by the Laws of the United States, in pursuance of the trust reposed in you, and for so doing this shall be your **COMMISSION.**

In Testimony Whereof, I have caused our seal for Military Commissions to be hereunto affixed. Witness *Horatio Seymour* Governor of our said State, Commander-in-Chief of the Military and Naval Forces of the same, at our City of Albany, the *Fourteenth* day of *September* one thousand eight hundred and sixty-*Two*

(Signed) *John T. Sprague*
Adjutant-General

(Signed) *Horatio Seymour*

L.S.

A COPY OF WILLIAM CORBY'S COMMISSION AS CHAPLAIN OF THE 88TH NEW YORK VOLUNTEER INFANTRY. ORIGINAL DATED SEPTEMBER 14, 1862; COPY DATED JANUARY 20, 1897. (PROVINCE ARCHIVES CENTER, PRIESTS OF HOLY CROSS: INDIANA PROVINCE, NOTRE DAME, INDIANA)

LETTER FROM COL. RICHARD BYRNES TO HIS WIFE, ELLEN, DATED MAY 17, 1864, ENTRUSTED TO FATHER CORBY. SEE P. 238. (PROVINCE ARCHIVES CENTER, PRIESTS OF HOLY CROSS: INDIANA PROVINCE)

WILLIAM CORBY'S LETTER OF RESIGNATION FROM THE ARMY, DATED
SEPTEMBER 20, 1864. (UNDA)

WILLIAM CORBY'S HONORABLE DISCHARGE FROM THE ARMY, DATED SEPTEMBER 27, 1864. (UNDA)

PASSES THROUGH THE LINES ISSUED TO FATHER CORBY IN 1865. SEE
P. 270. (PROVINCE ARCHIVES CENTER, PRIESTS OF HOLY CROSS: INDI-
ANA PROVINCE)

ORDER OF

Memorial Ceremonies

AT

GETTYSBURG, JULY 2d, 1888,

ON THE

UNVEILING OF A MONUMENT

—☙‖ **TO THE MEMORY OF THE DEAD** ‖☙—

OF THE

Three New York Regiments

(63d, 69th, and 88th)

OF THE

IRISH BRIGADE

Who Fell in the Three Great Battles of July 1st,
2d, and 3d, 1863.

✣

"AS LONG AS VALOUR SHINETH
OR MERCY'S SOUL AT WAR REPINETH,
SO LONG SHALL ERIN'S PRIDE
TELL HOW THEY LIVED AND DIED."

COVER OF "ORDER OF MEMORIAL CEREMONIES," GETTYSBURG, PA.
JULY 2, 1888. SEE PP. 187–200. (PROVINCE ARCHIVES CENTER, PRIESTS
OF HOLY CROSS: INDIANA PROVINCE)

PROGRAMME

—OF—

MEMORIAL CEREMONIES, JULY 2d, 1888,

OF THE SURVIVORS

OF THE

IRISH BRIGADE,

In dedicating and presenting to the Gettysburg Battlefield
Association, on behalf of the State of New York,

A MONUMENT

To the Memory of the Members of New York Commands

of the Brigade who fought on many well-stricken fields

for the preservation of the Union, and in the

CAUSE OF UNIVERSAL LIBERTY.

COVER OF "PROGRAMME OF MEMORIAL CEREMONIES," GETTYSBURG,
PA. JULY 2, 1888. SEE PP. 187–200. (PROVINCE ARCHIVES CENTER,
PRIESTS OF HOLY CROSS: INDIANA PROVINCE)

In The Name of God. Amen I William Corby now residing at the University of Notre Dame in the County of St Joseph, State of Indiana a Son of Daniel Corby who resides in the county of Wayne township of Gross-Point state of Michigan, being of sound mind & memory and considering the uncertainty of this frail and transitory life do therefore make, ordain, publish and declare this to be my Last Will and Testament. That is to say: First after all my lawful debts (if I have any) are paid and discharged the residue of all the real or personal estate which may come into my possession as lawful heir or which may be bequeathed to me by friend I give bequeath and dispose of as follows— To the Congregation of Holy Cross and at the disposal of the provincial General of said Congregation — but if my relations should be in need some assistance should be given them —
This 9th day of Sept 1858 — William Corby

The within written instrument was subscribed by the said Wm Corby and acknowledged by him to each of us — and he at the same published & declared the said instrument to be his last will and testament

Patk Dillon
N Gorney
Thos Carroll

WILLIAM CORBY'S WILL, LEAVING HIS ESTATE TO THE CONGREGATION OF HOLY CROSS, DATED SEPTEMBER 9, 1858. (PROVINCE ARCHIEVES CENTER, PRIESTS OF HOLY CROSS: INDIANA PROVINCE)

MEMOIRS OF CHAPLAIN LIFE

VERY REVEREND EDWARD SORIN,
SUPERIOR-GENERAL OF THE CONGREGATION OF HOLY CROSS.

J. Card. Gibbons,

Filially and Respectfully Dedicated to

His Eminence,

James Cardinal Gibbons,

The Great Major-General of Christ's Army

in America.

PREFACE.

This little book embraces the experience of three years spent in active service during the great Civil War. The subject deserves an abler pen, more consideration and time than I can bestow upon it. I have written these pages in hours, and half-hours, snatched from my official duties, which frequently demanded my attention, and so engrossed my thoughts that it became difficult to bring them back to the work on hand.

The chief merit, if any, will be found in the subject itself. It will suggest more than is written. I have tried to give a realistic account of every-day life in the army, and have recorded, chronologically, incidents, exactly as they occurred under my notice. I have purposely avoided lengthy descriptions of battles, since these have been written over and over; in fact, every school-book is full of them. The movements of the army, however, are given, so that one who takes time to read the following pages will have a comprehensive idea of the various campaigns made by the great "Army of the Potomac," from the commencement, under McClellan, in 1861, up to the time of the surrender of Lee, under Grant, in 1865.

Besides a short sketch of Fathers Dillon, Ouellet, and Gillen, I give a valuable account, written by Father Egan, of his own experience and labors. Finally, an able article from the gifted pen of my friend and "companion in arms," Maj.-Gen. St.· Clair A. Mulholland, of Philadelphia, recounts the chivalry of the soldiers—and especially of the Irish soldiers—who won imperishable glory in the defense of right on innumerable battle-fields. No wonder the Irish soldier is so renowned, since he springs from a fearless race, whose valor has been tested in a war that was incessant for three hundred years, with the Danes and Normans, followed by contests, more or less fierce, for centuries, with England.

My object in presenting this book to the public has been to show the religious feature that existed in the army. In the presence of death, religion gives hope and strength. The Christian soldier realizes that his power comes from the "God of battles," not from man. Very valuable services have been rendered me in the preparation of this book by my esteemed friend, M. F. M. The retiring modesty of my friend will not allow me to say more.

THE COMTE DE PARIS.

I take great pleasure in giving first place in my memoirs to the following letter, which came to me through my esteemed friend, Maj.-Gen. St. Clair A. Mulholland, from Prince Philippe, Comte de Paris. This letter needs no comment. His Royal Highness speaks from personal observation.

Major General Mulholland

Stowe House,
Buckingham.

26. 6. 91

My dear general

I hear with pleasure that the Revd Father Corby, Catholic Chaplain in the Irish brigade of the Army of the Potomac during the Civil war, is writing his memoirs of chaplain life. This brings back to my memory the time I spent in that great war, I always remember with pleasure every incident of it. the. open air

Mass in the middle of the bivouac, the gallantry of the Irish soldiers on the field of battle, the devotion of the priests and the care they took of the sick and wounded I wish for the sake of the great catholic Community of the United States the best possible means to Father's Corby's book and I remain

yours truly

Philippo Comte de Bary

INTRODUCTION.

As with all old soldiers, it is an agreeable pastime for me to tell "War Stories," or incidents of the late war. Most persons, especially the young, listen with more than ordinary interest to such narratives coming from a veritable participant. I will try to give, in my own blunt way, for the benefit, and perhaps for the edification, of my readers, the reminiscences of three years spent, during the active campaigns of the late war, in the "Army of the Potomac," under McClellan, Burnside, Hooker, Meade, and Grant. I feel satisfied that there is no one who has tried to furnish such material for war history as I propose to relate. The subject is entirely new. Many of my companions, now dead, could have done much better in furnishing this information; and, had they lived, no doubt would have told very rich and interesting experiences during those years so full of thrilling events. Now, therefore, as God in His goodness has been pleased to spare my life amid the perils of the battle-field, the fevers of camp-life, the miasma of swamps, and, too, long after most of my companions, especially among the chaplains, have passed away to their reward, I will try to give my experience in as simple a form as possible.

The war, in 1861, particularly after the first "Bull Run," became the absorbing question throughout the nation. Young, active, patriotic, and even possessed (in my own conceit) of zeal for the salvation of those destined to fall in the pending stupendous contest between two powerful opposing armies, I volunteered my services as chaplain to an organization which was being formed in New York. This I did at the request of my superior, Very Rev. E. Sorin, now Superior-General. I resigned my professorial duties in the University of Notre Dame, Ind., and, taking up the lively sentiment expressed in an old song,

"I'll hang my harp on a willow tree,
I'll off to the wars again;
A peaceful home has no charm for me,
The battle-field no pain,"

away I went, took the train from Chicago on the Pittsburg & Fort Wayne Railway directly to Washington to meet the soldiers with whom I was to spend three years. It was much like getting married. We made the engagement "for better, for

worse; for richer, for poorer, till death do us part."
On my journey I thought over the problems of the
future — the chances of ever returning to my bright,
prosperous college home, of the dear ones I left
behind. Occasionally, my meditation was broken by
the beauty of the scenery which attracted my attention along the route.

I had never been East before, and I need not say
that, like "Our Country Cousin," I was not a little
surprised at the features of its landscapes. The
beautiful valleys, the lofty mountains, the ravines
dipping down to a frightful depth—the ravine below
me seeming as deep as the mountain was high above
me—the rugged old gray rocks standing out in huge
bulk, cutting their monster figures in bold relief
against the blue vaults of heaven, filled my mind with
sentiments of awe. The sun glittered on the mountain tops, which cast their long shadows over us, and,
as we passed rapidly along, we crossed rivers which
seemed to be rushing away from the bloody strife
ahead of us. In these waters the sunlight dances, so
to speak, with never-ceasing motion. I felt alone, as
space widened between me and home. I felt strange,
in new lands, among new people. Then, as the evening came on, and the sun gave place to the pale moon,
my meditation on the doubtful future came back to

me, and I mused on the life, as yet untried, amidst
soldiers and great armies. Finally, tired of what I
had seen, heard, and imagined, I tried to forget all
and rest. But soon appeared long lines of soldiers,
marching to the sound of drum and fife; officers (on
horseback) dashing at breakneck speed, their scab-
bards rattling at their sides, while the glistening
blades flourished in the air, beckoned their commands of "Forward!" Then came up the flying artillery, breaking through every obstacle; while, on the
flanks, the swift cavalry men, mounted on well-capar-
isoned horses, fresh for the wild sport, flew past the
infantry, to cover dangerous advances of the enemy
on either side. The words, "Forward!" "Double-
quick!" "Load!" "Prime!" "Aim!" "Fire!"
resounded in war-like tones, and the great battle-field
presented a scene panorama-like — muskets crashing,
cannons booming, shells bursting — then a sudden
loud, crashing sound, as if half the earth had
exploded! The train had stopped with a terribly
uncomfortable jerk. Just then I awoke. I arrived
in Washington, late in the night, in the fall of 1861.
I made inquiry for a Catholic church, and was
directed to old St. Peter's, on East Capitol Hill.
Here I found hospitality for the night. The good
old pastor, long since gone to heaven, seemed at first

very uneasy. He had never seen me before; but after a short time he was convinced that I was not a fraud. I had rather a grave, honest face that was in my favor, and which, in many close places, during the war and afterward, proved a satisfactory introduction. In a short time we were in full confidence, and he asked me about my trip, where I came from and where I was going. I answered him, as best I could, and told him I was chaplain of the Irish Brigade.

" Oh!" said he, " the brigade has just arrived from New York. I met a Rev. James Dillon this morning who also came to be a chaplain."

" Where is he now, may I ask? "

" He is stopping with Rev. Father Walter, pastor of St. Patrick's Church in this city."

Next morning I said Mass, took a slight breakfast, and hastened to St. Patrick's. Father Dillon had just gone to camp. However Father Walter was able to give me all the necessary information, and during the forenoon I met good old Father Paul Gillen, C. S. C., who drove me in his " Rockaway " across the " long bridge " that passes over the Potomac River to Alexandria, Va. A short distance out from the city, I found the Irish Brigade in camp. Now I shall tell about chaplain life, beginning with that of the Irish Brigade, which has no mean record for devotedness and bravery.

CONTENTS.

(14)

CHAPTER I.

THE brigade known as the " Irish Brigade," composed largely of recruits from New York City, under the command of Gen. Thomas Francis Meagher, had the greatest number of Catholic chaplains. This brigade had, of course, its history. When President Lincoln called for 75,000 volunteers, the call was responded to promptly. The general impression at the time was that the disturbance at the South would not last long, and the volunteers were enlisted for ninety days only. Under this call the Sixty-ninth New York Infantry, a militia regiment which so distinguished itself at the first battle of Bull Run, in July, 1861, offered its services, which were accepted, and the regiment, accompanied by Capt. (afterward Brig.-Gen.) T. F. Meagher and his Zouaves, all under the command of Col. Michael Corcoran, "went to the front." At this first Bull Run battle, the Sixty-ninth New York fought desperately; but the gallant Col. Corcoran was captured with several of his command, and was carried off to Richmond, where he was kept prisoner for thirteen months.

Rev. Thomas F. Mooney, of New York, went out as the chaplain of the Sixty-ninth, but was obliged, in a short time, to return home to attend to very important duties assigned him by his ordinary, Most Rev. Archbishop Hughes.* The soldiers, at the President's call, had enlisted for ninety days only; and before the memorable battle of the first Bull Run, which took place July 21, 1861, the term having expired in the case of several regiments, on the 20th, many militia regiments from Massachusetts, Connecticut, Pennsylvania, and one from New York, besides a battery, returned home. The Sixty-ninth agreed to continue. They did so, and "fought like Turks." After this battle was over, the Sixty-ninth was disbanded in New York, the time having expired sometime before. Here we start. We leave Col. Corcoran a prisoner in Richmond, and the old Sixty-ninth, with Meagher's Zouaves, mustered out of the service, with honor to both officers and men.

Thomas Francis Meagher, who distinguished himself at Bull Run, set about recruiting, not a single regiment, but a brigade. In a short time, with the help of other efficient persons, he organized three Irish regiments. The old Sixty-ninth re-enlisted, and was joined by the Eighty-eighth and Sixty-third New York regiments. Each of these enlisted for "three years, or during the war." To this brigade of three New York regiments were subsequently

---

* Rev. Bernard O'Riley, S. J., replaced Father Mooney for a few weeks, until the Bull Run battle terminated that campaign.

added the Twenty-eighth Massachusetts Infantry,
the Sixty-ninth* and One Hundred and Sixteenth
Pennsylvania Infantry, and Hogan's and McMahon's
batteries. The brigade in question was ever after
known as the Irish Brigade, and was commanded
by Gen. Thomas Francis Meagher. The six regiments composing this brigade had five Catholic
priests as chaplains. Rev. James Dillon, C. S. C.,
chaplain of the Sixty-third; Rev. Thomas Ouellet,
S. J., chaplain of the new Sixty-ninth, and the writer,
chaplain of the Eighty-eighth. Rev. Father McKee,
chaplain of the One Hundred and Sixteenth Pennsylvania, soon fell sick and resigned; he was replaced
by Rev. Father McCullum. The latter, unable to
endure the hardships of campaign life, also resigned,
leaving the brigade with three Catholic chaplains,
namely, Dillon, Ouellet, and Corby. Besides these,
there were other Catholic chaplains in the Army of
the Potomac. Paul E. Gillen, C. S. C.; Father
O'Hagan, S. J.; Father Martin, of Philadelphia;
Father C. L. Egan, O. P.; Father Thomas Scully,
of Massachusetts, and Rev. Doctor Kilroy. These I
mention with no regard to precedence, excepting as
they come to my mind. Most of those mentioned in
this last list remained only a short time in the army.
Some were taken sick, others were too old and could
not endure the fatigues and privations, others belonging to religious orders were called home for special

* The Sixty-ninth Pennsylvania was aft r a time assigned
to another brigade in the same corps.

duty. Of this number, however, Father Paul E. Gillen, C. S. C., was a veteran. Father Egan entered the service about the last of August, 1863, and remained to the very end of the war. Father Gillen started at the beginning and stayed until the end of the war. Other chaplains, known as "Post Chaplains," rendered valuable services in the hospitals, encouraging the sick and wounded, and administering the sacraments to the dying; but here I intend to speak principally of those connected with the Army of the Potomac, in the "field" and at the "front."

CHAPTER II.

TO make a starting point for the reader, we shall commence with the Irish Brigade located near Alexandria, Va., across the Potomac from Washington, in the fall of 1861. This brigade will form the most important center of our ecclesiastical labors during the war, in the Army of the Potomac, and of this narration. First, because, as I have said, it had the greatest number of priests, and second, because the Sixty-third, Sixty-ninth and Eighty-eighth New York regiments, forming the principal part of the brigade, were almost exclusively Catholic, both officers and privates. At no time during the war, from the organization of the brigade till after the "surrender of Lee," was it without a priest; and men from various sections of the army, during the active campaign, when they needed the services of a priest, directed their steps to the Irish Brigade, where they were sure to find one. To this brigade, as a rule, were the generals also referred, when a priest was needed to assist men sentenced to death by court-martial. The

(21)

brigade was quartered on elevated ground about two miles from Alexandria, where it remained from the early fall of 1861 until the spring of 1862. No fighting worthy of notice was done during the winter, but picket duty, drilling, police and other camp duties, kept the men busy.

Our camp was called Camp California, in honor of our Maj.-Gen. Sumner, who commanded the division, and who had recently been in command of regular troops in California. I am amused when I read the works of some historians, who, looking entirely on the bright side of the picture, try to impress their readers with the beauty of this camp, and who draw largely on their powers of imagination to give a poetic touch to the scene. No doubt, the scenery on the south side of the Potomac, where we were, is very picturesque, with its lofty hills, fertile valleys, and the majestic river flowing into the Chesapeake Bay. But let us look on the other side of this poetically described camp—when poetry is forgotten in the presence of stern reality. Everyone who campaigned in Virginia will agree with me in the statement that the Virginia mud, after winter rains, is the worst mud he ever encountered, except, perhaps, the "gumbo" of Dakota and parts of Texas. The soil is a reddish clay, and very porous. I have pushed down a pole, with my hands, nearly ten feet in Virginia soil, and have had my powerful horse bogged in an ordinary highland corn-field. (No wonder Burnside "stuck in the mud"!) Our camp was laid out in streets, and the army regulations, fully carried out, conduced to make the men as comfortable as possible; but these streets, rained on continually, worked up by the tramping of the horses and the heavy wheels of the loaded army wagons, were a sight! They resembled exactly, except as to color, the mud-pits where clay is mixed for the manufacture of brick. Then, too, the roads passing back to Alexandria from the camp, and toward Washington, and even in Washington, on all the unpaved streets (and there were few paved streets in Washington in those days), were in a most terrible condition. One day I saw an officer attempt to cross the street in front of my tent in Camp California. When he reached the center, his boots sank so deep in the tough clay that he was obliged to call a soldier to dig him out with a spade. Even then, as he attempted to pull out one leg the other would sink, and so on, till it became impossible for him to extricate himself except by pulling his feet out of his boots and escaping in his stocking feet.

Anyone who has spent considerable time in an active campaign knows how quickly trees, fences, and all adornments, disappear before an army enlisted for war. As Gen. Sherman is reported to have said to a female citizen who complained of the cruel injuries the soldiers were inflicting on her property: "Why, madam, war means cruelty!" so it is needless to say that Camp California and all the other camps soon presented anything but the appearance of Elysian Fields. The scene was one of dreary waste, tented with "houses of canvas," which was white when it left the factory, but smoke and Virginia mud had changed its color somewhat. This was nobody's fault; it was the fault of circumstances; it was the fault of war. Here Rev. James Dillon, C. S. C., Rev. Thos. Ouellet, S. J., and the writer, spent the winter of 1861-1862. We were prisoners in tents on the hill; for from these tents we could make no egress, except to plunge into the mud so deeply that it became a question of losing our boots. All the officers, chaplains included, wore boots with long legs, and it was only with great difficulty that they were made fit for use, after even a short tramp in Virginia mud. This reminds me of a boot-black, who was called upon to clean the boots of an officer entering Washington. He worked diligently for a long time, and finally called out to a companion in his profession:

"Jim!"

"What d'you want?" was the laconic reply.

"Lend me a spit! I've got an army contract!"

Our tents were as good as could be expected, and both officers and men were very kind to us; but imagine a man living in a tent all winter, with less accommodations than lumber-men find in the wilds of Minnesota! No beds except some army blankets placed on boards, conveniently arranged, and some of us enjoyed the luxury of a buffalo robe. In these tents we had small stoves; and our fuel was green pine, which, in many cases, furnished more smoke than heat; so that frequently we were obliged to open all the doors — that is, turn back a flap of the canvas at either end of the tent, and let the cold, damp wind of Virginia pass through and dispel the pungent vapor. However, all these discomforts were luxury in comparison with life during an active campaign. Wait until we go farther!

I shall make it a special point to write of every-day life, and the hardships and privations which necessarily attend such a life. Most authors, in writing of war, confine themselves to descriptions of battles, thereby gratifying the morbid taste of the masses who wish to read of carnage and strife; but there is more interest in the real every-day life of the soldier. From a candid account the reader will understand that a soldier suffers a thousand times more from every-day hardships in war than from the simple fact of entering a battle-field, where, for a few hours, he is in the midst of bloody strife, and, perhaps, at last receives a flesh wound — "good for ninety days" — or drops to speak no more. The mother, the sister, the loving ones at home, when retiring at night, or when enjoying a good warm dinner, sigh and ask:

"Where is Thomas, or James, or William, now? Have they any comforts? Is there anyone to care for them?"

Oh, you of a younger generation, think what it cost your forefathers to save our glorious inheritance of union and liberty! If you let it slip from your hands you will deserve to be branded as ungrateful cowards and undutiful sons. But, no! you will not fail to cherish the prize—it is too sacred a trust—too dearly purchased.

Horses, used for drawing provisions, fuel, and other necessaries, died in the camp during that winter, in great numbers, and had to be replaced entirely by mules, that could sleep in mud and live on chips!

CHAPTER III.

CHAPLAINS — THEIR WORK — CHARACTER OF THE SOLDIERS, AND ESPECIALLY OF GENERAL THOMAS FRANCIS MEAGHER.

FATHERS Dillon and Ouellet, being in New York when the brigade started for Camp California, Virginia, went on with it; but I, who enlisted and was "mustered in the service" at the same time with the above Fathers, could not, and did not, reach Camp California till sometime later. I was transacting business in the interest of Notre Dame in Illinois and Wisconsin when the news of my appointment by the Governor of New York reached me, and as soon as I could dispose of the business matter, I started directly for Washington, D. C., where I arrived, ready to "report for duty," in the fall of 1861. As mentioned above, Fathers Dillon, Ouellet, and Corby were in charge of three regiments, each forming, as it were, a congregation. During the winter we spent our time in much the same way as parish priests do, except in this—we had no old women to bother us, or pew rent to collect. We celebrated Mass, heard confessions, preached on Sundays and

(27)

holydays. During the week, many minor duties occupied us. We were called on at times to administer the pledge to a few who had been indulging too freely, to settle little difficulties, and encourage harmony and good-will; to instruct such as needed private lessons on special points of religion, and everywhere to elevate the standard of religion, morality, and true patriotism. This formed the winter's work, not only for the chaplains of the Irish Brigade, but also for all Catholic priests so engaged. But as I started out with the idea that the Irish Brigade was, as it were, "headquarters" for Catholic labors, I must keep to it.

Here let me say a word about Gen. Thomas Francis Meagher, whose character is, I think, not well understood by many. Gen Meagher was more than an ordinary gentleman He possessed high-toned sentiments and manners, and the bearing of a prince. He had a superior intellect, a liberal education, was a fine classical writer, and a born orator. He was very witty, but more inclined to humor; was fond of witty or humorous persons, and admired those who possessed such gifts. He was a great lover of his native land, and passionately opposed to its enemies; strong in his faith, which he never concealed, but, on the contrary, published it above-board; and, wherever he went he made himself known as a "Catholic and an Irishman." He was well instructed in his religion, and I should have pitied the one who had the temerity to speak disparagingly of it in his presence.

Although not what we would call a pious man, he loved his faith, and assisted in making religion take a front rank. For example: With his natural fondness for sports, and with a desire to keep up life and energy in his command, he would make elaborate preparations for the celebration of St. Patrick's Day; and while organizing steeple chases, hurdle races, etc., in the morning, all attended Mass and listened to the sermon; he, in person, acting as master of ceremonies, directing the band when to play during the divine service; but this will be noticed more *in extenso* in a future chapter. The above shows something of the character of the man. Besides being, as we all know, as brave as a lion, he did not neglect going to confession from time to time, especially before battles. It is to be regretted that, at times, especially when no fighting was going on, and time grew heavy on his hands, his convivial spirit would lead him too far. But by no means must it be concluded from this that he was a drunkard. It was not for love of liquor, but for the love of sport and joviality that he thus gave way, and these occasions were few and far between.* Besides, he was polite and gentlemanly, even when under the influence of liquor; never sinking to anything low or mean, beyond indulging too freely in unguarded moments.

---

* It has been insinuated that he was in liquor when he was drowned in the Missouri River; but this is contradicted by the Rev. J. St. Onge, then missionary out West among the Indians, and now pastor in Troy, N. Y.

His appearance was very much in his favor, being one of the finest-looking officers in the whole army; and, mounted on a magnificent horse, surrounded by a "brilliant staff" of young officers, he was a fit representative of any nation on earth. It is not surprising, then, that a man of his intellect and noble personal character drew around him, not a low, uneducated class, but rather refined and gentlemanly officers and men, recruited mostly from New York; while many came from Boston, Philadelphia, Jersey, and even from Europe, to join his standard.

The officers of his command were, for the most part, men of superior education, gallant beyond any around them in the army; and as for bravery, this they imbibed with their mother's milk, yea, it was born in them."* The "rank and file" was composed of healthy, intelligent men, far above the average, and in many cases of liberal education. Here I would state that I frequently noticed superior men on guard, and engaged in other inferior duties. In my regiment, as private soldiers, there were seven first-class lawyers! Last, but not least, the surgeons of this brigade were among the first in the army—Dr. Reynolds had no superior. This little bit of personal history is necessary to show that the Irish Brigade was not entirely unworthy the title of "Headquarters of the Church in the Army of the Potomac." Moreover, it shows with

---

* Note on page 31.

what material the chaplains had to deal. Remember, too, that this great body of officers and men was, I might say, entirely Catholic, and one may easily infer that the influence, for good or evil, was considerable. When, later, the brigade was joined by the Twenty-eighth Massachusetts and the One Hundred and Sixteenth Pennsylvania regiments, besides McMahon's Battery and the Sixty-ninth Pennsylvania—many of the four last being Catholic—there was a body of about 4,000 Catholic men marching—most of them—to death, but also to the glory of their Church and country. I regret that I have not môre data concerning the illustrious Corcoran Legion. But were we to count in the Legion composed of 3,000 Irish Catholics; the Ninth Massachusetts, with 800; the Third Brigade (known as the "Excelsior," with Father O'Hagan as chaplain), in which there were no less than 1,300 of the same faith, we should number, in solid bodies alone, in the Army of the Potomac, over 9,000 Catholic soldiers, not to mention odd numbers in every regiment in the army. A full page of history, in all justice, should be given to such a respectable body of Christian soldiers—unique in character, unique in faith, unique in nationality; but ever brave and true in support of their adopted country.

[NOTE.]—Several officers who served in the Austrian Army, and in various other armies, figured later on in the Irish Brigade, and many distinguished Irish-Catholic officers and men who served in the Papal Brigade in defense of the temporal power of His Holiness, subsequently joined the Irish Brigade here. Many others from the sâme organization were to be found in various parts of the Army of the Potomac.

CHAPTER IV.

THE IRISH BRIGADE TAKES THE FIELD.

IT is not the object of this narrative to write a history of the war, or of a part of it even, but I must give sketches, here and there, to bring out the part taken in the movements by the chaplains. On March 5, 1862, general orders were given to "strike tents" and "march!" This put the whole Army of the Potomac in motion. The Irish Brigade was up and doing at three o'clock in the morning. Oh, I remember well that dreary morning! It was not frosty, but a raw wind, and a miserable, drizzling rain chilled us as we were hastily preparing to depart on our first march — our first campaign. It took a long time to get everything ready. We, the chaplains, had more than ordinary preparations to make; for, besides the ordinary "traps" required, we had to take all the necessary vestments, altar stones, missals, etc., for the celebration of Mass. At last, about seven or eight o'clock, all were in motion. Father Dillon and myself, being of the same order, generally went in the same boat, so to speak. When everything was ready, we thought of something to eat.

I took a small sack and put into it a few pounds of "hard tack" crackers hard as pieces of brick. This I suspended from the pommel of my saddle, and it rested against the shoulder of my horse. He was a poor, old, gray horse. One of the officers, a colonel, who was in constant motion, borrowed my horse—an active, strong animal—and the quarter-master furnished me with this as a substitute. Now I wished to appear in such style as befitted my position in the regiment on the first march; but on this animal I made a very sorry figure. Moreover, when all the troops were crossing a small stream of water, this brute got into the middle of the creek and would go no farther. Here the gallant chaplain of the Eighty-eighth sat, trying to persuade the old gray to proceed, but to no purpose, while officers and men were passing and looking on. Finally, one of the men, by the gentle use of his bayonet, encouraged the animal to move. I had my own horse next day.

The roads were in a terrible condition, and the poor men who loaded themselves before starting from camp, with boots, stockings, underwear, etc., kept casting them off on the roadside as they felt themselves unable to carry them any longer. It was a sight to behold the variety of articles along the road for miles, and many of these very articles had been sent to the soldiers for their comfort by tender-hearted wives, mothers, and sisters. We marched all day till late at night, then halted on a bleak corn-field. It still rained, and a cold March wind blew dismally.

3

Father Dillon and myself were very tired, and we tried the "hard-tack"; but, resting against· the horse all day, the sack of crackers had absorbed the rain and the perspiration, and they smelt of "old gray horse," and, in fact, tasted of "old gray horse." We had nothing else. In the morning we had placed everything in an army wagon, even our buffalo robes and army blankets, so that we were now left without anything to eat and with nothing to sleep on. Father Dillon got off in the shelter of some brush, and, after the fatigues of the day, slept a little. Some men wanted to go to confession, as we expected to be in battle next day, and I sat on the roots of an old tree and heard all who came; but most of the men were entirely exhausted, and they soon fell asleep on their gum blankets, while I sat on some sticks the rest of that night, near the fire which the soldiers had started. The wind, now blowing a gale, drove the smoke into my face, and when I moved to the opposite side, the shifting wind drove me back to my former position. Thus I spent that night, after marching the previous day about eighteen miles in rain and mud, with no dinner and no supper, followed by no sleep.

But, you may ask, where are the materials that were put into the army wagon? They are there, but the wagons are "stuck in the mud" — Virginia mud — ten or fifteen miles behind. Next morning we rose from the ground! — to march! No breakfast, and, as we advanced, we left the army wagons still farther behind us. The soldiers always carried a small quantity of coffee, army crackers, "hard-tack," and a chunk of pork, so they had something "to keep life in them"; but the chaplains depended upon the army wagons, which they did not see for five or six days after leaving Camp California. Notwithstanding these discomforts, all moved on. It is a mistake to think that the soldiers, even the line officers, know where the army is going, and just where the enemy will be found. These things are known only to a few of the principal officers in command, and not always to them. They frequently have to find the enemy in much the same manner as hunters find the location of lions and tigers in a Bengal jungle. But this much we knew—we were going toward Manassas and old Bull Run battle-field; and this had something to do with the condition of our nerves, especially in the case of those who had never had a chance to "smell powder."

That same evening we reached Manassas, and we found that the enemy had retreated hurriedly and left behind them valuable stores. Here the men found some "jerked beef." They called it "junk"; but, no matter, it was sweet to starving, green chaplains, who had never campaigned before, and did not know how to take care of themselves. We got some fresh "hard-tack"—not that which "smelled of horse and tasted of horse"—and some black, but hot, coffee. We were new men for awhile. Shortly afterward it began to rain, in the usual dreary

Southern fashion of raining. Some of us were partly sheltered by an old tent that had been left by the enemy, and, as the ground was nothing but mud, the soldiers piled in the tent some brush, and on this brush-pile we sat, "*Sicut nycticorax in domicilio.*" For about two days after, we had no food; but, finally, on a countermarch, we met a Suttler who was selling, in limited numbers, small cakes at from 25 cents to $1.00 apiece—for money was not considered by the hungry men, and the kindness on this march of Lieut. J. J. McCormick and Capt. Moore I will never forget. On the 13th, or thereabouts, having accomplished our mission—namely, to find out all about the enemy, his location, movements, etc.—we expected to return to Alexandria at once, and take shipping for the Peninsula. I, being the youngest of the chaplains, was started back in advance to secure altar-breads, altar-wines, etc., for the Peninsular Campaign. In the meantime the enemy made a show of fighting. Our troops were ordered back. When I heard this in Alexandria I started at once for the "front"; and on my way, while passing over the old Bull Run battle-field, I found myself in the dark, amidst dead men's bones, and a stillness that was death-like. Nothing was heard, except, now and then, a piercing sound from a screech owl. I pushed on, however, and after some miles, heard a shrill, frightful voice cry out: "Halt! Who comes there?"

"A friend," I replied.

"Advance, friend, and give the countersign."

But, not knowing the countersign of course, I entered into an explanation; but it was of no use, I had to dismount and surrender. Soldiers on picket duty must obey orders, and I was made a prisoner. Fortunately, I was captured by soldiers of my own *corps d'armée*, and, after being brought to headquarters, the general in command, Maj.-Gen. Richardson, being from my native State, Michigan, identified me, and directed the soldiers to "take good care of the chaplain of the Irish Brigade, and escort him to his command." This they did with much courtesy. Next day was Sunday, and the chaplains did all they could to sanctify the day. I do not remember what other chaplains provided, but I remember very distinctly the altar constructed under my supervision, for I was determined to say Mass. There were no boards, no boxes, no tables, in the entire camp, and the camp was in a dense woods. The soldiers cut some pine branches and fastened them to a tree, as a slight shelter for the future altar. Then they drove four crotched sticks in the ground and put two short pieces, about two and a half feet in length, from one crotch across to the other; they then cut down a tree, and having cut off a length about six feet, split the log in two, and placed the pieces of split timber, flat side up, lengthwise, to form the table of the altar. This, the rudest of altars, I dressed, as best I could, with the altar linens. Two candles were lighted, and

Mass was celebrated in the forest of Virginia, after a fashion to rival that of the most destitute Indian missionary that ever put foot on the soil of the Huron Nation.

CHAPTER V.

ABOUT the end of March, 1862, all the troops
were ordered back from the movement on Manassas (the enemy having retreated toward Richmond), to take shipping on the Potomac and be
transported to the Chesapeake Bay, and, finally, to
the Peninsula. About 1500 of the Irish Brigade
were placed on the *Ocean Queen* — about which
there was plenty of ocean but not much queen! The
vessel was certainly a fine one; but, hired by the
Government simply to convey troops, its management
had no responsibility in regard to beds, food, or any
of these necessities of life, and our trip to the Peninsula was one of considerable deprivation. The
chaplains said their office, and the other officers
fasted. Thus we might say, with "Jack," the servant of
Dean Swift, "we were on the road to heaven." "My
master," said he, "is praying and I am fasting, and
if fasting and prayer is not the road to heaven, I
know no theology." The troops in the other ships

(39)

were not even as well cared for as we were. Finally, after leaving Fortress Monroe, we landed at Ship Point, Virginia.

The weather was bad; no end to cold rain, sleet, and mud. We had no fresh meat, no vegetables; nothing but fat pork, black coffee, and "hard-tack" three times a day. We found here many small huts, which had been occupied by the Confederate soldiers during the previous winter. Into these we were glad to go, since we had no tents. I had, in my supply of clothing, three fine new flannel shirts, and at this time I thought I would take the advice of the kind-hearted Sister who had sent them, and put one on. I opened the box in which they had been packed, and put one on for the first time. Next morning I felt a queer kind of itching all over. I said nothing, but pulled out another new shirt, went to the river and took a good wash, and put on another of the new shirts. Now curiosity got the better of me, and looking at the shirt I had just removed, I found it full of—excuse the word—clothes lice, or "greybacks." I flung the shirt into the river, and returned, feeling all right. Next morning I had to do the same, and still the third morning did the same. Thinking that the soft flannel was the attraction for these miserable tortures of military life, I flung all my flannel goods into the river and contented myself with cold linen. After awhile it leaked out that all the officers were in the same condition.

This, however, was our first experience with "grey-backs." They had been left to us as a legacy, and were the sole inhabitants of the huts that had been evacuated by the routed enemy. Let me say here that many a poor soldier who could not procure entire suits of new clothes at will, was subjected, not only to sufferings from want of good, fresh food, long, tedious marches under a scorching sun, with dust penetrating every particle of his clothing, or under pelting rain and through mud knee-deep, but to incredible tortures from these "greybacks." It is easy to laugh about this now, but sensitive persons fairly shudder at the thought of this pestilence, worse in nature than many of the Egyptian plagues. To face this kind of life requires more courage than to face the belching cannon and the smoke of battle. It is all very well to write war history so that it may read like a novel or a romance. You will find some writers telling of the Elysian Fields, the beautiful mountains, the prancing war-horse, and the shining swords and bright bayonets, glittering in the sun. While all this is true, it is well to give some of the ordinary reality, and do away with some of the poetry. It has a good effect, because it brings out the true and full historical character of warfare, and teaches a lesson to rising generations. From a knowledge of the hardships of their fellow-citizens and forefathers, they set a higher value on the freedom and prosperity thereby secured for them, and the consideration of the many evils of war, will

prevent them, in future political contests, from rashly
provoking the spirit of war, either civil or interna-
tional. There are times when war can not be avoided;
but it should be resorted to only after all other
means have been tried, tried again, and in vain.
Henry the Great, of France, once ordered some
bronze cannon of immense size, and caused to be
engraved on them this terrible motto: "The last
argument of Kings."

This may seem to be a slight deviation from my
narrative, but it is certainly pertinent since it gives
an insight into the life and labors of the now bellig-
erent chaplain, under trying circumstances. Moved,
as he is, by true patriotism, he faces war and its evils,
but regards it always as a primary duty to attend to
the spiritual wants of his charge. Just here I recall
a poor soldier who was accidentally shot through the
left lung. I happened to be near by, had just time
to hear his confession, and he breathed his last. All
the aforesaid labors, trials, and fastings were well
rewarded by the chance given to save that one soul.
We have now arrived at May 1, 1862, the chaplains
"in front" with their commands. A huge tent,
which belonged, principally, to the Sixty-third, was
used for a church, and in it we opened the May devotions. This tent was like a circus tent (very large),
and many persons could stand under it. When
prayers commenced, the soldiers dropped down on
their knees, mud or no mud. Many, however, were
sharp enough to provide at least a chip to put under

their knees, to keep them from sinking too deep in the
mud caused by recent rains. About the camp altar
the condition was a little better, as the boards taken
from cracker boxes formed a sort of floor. In this
tent Mass was celebrated every morning, and prayers
were said every evening, to which the boys were
called by the ringing of a small bell through the
camp, by a drummer boy. Confessions were heard
also. Many officers and soldiers came here, from
various parts of the army, and it was like a parish
service—all except the collection. The Catholic soldier is glad to find a priest in the army, or even to
see one in the distance, and it always gives him new
courage. It is an inestimable privilege for him to
make his confession, receive Holy Communion, and
attend Mass, especially when it may be for the last
time. Soldiers thus prepared go into battle full of
courage and confidence. I had occasion to go down
to the landing where the hospital was located, several
miles from the camp. Here I met a cavalry soldier
who had not seen a priest since he entered the army,
nearly a year previous to this date, May 3, 1862.
He made preparations at once, dropping down on his
knees on the ground, while I sat on a cracker box
and heard the confession of the delighted trooper.
After confession, he arose, and, regardless of his soiled
knees, expressed his joy, by crying out: "O Father!
I feel so light!" From that moment he seemed to
have new life and courage. This soldier lived to pass
through many battles with brave Phil. Sheridan,

who was no braver than the soldier herein mentioned. There is no more consoling sacrament established by our Lord, than the Sacrament of Penance — confession. It seems to have for those who rarely find opportunity to receive it, an infinite charm when unexpectedly brought within their reach. The cavalry man mentioned is, at this writing — January 20, 1890 — still alive, at Notre Dame, in the same community with me, leading a good Christian life, but much disabled by two large bullets which he carries buried deep in his body — bullets which he must, of necessity, carry with him to the grave. What a coincidence, after nearly thirty years! What kindness on the part of Divine Providence, "without whose care not even a sparrow falls to the ground!" God protects His own; He favors those who trust in Him; He glories in those brave servants who are faithful and do not run after false doctrines. "So spake the Lord," said the Prophet Elias, and quoted by St. Paul: "I have left me seven thousand men that have not bowed their knees to Baal."—*Romans, xi.* Thus did the Lord, exulting, so to speak, proclaim the number of His servants and friends, men faithful to His service, and confident in His loving and paternal care.

CHAPTER VI.

SHORT DESCRIPTION OF THE LOCALITY—A FEW HISTOR-
ICAL NOTES—PRINCE OF THE "HOUSE OF ORLEANS"
—MASS.

HERE may be made a note which, I am sure, will
be interesting to the reader. As I have said,
our troops embarked and passed on to the Chesapeake
Bay, the greatest inlet on the United States Atlantic
Coast—a mighty arm of the sea, about 200 miles long
and very wide. On its bosom floated the ships that
bore the *notorious* Cornwallis, with his troops, to the
coasts of the Carolinas and Virginia. On its bosom
also floated the ships that bore George Washington,
his troops, and the French allies under Rochambeau,
to the victory of Yorktown and the final termination
of the war with England. On these waters, Hamp-
ton Roads, forming the estuary of the James River,
took place the memorable naval battle in which the
novel and famous *Merrimac* and the *Monitor* figured,
revolutionizing naval warfare throughout the world.
The Chesapeake receives the Potomac, the Rappahannock, the York, and the James rivers, each made
famous by battles which took place on their waters

(45)

and on their banks, during the Civil War. The
Potomac passed between union and secession. From
it McClellan's army borrowed its name. On the
Rappahannock is located the city of Fredericksburg,
made historic by the contests which took place there,
especially the disastrous battle under Burnside. On
the James is located the city of Richmond, celebrated as being the capital of the Confederacy. Coming back to the York River, we notice on its banks
Yorktown, known by every schoolboy in the United
States as the place where Cornwallis surrendered his
entire command of 7,000, and capitulated to George
Washington, in 1781, after marauding along the
shores of the Carolinas, and destroying $15,000,000
worth of American property. But Yorktown obtains
additional notoriety from the fact that the Confederates revived the old works of Cornwallis, and fortified an army there, so that it was considered by them
impregnable; and, finally, in May, 1862, after spiking
their guns, about seventy-two in number, they evacuated a fort which, if held, might have been instrumental in preventing McClellan's march to Richmond.
This action was a surprise to all, and I think very
much against their own interests.

A few miles from Yorktown is Williamsburg, full
of historical reminiscences. It was the capital of
Virginia and the seat of the colonial government
prior to the Revolution. Therefore, who, possessed of
any patriotism, could pass over the renowned Chesapeake, whose shores have living voices, echoing and

re-echoing the mighty deeds of heroic men, without feeling a thrill of enthusiasm? Yes, in passing along these shores, one should lift his hat in reverence to the past, or in memory of the brave soldiers who lie in forgotten graves along its shores, and of many other fellowmen who have perished, either by the sword or by starvation, during the two centuries since the colonial days of Sir Walter Raleigh. This may seem to be too much of a digression from our main point, but I make it for two reasons: First, I could not resist the temptation of recalling what made such a deep impression on the writer during his campaign life of three years in the Army of the Potomac, in these memorable places; secondly, because lovers of history will gladly read a few lines that recall such an impression, and find the narrative of chaplain life more interesting.

Now we will go back and start from the camp in front of Yorktown, just before the evacuation of that town by the Confederates in May, 1862. Our camp was called Camp Winfield Scott, in honor of the old general. Owing to the many preparations necessary for storming Yorktown, strongly fortified as it was, also for the building of bridges over the creeks and swamps, considerable time was consumed. This gave us opportunity to look around, and to provide clean, new garments, to fix up neat quarters, and to get accustomed to real soldier life. Here might be mentioned the fact that all tried to make the best of a life necessarily exposed to many inconveniences.

The real chivalry of our army was kept alive by the example of our brave and brilliant officers. None excelled, and few equalled in this respect, Gen. Thomas Francis Meagher, commander of the Irish Brigade, while Gen. McClellan, in his capacity of commander-in-chief, held the very highest possible position in the affection, confidence and respect of both officers and men. He was honored, too, by distinguished noblemen from Europe, some of whom acted as *aids-de-camp;* the most noted being the Princes of the House of Orleans. The Prince de Joinville also accompanied McClellan, but not as an aid. We found these gentlemen, with others of distinguished family, very agreeable; in fact, they endeared themselves to many of us by their kind and gentle manners. They came to participate in the active campaign life, from a desire of perfecting themselves, by experience, in the use of arms and the strategies of war. They seemed to have a genuine love for soldier life. McClellan had the faculty of surrounding himself with men of distinction, both of this country and of Europe. In the center and at the head of the great army, he looked and acted a prince of princes, and we may be permitted to borrow words from Shakespeare to give expression to his magnetic character:

> " By his light
> Did all the chivalry of England move
> To do brave acts."

Amid all the inconveniences of war life there is

much of that truly chivalrous spirit which lifts the mind from the every-day routine and sends it flying back over the dusty pages of history to call up the heroic deeds of the great men of the mighty past. Many preparations were made in our camp for the siege of Yorktown. Our men confessed their sins, received Holy Communion, and spent their spare time in much serious reflection on the past and the very doubtful future, with its possibilities in the coming battle or battles. Fathers Dillon, Ouellet, and myself were always ready to assist them in their anxious preparations.

As I have said, Yorktown was unexpectedly evacuated by the Confederates, on May 4, 1862. At once we were ordered to advance. We abandoned our quarters, leaving the rustic decoration made for the devotions of May behind us, and marched on. The roads were in a frightful condition, so much so that our cannon became imbedded in the mud; the horses could do nothing in the face of such difficulties; they could only pull out one leg, and thereby sink the other deeper. At length, long ropes were tied to the cannon carriages, and a few hundred soldiers, with a "long pull, a strong pull, and a pull altogether," succeeded in extricating the guns. This was very slow work. We finally passed through Yorktown, which was filled with concealed torpedoes. No one knew at what moment he might be blown "sky high." I took care to keep in the center of the well-beaten road, watching every step my horse made,

4

fearing to encounter a hidden explosive that would settle all doubts concerning the future army life as far as my horse and I were concerned. Army wagons with provisions, tents, ammunition, etc., brought up the rear, as usual.

A certain driver, who was driving six mules with a single line, was whipping and cursing away "like sixty," as the saying is, when a lean, long-necked minister came along, on a horse covered with cooking utensils and stores. The minister, feeling it his duty, called out:

"Young man, do you know who made you?"

"What?" said the driver, stopping a moment from his whipping and cursing.

"Do you know who made you?" repeated the minister, this time in a very loud voice.

"Oh!" said the driver, "this is no time for conundrums!"

And lifting his great army whip, he struck the leading mule on the ear with a snap that sent the blood flying.

"Go on there!" he cried, "you cursed descendant of Pluto!"

He had heard some one say Pluto, and he thought it must mean some very bad beast—bad enough to be the origin of mules. Anyhow, the minister retired.

McClellan pushed on as rapidly as possible, and a wing of our army came in contact with a portion of the Confederate forces at Williamsburg, and repulsed them there. In order to follow orders received from

Washington, several divisions, including the Irish Brigade, were rapidly pushed up the York River and to Cumberland, landing on the right bank of the Pamunkey River. The other divisions, with the trains and artillery, moved in the same direction by land. Sunday, May 11, before starting up the river, we had a few hours' free time early in the morning. The night previous I had caused to be constructed, under a small tent, a rude altar, composed, not of carved walnut, or of costly cypress, or bird's-eye maple, but of cracker boxes, supported by a light frame-work, forming a quasi-table, with room enough to place on it the altar stone, cards, missal, etc. Here I celebrated the Holy Sacrifice — *Coram populo, vel militibus presentibus.* This Mass was attended with much devotion, perhaps more than the general public would be willing to ascribe to soldiers. But a true Christian soldier has for motto: "Fidelity to God *first,* and to his country next;" and no man can be a true, reliable patriot who is a traitor to his Maker. The sermon on this occasion was short: "My dear brethren, never forget your duty to God." Scarcely was the last word of the short sermon heard, when the command resounded through the camp: "Fall in!" and while the servants hastily folded up the small tent, I swallowed from a tin cup my coffee, then mounted my horse. While hundreds of thousands in cities, towns, and hamlets were slowly walking to church, and, later on in the day, listening to the grand tones of the inspiring organ, the charms of classic music, and the eloquence of the pulpit, your humble servant was marching on with his command, which he never allowed to go alone, fearing that his official services might be wanted at any moment. Thus I spent that Sunday, but not without fruit. A soldier was suddenly taken ill, and I was summoned immediately. I had but a short distance to go, which was fortunate, for the poor soldier was sinking very rapidly. These opportunities for doing good were great consolations, and recompensed the chaplains for their fatigues and privations, since they brought the consciousness that their labors and time were not lost. Thus, unknown to nineteen-twentieths of the command, good was being done, and the soldiers felt a security in knowing that their priest was always quite near—in fact, "within gun-shot," and ready to serve them at a moment's notice.

CHAPTER VII.

HOME OF MRS. GEORGE WASHINGTON—NOTED RIVERS —LAND OF THE RED-MAN IN CAPTAIN SMITH'S TIME—ETC.

OUR move up the York River brought us to the "White House," as it was called. This at once marked a spot of much interest to our troops, and revealed to our admiring eyes the home of the pretty widow, Mrs. Custis, who became the wife of George Washington. It was a two-and-a-half story frame building, having only six rooms, surrounded, however, by several out-offices. The grounds were nicely kept, and the parterre in front was particularly charming. Gen. McClellan placed a guard on the premises to protect the property; but later on during the war the building was burned and the entire surroundings assumed a desolate aspect. Even the fine pines and cedars that gave a tone of poetic fancy to this historic spot were destroyed by the ruthless hand of Mars. The property belonged to the Lee family, who inherited it in a direct line, Gen. Lee's mother being a Miss Custis.

This spot marked a stopping place in our march,

and in our life, which resembled very much that of
Gypsies. It also reminded us that we were drawing
nearer and nearer to the great contest that would end
in many horrors — bleeding wounds, groaning suf-
ferers, death to thousands, and tears to the eyes of
innumerable widows, orphans, and dear ones at home.
In anticipation of this the chaplains had their places
of worship arranged as best they could, where, in
the evenings, men could go to confession and receive
Holy Communion next morning. With lively faith
they gathered around the altars, assisted at Mass;
and as they watched the priest lift the Sacred Host
on high, many a one said in his heart: "Perhaps
this is the last time I will see Jesus till I meet Him
in the life to come." O how many war States, but
especially Virginia, were sanctified in this way!*
Thousands of soldiers, looking up to heaven into the
eyes of the Deity, asking help; the priest, lifting
up the "Spotless Lamb," calling out to man and
to the eternal Father: *Ecce Agnus Dei* —"Behold
the Lamb of God, who taketh away the sins of the
world." A good minister met me on the march one
day and asked, in all simplicity and earnestness:

"Chaplain, how do you bring your men to Divine
service? I see them as I pass your quarters attending by the hundreds, if not thousands, every Sabbath, especially, and often during the week. I can

---

* Altars erected on hundreds of spots, dotting the land as
bright stars do the firmament.

not induce my men to attend that way; in fact, very few take any interest in religious services."

"Why, my dear sir, I do not bring them," I replied; "their faith brings them."

A little to the northeast of this location was the Mattapony River, which figured on our war maps. This river has three small forks, called, respectively, the "Mat," "Ta," "Po," and the "Ny," which, united, form the name referred to—the "Mattapony." Between us and Richmond was the well-known Chickahominy River, whose stream, in many places, is not more than forty to fifty feet in width, but whose shores are marshes or swamps, varying from one-half to one mile wide. Heavy forest trees grow in the marshes, and make them similar in appearances to the great cypress swamps of Louisiana. After passing over these marshes one reaches *terra firma* again.

Here we found ourselves on the once rich hunting grounds of the red-man, which were so much desired by the whites. It was while the famous Capt. John Smith was passing up this Chickahominy River that he was captured by the Indians, and would have been sacrificed to the "Great Spirit," but for the intervention of the gentle and kind-hearted Pocahontas, who, moved by compassion, saved his life at the risk of her own. Our minds were carried back to the time of this gentle "child of nature" (over three hundred years ago), and we reflected what changes had taken place in the lands where she exercised a chastening and refining influence over the brave but

savage warriors of those days. This place was at that
time filled with red-men, and innumerable wild beasts
roamed at will and furnished an abundant supply of
food for the children of the forest. Here could be
seen the elk, wild deer, the cinnamon bear, the coon,
wild turkey and fowls of infinite variety. Now what
do we see? Two great armies on either side of the
river — descendants of civilized European stock, children of Christians — making ready, with all the most
destructive engines of war, to slaughter each other, to
cause human blood, brother's blood, to flow in
streams! Alas, for the errors of poor human nature!
But, *humanum est errare* — "it is human to err."
We can understand this savage inclination in the
untrained barbarian, but not in the enlightened
Christians of the nineteenth century! "*O tempora! O
mores!*" If at this time the sweet, gentle Pocahontas
could return as an angel of peace to her old home
and cast herself between the belligerents, doubtless
their passions would be cooled and the bright vision
would kindle fraternal charity in every heart.

We have not yet, however, reached the Chickahominy River. We are still on the banks of the
Pamunkey, up which are coming the army supplies—
men and material pretty well mixed. As the men
land, we notice a wonderful variety. Here comes a
regiment of Zouaves, known by their red dress-caps,
white leggings, and baggy trousers. Now we see a
company of cavalry, their short jackets and well-
fitting trousers trimmed with yellow. Next come the

engineers, who wear dark blue trimmed with orange; and, finally, the regular infantry men, attired in the ordinary blue uniforms with dark trimmings. These soldiers, constantly coming in from the ships, soon became very busy unloading the necessaries of war in infinite variety. It would remind one of the slight-of-hand man or prestidigitator, who, from one hat, may take a sponge cake two feet in diameter, a pair of live rabbits, a lady's costume, and a bottle or two of wine. From the vessels our men took the indomitable army mule, army wagons, corn, baled hay, flour, pork, "hard-tack," suttlers, with all their traps, cartridges, cannon caissons, cannon balls, cannon shells, powder, crow bars, and perhaps a few toothpicks. The latter were hardly essential. While all this necessary work was going on, many of our men were engaged in building eleven new bridges, found indispensable for crossing the swamps and the Chickahominy River.

In the meantime the chaplains kept up the Christian fervor of their men by celebrating Mass and hearing confessions. Frequently, also, some good soldier, who had not the time or the facilities for writing, requested the priest to do so for him. Such letters would, invariably, be addressed to a dear wife, mother, sister, or brother, who was only too anxious to know how John or James fared at the "front." Hundreds of such letters passed homeward, and in time the dear ones would write to the chaplains of the brigade, asking for more information.

At the time, such letters passed for what they were worth then and there; but now, over a quarter of a century since, these letters would be worth an incalculable amount of money. They were generally very simple and straight to the point; and oh, how full of heartfelt interest! And the answers! What an infinite variety of expressions, prompted by maternal love and solicitude, or by the fraternal anxiety, but hopeful courage, would fill pages; and then the affectionate and tender-hearted sister could not suppress the wail of grief that filled her soul at the thought of the privations, hardships, and exposures to which her dear brother was subject. The priest was a go-between, exercising, as best he could, his offices of Christian charity in numerous ways. It was touching to see how those who had never seen us wrote confidingly of their family affairs; just as children to their fathers, not only Catholics, but also non-Catholics. What a proof of an unconscious but divine faith!

CHAPTER VIII.

PASTIMES AND REALITIES—BATTLE OF FAIR OAKS OR
SEVEN PINES.

ON May 31, 1862, Gen. Meagher, wishing to keep up the spirits of his men, organized a steeple chase and a mule race, and numerous prizes were offered. Steeple chases, as a sport, are not extensively known or practised in this country. The preparations are made by building hedge or brush fences, digging ditches six to eight feet wide, etc. Then the gentlemen (in this case officers exclusively), mounted in jockey dress, ride over this ground, and, with their horses, jump the fences and ditches they come to throughout the course. Six, or perhaps as many as eight, enter for the contest and go abreast. As the jumping is very hazardous, it becomes exceedingly exciting. Not unfrequently when a horse and rider had unfortunately fallen into a ditch another horse and rider, coming close behind at full speed, and unable to stop, would go down to join the *melée*, or, in some extraordinary cases, jumping over the fallen horse and rider, keep on, bent on winning the prize. It was certainly a great novelty to many of us, who,

(59)

born in the States, had never before seen such recreation, which must unquestionably have been the invention of wild Irishmen, who did not know what fear is! It was an ordinary occurrence to see men with dislocated arms, broken shoulder-blades, and black eyes; and, in some cases, the horses were killed outright, or disabled so that they were shot to put them out of pain.

The mule race was laughable beyond expression. Each teamster rode his adversary's mule, and the mule "in last" was the one that took the prize; consequently no one wanted to get in last, because it would give the prize to his opponent. Such whipping and roaring I never heard. It made all wild with jollity. When several of the obstinate brutes ran and stuck their heads into shanty windows on the route, and performed many still more ridiculous freaks, the merriment grew almost into a craze.

In the midst of all this, the cannon opened their brazen mouths and belched at our troops the missiles of death. These were quickly responded to by those of our troops who were in the vicinity of the attack. The drums beat the "long roll," and a cry "To arms!" flew along our lines. Lieutenants, adjutants of various rank, and orderlies came with reckless speed, their horses covered with sweat and panting with fatigue and excitement, which they seemed to have caught instinctively from the surroundings and from their earnest riders. In a few moments we were marching to the scene of contest.

Now we had to test the Chickahominy swamps. We marched all night till about two o'clock in the morning, over the corduroy roads that kept some of us out of the swamps; but when it came the turn of the cavalry and artillery to cross the swamps and river, there were scenes that beggar description. The rain, which had fallen in torrents a short time previously, had swollen the river and filled the swamps to such a degree that the logs forming the corduroy roads were partly floating, and some of the eleven bridges that had been built by the troops were swept entirely away. The night was dark, and the bridge we had to cross was at first called the " Grape-vine Bridge "; but before the cavalry and artillery passed over, it was given a new name, more appropriate to the dilapidated, unsafe condition in which we found it in the darkness of the night. It was renamed the " Devil's Bridge." Horses fell in vain attempts to plunge their way; the artillery got stuck; harmony of action and voice left the ranks, and we were bogged in the dark, dismal swamps of the Chickahominy.

In the midst of all this distressing confusion and real hardship, we mused over the New York, Philadelphia, and other gentle, innocent heroes, who would awaken that morning from a sound, refreshing sleep, get up at eight o'clock, or later, come down to breakfast, pick up the morning paper, and glance over the " army movements," and, thinking that the army should rush to the " front" as the firemen go over Broadway and other well-paved streets to a destructive fire, remark: "How slowly that army moves!" I can not dwell on this point now, nor is it to my purpose; but I must say that many well-meaning men passed criticisms on the conduct of the war, who would have formed very different opinions had they known one-tenth of the difficulties such as I have simply alluded to above, *en passant.* These great difficulties were to be met with on all occasions when anything like a general move had to be made. To mobilize a great army, taking into account the hundred thousand details, contingencies, etc., is an undertaking but partially comprehended by men having a military education, but with no practical experience, and fully comprehended even by few experienced military men. From this standpoint one may easily see how absurd it is for men with no experience and no military education, hundreds of miles away from danger of bullets, to pass judgments off-hand, and vehemently condemn seeming mistakes, which may, in reality, be great military manœuvres.

As I have said, we passed most of the night reaching the scene of contest, called Fair Oaks or Seven Pines. We halted in the dark on a field nearly surrounded by woods, and tried to rest for a short time on the wet ground, to recover some of the strength lost by the fatigues of the night. In the morning when we opened our eyes we found that we had been sleeping with the dead! Many a poor soldier lay cold in death just where he fell in the battle of the previous evening, and we saw the ghastly appearance

of their bodies, which had been, as it were, our bed-
fellows, and a shudder passed through our hearts.
In this situation we could see the effects of the
desperate struggle of the previous day, May 31, 1862.
We were told that had it not been for the Thirty-
seventh New York "Irish Rifles" and three brave
Michigan regiments forming Berry's Brigade, the
Confederates could have called the day entirely their
own; but these regiments repulsed the enemy with
considerable loss. Taking a hasty look over the
locality, I saw on every side dead men, dead horses,
broken muskets, caissons smashed to pieces, and
general destruction of life and property. The
impression made on my mind then, about twenty-eight
years ago, is still as fresh as if it were only yesterday
that I witnessed the scene.

An inspection of a battle-field immediately after
the battle has a very depressing effect on the mind,
more so even than the battle itself. In sequestered
places were a number of wounded and dying. The
priests of the Irish Brigade visited them and rendered
such assistance as Catholic soldiers were in need of,
and then passed through our mind forebodings of
what the day might bring forth. I must say that the
outlook was not an exhilarating one. By this time,
full daylight, June 1, 1862, we noticed the advance
of the Confederate troops. They came en masse,
presenting a bold front. All the faith and piety
preached during the few previous months must now
be put into practice. Our men of the Irish Brigade

blessed themselves with more than ordinary fervor, offered a few fervent prayers to God and His Blessed Mother, and then, resigned to fate, they passed, even in the face of impending perils, an occasional joke, or quoted a line of poetry. A balloon which had appeared above the raging conflict on the previous day, had informed Gen. McClellan of the movements of the Confederates, and he knew that they were taking advantage of our critical position — our right wing being unprotected — a failure on the part of McDowell to fill that vacancy with his 40,000 men, as he was expected to do. Besides this failure, the recent rains had swollen the small stream of the Chickahominy until it was a raging torrent, and the marshes had become expansive lakes, with part of the Union troops on one side and part on the other! This rendered McClellan's position extremely hazardous, and the Confederates were fully confident of an easy victory, knowing, as they did, that McDowell with his great command was not near to assist McClellan in any way. They took into consideration, also, the embarrassment caused by the unprecedented floods in and along the shores and marshes of the Chickahominy.

At daylight the Confederates advanced, and the "long roll" had already called to arms all the Union men then on the ground. The conflict commenced early, and increased in fury until a "tenderfoot" felt that hell had opened its gates and let loose hundreds of thousands of demons, "shapes hot from Tartarus," whose ferocity knew no bounds, and whose single aim was destruction, without mercy to friend or foe. While the battle increased in violence and pressed the Union front, Gen. Thomas Francis Meagher's action, with his Irish Brigade of infantry and his battery of eighteen ten-pound Parrot guns, is thus described by Dr. James Moore, United States surgeon, in his complete history of the war: "Gen. Meagher, at the head of his famous Irish Brigade, advanced gallantly, and, charging with great fierceness, mowed down the rebels by platoons. They were compelled to retreat, while a storm of shells from the Parrot guns accelerated their flight." (Page 172.) Healy, in his history, speaking of the same battle, says: "Meagher's gallant brigade was then brought up to relieve the hard-pressed regiment. Advancing with their well-known war-shout, they closed with fearful ferocity on the foe, and for an hour mowed them down almost by companies."

CHAPTER IX.

BIGOTS—TRUE FREEDOM, ETC.

WHAT has all the last chapter to do with the chaplains? some reader may ask. It has everything to do with them. It shows that the doctrines they preached did not make cowards. It furnishes one more grand historical fact to shut the mouths of bigots who wantonly take every occasion to stir up animosity, quite unnecessarily, against Catholics. The press holds out to the American people the great power of the Pope, and tells them that by his power and office he directs Catholic politics in the United States, and that our great American free institutions are in danger! " The Pope and the Catholic Church will be their ruin! " In the first place, let me ask, should we have any free institutions or any free country at all, were it not for Catholics? I write not as a foreigner but as a native-born American citizen. Was it not a Catholic— Columbus—who discovered this country? Was it not Catholic Spain that encouraged him, and furnished him the means? Consult history. Wherein have the Catholic Church and the Catholic people in this country failed in patriotism? Tell me that! and do not try to frighten good people with the ghost of a Pope coming over here to destroy our free institutions. The Pope loves the United States, as he has frequently asserted, and he has other occupations, besides uprooting national institutions within her borders. The Catholics of various nations showed their love for this country during the struggle for independence, for national freedom.

Many civilized nations seemed ripe for liberty when the superhuman blow was struck over a century ago and the glorious fruit fell at the feet of America. Like birds let out of a cage, the people who had come over here from Europe felt that they had left behind them a prison life. They left behind them oppressive laws. They left behind them an overbearing aristocracy; and as new generations sprang up, the very thought of being kept on their native soil, unwilling servants of worn-out social systems and ungrateful masters, caused a deep, strong desire to spring up in their hearts for absolute, unconditional, and everlasting freedom. The great lakes, the beautiful, inspiring torrents that continually rush to the sea, the extensive and fertile prairies; yes, even the rich and impenetrable forests, homes for the wild man, homes for birds and beasts, had fired the minds of Americans and told them by the voice of nature: "You are our sons, and you must be sons of freedom, now and forever." A voice was lifted; it was wafted over the Atlantic. A favorable response came from

various nations of Europe. From every city on this
continent, from every town in the country, from
every village and hamlet on the plain, from every
ship in the harbors, from every cabin in the forests,
and from the living hearts of millions of men, went
up that same cry for liberty. In response to this
universal demand, Ireland sent her brave sons to
do battle in the cause of liberty. Poland sent an
illustrious Kosciusko. Alsace sent a noble DeKalb.
From France and her Catholic king came the great
and patriotic Lafayette and the noted Rochambeau,
with thousands of French Catholic soldiers. Without the aid of these truly brave, talented, and gallant
men of the Catholic faith the United States could
not have gained her independence, and would be to-
day, in all probability, a humble colony of England,
just as we see our neighbor Canada. Not to speak
now of the friendly reception given to Lafayette by
Marie Antoinette, nor the favorable disposition of the
king to the American cause in promising an army
and a fleet, nor of Rochambeau at the head of 6,000
French Catholic soldiers, let us simply refer to Yorktown. Behold, rapidly advancing on the historic
waters of the Chesapeake Bay, Count de Grasse with
a powerful French fleet. He joins Washington, the
two forming an army of 12,000 heroes. Washington
takes one redoubt and the French take another.
Cornwallis, with his 7,000 well-trained British soldiers,
is compelled to surrender to the combined American
and French armies. This virtually ended the war

with England, and secured that greatest boon of
liberty. The joy that passed through the nation was
never before equaled. In no struggle into which
our dear country has been precipitated, either with
England, Mexico, or the late conflict of the rebellion,
can you find a lack of gallant generals, officers of
every rank, with tens of thousands of brave, hardy
sons of the Catholic Church in the ranks and at the
front, the place of peril, called in war times the "post
of honor."

Yes, wellnigh on every page of the history of the
United States you find recorded the brave deeds
of Irish Catholics, and Catholics of all nations,
including American Catholics, who labored zealously
in the cause of American liberty; and still we have
the mortification of hearing, through the press, from
the pulpit, and even in legislative halls, the hue and
cry: "Catholics will destroy our free institutions!"
Did not Catholics furnish the material to make them?
And why should they destroy their own work? Why
should they be debarred rights purchased by the
purest blood of their noblest sons? Shame on bigots
for their ingratitude! Shame on bigots for this lack
of a sense of justice! Shame on bigots for casting
dishonor on the memories of the men who saved their
lives and the honor of this country! Shame on
bigots for vomiting out spleen on the very men who,
shoulder to shoulder with their own forefathers, won
for them, on bloody battle-fields, the liberty they now
enjoy. Hold! Enough! Thank God, it is only from

bigots any cause of complaint comes. The national finger of scorn should be pointed at such men till they hide their diminished heads behind the mountains of some remote island far beyond the borders of a free and fraternal nation. These few remarks are not intended for a general fault-finding with men not of the Catholic faith in this country. No, we have reason to be thankful to all, excepting always the bigots. Some of the finest tributes I ever read to our faith came from Protestant pens—from honest, well-meaning men. Men of this kind are more numerous in our happy and prosperous country than in any other country in the world. Once more, let bigots cease their useless vituperation; let the Gospel, not scandal, be preached from the pulpit. Let the press temper its language and be inspired by the noble, manly spirit of our forefathers. Let the legislative bodies allow no bigotry, but deal only in justice, equity, and truth with all men. Then, and not till then, can we call ourselves a free people, bound together by the most sacred ties that patriotic blood is able to cement.

CHAPTER X.

THE battle of Fair Oaks was over and night spread
its dark mantle over the bloody scene, but could
not hush the groans of wounded men. Neither could
it bring the desired refreshment and comfort to those
nearly dead from fatigue, hunger, thirst, loss of blood,
and excruciating pain. Those who lost much blood
by severe wounds suffered terribly from the cold
night air—a natural consequence. Here I may
remark that in the early part of the war the provisions for the sick and wounded were very imperfect.
Not because of a want of necessary supplies by the
Government, which desired to see all the men in the
service provided with necessaries, and even with
luxuries, but from want of organization on the part
of those officers whose duty it was to attend to this
branch. Neither was it their fault. It must be
remembered that most of our officers, while brave and
attentive to duty, still lacked experience. Nearly all
were novices. On this occasion, especially, circumstances precluded the possibility of having everything

as it should be. For instance, to have hospital tents, cots, and a hundred and one other things required for alleviating the sufferings of the wounded. Many of the severely wounded lost everything — blankets, utensils, and provisions.* The country was in a terrible condition, covered to a great extent, as we have seen, with water, and to convey by wagons the thousands of tons necessary on such occasions was no small task. Later on during the war, with more experience and better organization, the surgeons were able to give better and more prompt attention and assistance to those in need. But, no matter how well organized, no matter how attentive all are, on such occasions there are inevitable sufferings. At times it is impossible to furnish even a drink of water to the soldier, bravely trying to endure not only the torturing pain of his wounds, but also the hunger and thirst that can not be assuaged by the best will of the best friends. Such are the contingencies of the battle-field. During the battle and after it, as fast as our men dropped, they were seen first by the priest, at the request of the sufferer, and if his wound was fatal, the priest heard his confession on the spot,

---

* Just after the battle of Fair Oaks, I wished to send word home to Notre Dame. I had no paper, but, after much searching, I found an old envelope, which had no paste or mucilage to fasten it. I found a stamp, however, and on the inside of the envelope I wrote: "The battle is over, and we are safe." I sealed the letter by pasting the stamp on the laps of the envelope. This I addressed to my dear sister, who handed it to Very Rev. E. Sorin, then the President of Notre Dame. He was so pleased with the real war-like message that he had it read in public to the faculty and students of the university.

and then he was conveyed to a place called a hospital. The surgeons, assisted by their hospital stewards, worked, not "eight-hour labor," but night and day, from fifteen to twenty-four hours, according to circumstances.

Here let me say a word on the position of Catholic chaplains. All know that Catholics, when about to die especially, desire to become reconciled to God, not merely by contrition for sins, but also by the use of the Sacrament of Penance, which was instituted by our Blessed Saviour, who, when He instituted it, gave to His apostles and their successors a special power to be exercised in its administration. We find in St. Matthew (xvi.), Christ addressing Peter thus: "Whatsoever thou shalt bind on earth shall be bound in heaven; and whatsoever thou shalt loose on earth shall be loosed in heaven." And in St. John (xx.), Christ, speaking to all His disciples, says: "Receive ye the Holy Ghost; whose sins ye shall forgive, they are forgiven them." Now, the priests were not obliged to fight in the ranks; but, by reason of the functions of their office, especially regarding confession, they were found at hand when one of their men desired, or was in need of, immediate attention. While Father Dillon and I were riding close up, and the battle raging at the time, we met a thin, lank soldier, rushing out of the battle in a terribly frightened condition. He had no musket, no haversack, no "impediments of war" on his person. Father Dillon demanded, in rather an official tone:

" Where are you going, sir? "

" B-a-a-back."

" Are you wounded?

" N-n-no."

" Where is your musket? "

" L-o-o-st."

"Oh," said he, " do not send me back! I am not
wounded, but I'm fearfully demoralized! "

And indeed his appearance showed that. As he
passed rapidly back through the woods and brush,
he was losing, not only his courage, but also everything most useful to him, even his hat; and the brush
lifted his hair, which literally "stood on end."   His
hair was of a yellowish color and very much sun-
burned, and his face was absolutely colorless.   The
picture he presented would baffle the descriptive
powers of Charles Dickens. He looked worse than
" Sir John Falstaff," when he emerged from the River
Thames, into which he had been thrown, with the
soiled clothing, by " Mrs. Ford's " men. We knew it
was useless to send him back, and we had no time to
waste. As we passed on, he kept looking back with
nervous twitches, and he sloped to the rear quite as
badly demoralized as a half-drowned hen.   But, one
may ask, were you not afraid yourself? Yes, indeed,
but withal we could not help laughing. If there is
anything, even in the face of the greatest dangers,
that will cause a man to laugh, it is to see a coward
badly scared, so that all his manhood seems to ooze
from his toes and the tips of his fingers.

As I passed over to the left wing of our brigade, I came up with Gen. Meagher, who was constantly passing from one part of the brigade to another. Gen. Meagher's staff was known as a "brilliant staff." It was composed of gallant young officers, who were decked out not only with the regulation gold straps, stripes and cords on their coats, trousers, and hats, but they had also great Austrian knots of gold on their shoulders, besides numerous other ornamentations in gold, which glittered in the Virginia sun enough to dazzle one. With this crowd I rode along for some time. We could hear passing us the whiz and whir of occasional bullets; but, presently, the Confederates, being attracted by the general and his staff, and getting range of us, sent a perfect shower of bullets at us. They shot a little too high, and we passed unhurt. I confess that I was not sorry when I reached the north side of an old log house, and in the shade of this I attended to a poor, wounded soldier, who had been carried there by two of his companions a few moments before. While behind this building, a one-story structure, made of round logs, with the chinks filled with pine, split in triangular shape, and plastered over with Virginia mud, I could hear the bullets strike the roof, making a sound similar to that made by hailstones falling on a tin roof. The shingles of this roof were, by the way, of the old-fashioned kind — "hand-made." Large logs were first sawed into lengths of about two-and-one-half feet, and these were rived into flat forms, varying in thickness from one-half to three-fourths of an inch. They were rough, but strong; and the stronger, the better under the above circumstances. Having heard the confession of the poor man, his wounds were dressed by our faithful surgeon, Dr. Reynolds; but, in spite of all the attention bestowed on him, he died in a few hours. The history of this soldier is the history of thousands who fell on this bloody field on that day, in the memorable battle of Fair Oaks or Seven Pines.

The above allusion to some of the duties and positions of Catholic chaplains is made in answer to the question put to me a hundred times since the war, as to where the chaplains were and what they did during battles. I will have occasion to refer to this again later on. Many, too, have asked me about the hospitals and the care of the wounded. On this point I have found that most persons have a very erroneous conception of such institutions. As soon as a general engagement begins, the wounded are carried back from the front so far as it is possible to do so. Many poor fellows must lie where they fall for several hours, and, in some cases, even for several days. This is especially the case when one army drives back the other, and in turn is driven back itself, so that on the disputed ground between the two forces the wounded of both armies may be so situated that their comrades can not reach them until a flag of truce be sent over. It is not easy to do this, especially at night; and sometimes the fighting may begin so early on the following morning that there is no chance to do so. Want of transportation, also, often keeps them in the same position. When the conditions are favorable, the wounded are carried back, and the surgeons, with others in command, determine upon a place of safety, and here is located the hospital. Sometimes it may be in the shade of a straw-stack, if such a luxury is to be found within a reasonable distance. Sometimes they take advantage of a grove, where may be found at least shade from a broiling sun. Again, it may be in some old barn, and when it is possible to get wagons to the front, the hospital tents are erected. But temporarily, the wounded are placed in some improvised shelter, where the surgeons, under orders of higher officers, attend to them.

There were regimental, brigade, division, corps, and surgeon generals. A perfect system prevailed, each taking orders from a superior officer until the head was reached; or, in other words, orders came from the head, and were transmitted all along the line. In the hospitals the surgeons commenced at once to dress wounds, administer restoratives, in case of sinking spells, and, in cases of necessity, amputate feet, arms, or legs. When amputation had to be made (and this took place after every battle), the victim was placed on a table, or on some boards in that shape, chloroform was administered, then the knife and the saw made "short work" of a man's leg or arm. You might see outside the *quasi*-hospital, in one great pile, legs, arms, hands, and feet, covered with the fresh blood of the owners — a scene that would sicken most persons to such an extent as to make them hope never to see the like again. The picture can be compared with nothing but a butcher shop, or slaughter-house, where meat is cut and piled up. In many cases it was impossible to find a suitable place to locate a hospital — which occurred at this very battle of Fair Oaks — and the wounded were placed in old freight cars and sent to the rear. Dr. Ellis, who had charge of the wounded, thus describes a scene, which he reports in his book on the subject: "The rebels having destroyed the railroad bridge across the river, the cars were run down to the river side, filled with the wounded after the battle of Fair Oaks. It was here, lying around on the track as they had been taken out of the freight cars, that I found over three hundred wounded, many of them in a dying condition, and all of them more or less mutilated and still enveloped in their filthy and blood-stained clothing as they were found on the battle-field. In many instances, maggots were creeping out of their festering wounds." (Hist. Irish Brigade, page 159.)

These scenes I myself witnessed, not once, but many times. Great distress fills one's mind when obliged to behold such misery, with no possible means to apply an immediate remedy; but such are the fates of war. Whenever it was at all within the power of the doctors, every attention was given with tender devotedness, not only to the wounded Union soldiers, but also to such Confederate wounded as happened to fall into their hands. A young Confederate, who had been wounded, said to Dr. Laurence Reynolds: "The Irish fight like devils, but they are very kind in the hospital." The priests could not confine themselves to any one hospital; they had to pass from one to another—wherever there was to be found a dying man who stood in need of the sacraments. Those whose wounds were not fatal were sent as soon as possible back to the city or town, where they received special care till they were entirely cured and able to rejoin their regiments, unless they secured a "leave of absence" to visit their families for a specified time; this might be from thirty to sixty days. The entire loss on both sides, Union and Confederate, in the two days' battle of Fair Oaks, or Seven Pines, was put down at 12,520.

CHAPTER XI.

MALARIA IN THE CAMP.

AFTER the battle of Fair Oaks, the Union troops were intrenched in front of Richmond, and waited some time for the necessary bridge-building, and constantly in the hope of receiving the promised re-enforcements. From some tall pines on our front we had a view of Richmond. The grounds were low and marshy, and malaria soon set in among our troops. Not being accustomed to the intense heat of the South, the Northern Union men died by hundreds. The priests were kept busy attending not only the men of the Irish Brigade, but calls came from far and near for their services. I often rode over twenty miles on a sick call. Every now and then, you would hear a brass band playing—strange to say— the peaceful Christmas hymn *Adeste Fideles* in slow measures, and by this all knew that there was a funeral. The band, playing slowly as the procession passed on, marched to each fresh grave, accompanied by a squad of soldiers under command of an officer. The men carried their guns reversed and loaded

(80)

with blank cartridges, and over the grave of each departed comrade the requiem vollies were fired.

Short and few were the prayers we said. The ceremony was short, and all returned to camp till another funeral had to be attended. A repetition of this occurred several times every day, until the ranks of the Northern Union men were decimated. We remained in this pestiferous swamp a long time, and the longer troops continue in a camp, the greater, of necessity, is the accumulation of offal and filth. Every effort was made by the officers to keep the premises clean, but much time was required to get rid of horses killed in battle that had swollen to a monstrous size under the Southern sun, and filled the air with a sickening odor. To bury them was no small nor pleasing job; but as many as possible were burned—400, if my memory serves me. Every other means to promote cleanliness was taken, but the malaria was beyond control.

June 15, or thereabouts, the Catholic priests present, namely, Rev. James Dillon, C. S. C.; Rev. Thomas Ouellet, S. J.; Father Martin, of West Philadelphia, and the writer, held a meeting to discuss various theological questions pertaining to our ministry. We. were all furnished with faculties by the saintly Archbishop of Baltimore, Francis Patrick Kenrick, D. D.; but being far removed from Baltimore, with no telegraph communication at our disposal (the wires in use at the time were all military ones, and were used exclusively for war purposes), and having no access to

6

the Bishop of Richmond, in whose diocese we were, we could not get Episcopal approbation on several cases that might require such approbation, and we came together to decide upon the best plan to adopt, under the circumstances. Among other things, we decided to stand by each other in case of sickness, and in case of death by sickness, or by a bullet, each chaplain agreed to say two Masses for the one who fell first. Shortly after this, Rev. Father Martin, who was very much older than the rest of us, in fact too old for such life, was obliged to resign and return home. In the midst of this sickness, continually on the increase, called by some "camp fever," but in reality malaria, the surgeon-general ordered each soldier to be furnished with a small quantity of whisky and quinine, mixed, every morning before going on daily duty. The regiments were drawn up in line, by companies, and as each man's name was called out by the adjutant or sergeant he stepped forward one step, took his medicine, and then stepped back into the ranks in perfect order. Some refused the whisky, but took the quinine. The chaplains neglected to take either. June 17 I felt very queerly, and being usually very healthy, I complained to my friends, particularly to Father Dillon, Quartermaster McCormick, and to Capt. Moore, of New York. Wishing to keep up my courage, they said my trouble came from imagination, and that I was influenced by seeing so many sick and dying. I did not give up, but kept on my feet, and one day, on or about June 18, I reeled

and fell to the ground. Good Father Dillon got me
a leave of absence (as officers we were always subject
to military laws), and managed to take me to White
House Landing. Here we found a sutler, and from
him we procured a pine-apple. I ate a slice of this,
but could do no more. Father Dillon also obtained
a bottle of beef tea. I was put on board an army
steamer, bound for Washington. Father Dillon saw
that I was placed in a berth (on the "soft side of a
plank") on board, with my coat for a pillow. This
was as near luxury as could be reached. He gave the
bottle of beef tea to a negro servant to warm — that
is, the tea, not the bottle — and went on deck, where
he became engaged in an interesting conversation
with an officer, a friend of ours, about the late battles
and future prospects. When he looked at his watch,
some time after, he found that several hours had
passed since he left me, and he came down to see
how I was. I was where I had been put, still on my
favorite plank.

"Did the beef tea do you any good?" he asked.

I told him that I had seen no beef tea.

He hunted up the darkey, and asked him:

"What did you do with that beef tea?"

"O, Massa, I done put the bottle in the hot water,
and it went all to pieces!"

The darkey was scared out of a year's growth, but
this did me no good. There I lay with absolutely
no nourishment until I reached Washington next day,
and was landed in the hospital of the Sisters of

Charity, where everything was offered me, but I was then too weak to take anything except a little medicine. This was nobody's fault. Army steamers were vessels hired simply for transportation of men in the service, and they were not expected to furnish beds or provisions. It may seem egotistical for me to write so much about a little personal experience; for, after all, I was incomparably better off than thousands of poor soldiers who had not and could not get even the care I received. I write this, as I said in the early pages of this narrative, to give a page of " unwritten history." Histories dwell principally on the exciting scenes of the battle-field, which constitute but a small portion of the horrors of war, in my humble opinion. Both sides of the picture must be shown. It required nearly twenty-four hours to get me to Washington, and there, under the care of the good Sisters of Charity, who were attending my sick officers and men, I lay insensible with a burning fever for three days. Persons were placed to watch me day and night. Thanks to the good medical treatment and excellent care of the " angels of sick and wounded soldiers"—the Sisters—I soon recovered. Being removed in good time from the malarial camp, no doubt helped, else I might have fallen a victim with the thousands of others who perished in the swamps of the Chickahominy. This was the only sickness I experienced during the entire campaign of three years, starting from Camp California, near Alexandria, Va., in the spring of 1862, and winding up at Petersburg, **Va.** In that time I was not absent one month, all told, from my post in the army. Meantime, I accompanied my brigade night and day, in heat and cold, in sunshine and rain; marching and counter-marching in Virginia, Pennsylvania, and Maryland, hundreds if not thousands of miles. Poor Father Dillon, who so kindly assisted me in my sickness, contracted in that army the disease that carried him to an early grave in 1868, and he now sleeps within gun-shot of where I write these lines. I recovered strength rapidly and returned to my post in time to witness the disasters of the " Seven Days' Fight," during which McClellan made his masterly retreat—than which no greater is recorded in history.

CHAPTER XII.

THE " SEVEN DAYS' FIGHT."

THE "Seven Days' Fight" commenced June 25, 1862, and lasted until July 2. McClellan was compelled to swing around his right wing twenty miles from the "White House Landing" to the James River, forming the new base of operations. This manœuvre required masterly skill and was made necessary by the failure of McDowell to protect (as was intimated in a previous chapter) McClellan's right wing with his 40,000 men. Our base of supplies was in great danger, and it required a whole division to protect the same. In making this move in front of the watchful enemy, McClellan was, moreover, obliged to protect and control a great herd of fat cattle, an immense train of army wagons, ambulances, and artillery, stretching in one line fully forty miles, and all to pass over one narrow road. During the "Seven Days' Fight," the Union soldiers moved by night toward the James River and during the day fought like tigers. This retreat from the front of Richmond was necessarily attended with a great deal of hardship; for the fighting by day

and the marching by night well-nigh exhausted the
Union soldiers. Day and night the priests accompanied their men, hearing confessions and administering the sacraments as far as possible, especially to
those who were mortally wounded. This gave great
security to the minds of the Catholic soldiers.
Everything concerning this move was kept secret at
first, lest the Confederates, learning of McClellan's
intention, should pounce upon him before he could
put in motion his great train. The Confederates did
learn his plans, and forced him to battle; but much of
the work was already accomplished, although many
of us were not and could not be ready. When the
enemy struck our ranks, we were forced to save what
we could and let the rest go. Many trunks, tents,
etc., were simply abandoned. There was time only
to fight, and no possibility of securing transportation,
as all the army wagons must get out of the way and
move rapidly toward the James River, laden with
the absolute essentials of war—ammunition and provisions. Here we abandoned our large chapel tent, the
canvas of which had cost us over $500. Here I
lost my trunk, in which I had a small quantity of
clothing, a few books, and all the sermons I had ever
written. They were in manuscript form, and I am
sure no publisher would make his fortune by publishing them.

At the battle of Savage Station, in the course of
the "Seven Days' Fight," the Union troops were hard
pressed and thrown into confusion, and at this point

McClellan ordered up Meagher's Brigade, with that of General French, to repulse Jackson, who moved on our right in massed columns, determined to wedge in between us and the river. Had he accomplished this, he would probably have captured a large portion of the Army of the Potomac; and he was in a fair way to do so, when the green flag was unfurled to the breeze. A desperate charge was made, and the hitherto victorious Confederates retired before the intrepid advance of the Irish Brigade, gallantly assisted by the brigade of General French. Both brigades charged with most extraordinary courage and gained a very important point. McClellan, speaking of this afterward, said: "This gave an opportunity to rally our men behind the brigades of French and Meagher, and they again marched up the hill ready to repulse another attack." Moore, in his "Complete History of the Rebellion," speaking of this same battle, says: "The Irish regiments fought bravely, charging at times up to the cannon's mouth, and once dragging off a battery and spiking the guns." * (Chapter XXI, Page 213.) At this very critical point it may be said, with no great degree of boasting, that, owing to the well-known bravery of the Irish Brigade and the confidence which their reputation inspired in others, the Army of the Potomac was saved. Had not the Confederates received that timely repulse, they would have

* Here the Irish Brigade received a new name, and was called, in local circles, "The Irish Blockade."

succeeded in pressing between the Union army and the river and passing round in the rear of McClellan. Thus they could have prevented his reaching his new base of supplies, which was in a place of safety, protected by the soldiers on the gunboats, who had been instructed as to the part they were expected to perform.

I can not pass over at this point the well-known humorous and somewhat witty reply of Capt. O'Shea, of the Tammany regiment, under peculiar circumstances. The captain had received orders with his command to repair a broken bridge over the Chickahominy. One of McClellan's *aides* rode up, full of anxiety, and demanded:

" Who commands here? "

The captain, who stuttered considerably at times, replied:

" I-I-d-do."

" I want to know, sir, can artillery pass over? "

"Ye-yes, s-s-sir, if they are f-f-flying artil-l-lery!" —casting a glance over the broken bridge as he made the answer.

It very much astonished many brave soldiers in the Army of the Potomac to know how it was possible that the men and officers of the Irish Brigade could be so light-hearted under grave and trying circumstances; but it is a characteristic of a great people, of sound morality and manly achievements, thus in peril and in the face of death to give these tokens of cheerful heart and vigor of mind. While the Irish Brigade was making its desperate charge, an occurrence took place worthy of notice here. The first regiment ordered up to check Jackson was the Ninth Massachusetts, then under command· of Col. Cass. This was a well-known Irish regiment, and had for its chaplains, first Father Scully and later Father Egan. It fought against fearful odds, Jackson having about 20,000 men. Col. Cass was almost in despair, when suddenly he saw the rush of the Irish Brigade to assist, and he cried out to Gen. Meagher:

"Is this the Irish Brigade, general?"

"Yes, colonel, we are here!"

"Thank God," said the colonel, "we are saved!"

The colonel, so encouraged, made another dash with what men he had left; but he soon fell to fight no more — fell at the "post of honor." Many of our men dropped in death during that battle, on the ground occupied later by the Confederates, and as night came, fighting ceased. A part of the night was spent by the Confederates in burying their dead and also ours who fell into their hands; but before doing this they "stripped our dead." Southern historians apologize for this by saying that the Confederates were in rags and could not secure a supply of clothing "for love or money." Many dead bodies were removed to make room to build camp fires for cooking purposes, and in many cases the dying and dead were placed in the same pile. Without doubt, many not yet dead were buried alive, as we have reason to know from some who revived enough to protest, just as they were about to be placed in the pit. The usual way is not to dig a grave for each man, but a long pit about six and a half feet wide and deep enough to hold all the dead in the immediate vicinity. The bodies are placed side by side and on top of each other in the pit, which is then covered over much the same as farmers cover potatoes and roots to preserve them from the frost of winter; with this exception, however: the vegetables really get more tender care. First, they are piled up in cone shape, and clean straw is placed over them so that the clay covering shall not touch them; and the shape given to the top, like the roof of a house, sheds all the rain. In the spring the vegetables are found as dry as if they had been kept in a room heated by steam. Circumstances prevent such tenderness from being extended to the fallen hero, for the time being at least. Immediately after a battle, the commanding generals take active measures for the contingencies of the following morning. Consequently, mounted *aides* and orderlies are sent flying in every direction with orders and instructions to the subordinate officers. In rain or cold, light or darkness, that might vie with that of his Satanic Majesty's kingdom, these devoted men dash off, and in the discharge of their duties often, unwillingly, trample on the dead and dying, who may be lying where they fell, on top of each other, the grey and the blue together. But what is worse, even the army wagons, and especially the ambulances, have often, in their hurry and rush, passed their heavy wheels over the dead bodies, and not infrequently over the bodies of men still tenaciously clinging to life in their prostrate and helpless condition. This is not an overdrawn picture, but one witnessed by hundreds of us during many battles.

As we retired, in our well-ordered retreat, toward our new position on the James River, we were obliged to abandon all our wounded who were not able to walk or to get transportation. All the ambulances were very soon full. Wounded men crawled on to army wagons; others hobbled along, their wounds still undressed, and from loss of blood becoming all the while weaker and fainter. Many held on till their last breath, to avoid capture and to be with their companions. From the wounded in the ambulances, from those clinging on to the rear ends of the army wagons, and from those limping along on foot, blood was dropping along the road, and thus the blood of heroes marked our way as the march continued to a position more suitable for a systematic and obstinate contest. On July 1, 1862, the Union soldiers reached their vantage ground on Malvern Hill, where a determined stand was taken by them. This battle was one of great carnage, and desperately fought by both armies. The Irish Brigade did its share during the day and expected that its day's task was done, when, at seven o'clock in the evening, it was found that Couch and Porter were hard pressed. Dr. James Moore, in his history (Chap. XXI, p. 216), thus describes the assistance rendered by Meagher's and Sickles' brigades:

"The brigades of Meagher and Sickles were sent to relieve the brave but exhausted troops of Couch, who had expended all their ammunition. These re-enforcements at this critical moment advanced upon the enemy, who recoiled. The tide of battle was rolled back." The battle ended with great losses on both sides, but the Confederates were completely routed. They gave up the conflict entirely and fell back, followed by the Union troops, and becoming, in their flight for safety, very much demoralized. Some think that McClellan should have followed the Confederates and captured Richmond, but there are conflicting opinions on the subject. The Army of the Potomac crowned the seventh day with a grand triumph—but our poor dead! We, the chaplains, had not the sad consolation of helping most of them to die well, neither had we an opportunity of seeing them consigned to their gory graves. Our heroic brigade left 700 of its bravest officers and men on the bloody fields behind; nearly every one of them Catholics, and we may almost say none without having shortly before received the sacraments. Let us hope that they met a favorable trial before the dread Judgment Seat; that their hardships, thirst, hunger, and the blood flowing from their painful, mortal wounds, cried for pardon for past sins, and found a favorable echo in the Sacred Wounds of a benign Saviour, who had shed the last drop of His blood for the salvation of their precious souls. We leave them, as a tear drops to their memory, to meet, we hope, in the Kingdom of Peace.

CHAPTER XIII.

THE "Seven Days' Fight" was over, and we were able to get a much-desired rest of mind and body, situated as we were, in a beautiful camp at Harrison's Landing on the banks of the James River. The Army of the Potomac reached this point July 2, 1862. Having left behind us the miserable swamps of the Chickahominy, where so much sickness prevailed, and where, as we have seen, many graves were made, we enjoyed beyond expression the new, clean camp, fresh water, sufficiently abundant for all purposes, and other conveniences, so much needed after fighting seven days and marching seven nights consecutively. The camp lay for miles and miles along the beautiful James River. Industry took possession of every soldier and officer, and each vied with his neighbor in beautifying his canvas house and immediate surroundings. By this time army life had grown upon us, and we felt more at home in it as we became more experienced in making ourselves comparatively comfortable. Our men were detailed by turns to build and construct lines of defense—trenches, breastworks, abatis, etc. Others were employed in making streets, policing the camp, and much time was given to dress parades, regimental and company drills. In this way time did not hang heavily on the soldiers so as to make them dull, uneasy, and discontented. After the day's work, the camp-fires were greatly enjoyed, and around them were many scenes of interest. At these fires were recounted tales of the bravery of companions who fell in the late terrific contests; the touching sight of James trying to save his wounded brother from the grasp of the enemy was described, or when Thomas fell, it was told how tenderly he spoke of his mother. It was a notable fact that most of the brave, good soldiers, expiring from the effects of gaping wounds, almost invariably mentioned most affectionately the one dearest to their hearts at that moment of sore distress, namely, the loved mother; while all devout Catholics called on the Queen of all mothers, Mary, Mother of Jesus, to assist them, by her most powerful intercession, to die well. This has been my experience and that of hundreds of others.

I remember, among innumerable escapes from death almost miraculous, a few which we frequently talked over by these camp-fires at Harrison's Landing. One was this: A young man, leaving Brooklyn, N. Y., received from his good mother a prayer-book. It was not bulky, but just the shape and size which could be easily carried in the vest pocket. The mother, full of solicitude for the life of her son's soul, even more than for that of his body, made him promise to say a few prayers every day out of this dear little book. It is not known that he did so every day, but it is known that he carried it in an inside pocket near his heart. In the battle of Malvern Hill a bullet struck the book in the center, passed through a portion of it, then glanced off without injuring the man in the least. This book was treasured ever after as a precious relic. Another soldier, from Philadelphia, wore the five scapulars given him by his kind sister. A bullet struck the scapulars on his breast and would have pierced his body had not the five thicknesses of the scapulars diverted its course. Hundreds of such instances could be told, and were told, over and over, at the camp-fires.

Good brass bands in the camp lent a most agreeable service. While the soldiers enjoyed their campfire chats, the bands were playing at various points and gave a romantic charm to the situation. Picture to yourself thousands of white tents among beautiful green trees, with the fires glimmering here and there for miles over an extended plain, furnishing light and comfort to over a hundred thousand armed men, while darkness gently spreads its mantle over all. As the hours creep into the night, the camp-fires show to more advantage, especially when you can imagine how the scene is animated by varied conversations — some droll and witty, some grave and touching, many concerning the great, sublime future.   In this you have a faint picture of our camp at night.

Here we spent about one month very profitably employed. Our new base of supplies was excellent, and we received a quantity of fresh food; we even got bread—real bread—in place of "hard-tack." Besides this, the soldiers were dressed in new suits, and everything was very clean. This was a good preparation for the hardship and privations that were to follow, as we shall see later on in this narrative.

Discipline in the army is very strict, especially in active campaigns. Soldiers were punished in various ways, according to the nature of the fault. Officers, too, came under the rule. For mean, unmanly acts— flagrant acts of immorality, and the like—hanging was generally the punishment. Military crimes, such as deserting the army when in front of the enemy, and especially passing over to the enemy, were punished by shooting; for murder, also, men were shot. Officers who openly disobeyed legitimate orders were tried by court-martial, and if the charge was proved against them, they were cashiered. Crimes of less gravity, in the eyes of military men, such as going out of camp without a pass, failure to perform certain tasks which had been assigned, giving insulting answers to officers, not keeping clean, not keeping guns and other military articles in perfect order, drunkenness, etc., were punished by imprisonment in the "guard-house," and in various other ways, as seemed best to those in command. These punishments were determined according to the frequency of the offence, and were

7

increased in severity when the individual concerned
showed a very incorrigible disposition. Sometimes
"drumming out of the army" was resorted to. My
attention was attracted one day to a scene, to me,
altogether novel. I saw at some distance our corps,
of perhaps fifteen or twenty thousand, manœuvring;
and, mounting my horse, started to see what was up.
The troops were forming into a hollow square, two
deep. Presently I saw two men, preceded by fifes
and drums, playing the "Rogue's March," and behind
them two soldiers with fixed bayonets pointed at
their backs. These men, who were private soldiers,
had one-half of their heads shaved close, and were
obliged to pass bareheaded within two feet of all
the soldiers in the ranks facing the hollow square.
Having passed entirely around the inside line of the
troops, they were expelled from the army in disgrace for all time. This is what is termed "drumming men out of the army." Their crime was, to
have been found dead-beats, or worthless as soldiers.
"Dead-beat," is the worst term that can be applied
to a soldier. It is a generic term, implying everything worthless and mean. Besides this, they had
been found guilty of theft. In all probability, they
had enlisted for that very purpose, at least so it was
alleged at the time, by those who knew them. I give
this instance now, and make reference to disciplinary
matters, because as I proceed with this narrative I
will have occasion to give an account, in the order of
occurrence, of some of these army customs and laws
put into actual practice.

CHAPTER XIV.

A "MILITARY MASS."

WE will now turn to the chaplains and see how they passed their time; but, first, let me say a word on the " Military Mass." Information on this subject has been frequently asked of me. It was not often we could celebrate Holy Mass with suitable or inspiring ceremonies. A first-class " Military Mass " is one celebrated in the ordinary solemn form, according to the rubrics; but the surroundings cause it to be styled by many a "Military Mass." First, it is in camp. Imagine the entire camp, the " church tent," and the great avenue leading to this tent lined on either side with green trees — put down for the occasion—all decorated with fresh branches, flags and other military emblems — a preparation like that made for a triumphal entry into a city. The congregation is composed exclusively of officers and soldiers, "rank and file," each one armed as for dress parade. The officers carry dress swords suspended from their belts, and wear the full insignia of their office. The cavalry men carry their heavy sabres in the same way, and on their boots the well-known

(99)

formidable spurs that rattle and click at every motion
of the foot. The infantry soldier, dressed in his
tidy uniform, carries his shining musket surmounted
by its sharp, glittering bayonet, that strikes terror
into the heart of the enemy when a desperate charge
is made by the intrepid men of arms. A military
signal, either by drum or bugle, is given at the
proper time, and orders are passed along the line to
" Fall in!" Once in ranks, all the regiments march
under orders of their respective officers to the
" church tent." As a result of careful drilling by
very intelligent officers, the movements are perfectly
regular and precise, and form a very pleasing sight.
The officers are justly proud of their men, while the
men are equally proud of their gentlemanly officers.
On they move, keeping step and time to the music, till
they reach the " church tent." Here the priests, vested
in rich silk vestments embroidered with gold and
artistic needle-work, begin Holy Mass, in presence of
the several thousand men and officers on whose bright,
neat uniforms the gold ornaments sparkle in the sunlight, while dress swords, many of them diamond
hilted, make a pleasing contrast to burnished sabre
and polished steel bayonet.

Here we have no organ on the " tented plain," nor
the shadow of a lady to supply the parts of alto, con-
tralto, mezzo-soprano, or soprano. All is stern manhood wrought up to its highest tension of honor and
duty; duty to fellowmen, duty to country, duty to
family and kindred; but, above all, duty to the great

God seated on the rock of ages directing the destinies of all nations. The music consists of the stirring, martial strains of the infantry and marine bands. During the more solemn parts of the Mass the soldiers " present arms " — an act of the highest respect — while outside, at the time of the Consecration (if we are not in the presence of the enemy), cannons boom in various directions; going forth like thunder in the heavens, to represent, as it were, the voice of God, or at least to speak of the presence of Him who rules from above, amid the crash of nations. Thus we see how God is served, even in camp. We behold the highest honors paid to Him by the solemn offering of the Holy Sacrifice, infinitely holier than that offered in the Temple of Solomon, amid the splendor of glittering gold and the flashing light of precious stones. No military equipage is too fine, no military honors too great, no music too sweet or too sublime, no respect too profound, in honor of the great God in the transcendent Mystery of His love and mercy — a Mystery offered on Mount Calvary, when Nature herself spoke in greatest reverence and covered her face in darkness, to hide it from the too great majesty of the Divine Being. The earth quaked in holy fear, rocks were rent in testimony of the Creator completing the sacrifice for the redemption of the world. Nature gave what men refused — testimony of Him who lifted rocks and mountains to embrace the clouds of heaven, and who spread out the mighty waters of the deep. This is more than I

intended to say on this point, but it is so in harmony
with the subject that has occupied the place of the
"Old Law," ever since its establishment, 1829 years
before our ministry in the army, I could scarcely say
less. When we chaplains could have a "Military Mass"
we were glad; but, as a rule, even on Sundays, the
Mass was less brilliant, in point of ceremonies, than
the one mentioned above. During the week we said
Holy Mass early in the morning, and through the
day said our office, attended sick calls, instructed
converts, and heard confessions, especially in the
evenings. Thus the time of comparative tranquillity,
for the space of about a month, was spent in preparation for the contingencies of the future, for days
ahead full of fatigue, hardships, and dangers to soul
and body.

CHAPTER XV.

OUR long rest of a little over a month was at an
end. It was well-timed, considering the work
before us. On August 16 and 17, 1862, the entire
Army of the Potomac was in motion. All we knew
at the time was that orders had come to march, and
we marched. Just where we were going, how long we
should be on the road, we could not know. McClellan,
general-in-chief, and perhaps a few major-generals,
knew, but no others. This was necessary, else the
Confederates might discover all about our movements,
and thwart our designs. It turned out that we were
ordered to help Pope, who boasted he knew no retreat.
Bad for him! A good retreat, when necessity requires,
is incomparably better than an injudicious advance,
and at times requires more skill — so say experienced
military men. We passed down the peninsula, com-
mencing our march on August 16, at eight in the
morning. We marched about eighteen miles that
day, and having crossed the Chickahominy River,
bivouacked for the night. This river widens out very

much toward its mouth. So, the ponton-bridge, on which all the infantry, artillery, etc., crossed, was over one thousand feet long, supported by 100 ponton-boats. A ponton, or pontoon, is used expressly for this purpose. The name is derived from the Latin, *pons*— a bridge. Pontons are made as light as possible, low and flat like a mud raft, and are not infrequently a simple frame with canvas bottom. These pontons are placed in lines parallel to the bank of the river, about ten feet apart, and then planked. This is quickly done by the pioneer corps. Leaving camp at Harrison's Landing, as I have said, we knew nothing of our destination, and I made no provision for the march, which proved to be one of seven days. We passed down the peninsula by Williamsburg and Yorktown to Newport News, where we took shipping for the Potomac once more The first day I got on pretty well. Col. Baker, my *compagnon de voyage*, had a small box of sardines, and I had a loaf of bread. We ate the bread freely, but, having an eye to economy, we were careful to take very small portions of the sardines each meal. The colonel said to me: "This reminds me of a story. A poor scholar, as such were called in Europe, very anxious to get an education, boarded here and there with poor but charitable people of the neighborhood. At one of these places the milk supply was short, and the good woman of the house said to the poor scholar: 'Now, Willie, you must take a big bite and a small sup.'" A good laugh followed, as we were then putting this very

principle into practice. As far as possible, we looked
on the bright side of all our privations, and, in fact,
this is the best way after all. When a man can keep
in good spirits, hardships do not prey on him. However, in spite of this philosophy, before we reached
our journey's end, both of us, and many others in our
condition, felt pretty *blue*. The first day the colonel
and I made our ·breakfast, dinner, and supper—six
meals—on one loaf of bread and a small box of
sardines, leaving nothing for the following day. Next
morning, after sleeping on the ground, we arose to
continue our march. We started without even a cup
of coffee. Riding on horse-back, in the fresh air,
gives one a fine appetite; but in our case it was the
worse for us. When noon came, we were almost
fainting with hunger. The men got their coffee and
" hard-tack " dinner, and Col. Baker and I slept a
little under the shade of a tree. After an hour's rest,
we marched on until we encamped for the night —
still very hungry and no food. The road for the most
part was through a "second growth" of pine, which
literally made a wall on either side. The ground
was dry, and the passage of the artillery, cavalry, and
infantry worked the road-bed into dust fully three
inches deep.

The soil of that country is clay, which makes
a very fine dust that penetrates everything. The
colonel and I rode along at the head of our regiment,
having other regiments before and behind us. The
dust was stirred up both by the feet of the soldiers

and those of the horses, and became so dense that it resembled, in a certain sense, a very heavy fog. Seated on my horse, I could not distinguish one man from another six feet ahead of me. Our hair, beards, and clothes were literally full of dust. In fact, we were all dust, and for anything we could see, were going back to the "dust from which we came." Add to this situation of hunger and dust, the terrible heat of the Southern sun in the middle of August, pouring down on our dusty heads as we passed along this road, walled in, as I have said, by the young pines growing as thick as "the hair on a dog's back," leaving no chance for a breeze to reach us. Thus suffocating from heat and dust, faint from hunger and thirst, we moved on, becoming more and more indifferent to past, present, and future. Next morning, the third day, we continued our journey, still fasting. When we had been on the way about two hours, a drummer-boy, belonging to our brigade, named Brinkworth, a real character, came galloping up to where the colonel and I were moving along. I gave him a few dollars and told him to try to purchase some food for us. As he was fearless in dashing here and there through the country, I knew he would have an opportunity for doing so. The morning passed on, and about ten o'clock inspiration moved a soldier, who noticed we had nothing to eat, to bring a small piece of raw pork and a "hard-tack" to each of us. As we have seen elsewhere, the men carried rations, but they were on foot, and delicacy would not allow us to ask any of these poor men to give us a part of their hard-earned stores, since we were on horseback and they were walking, loaded down with rations, musket, ammunition, etc. Even the raw pork and "hard-tack," which we accepted, tasted sweet, and we were very thankful for the kindness. We had lost so many meals, this bite only gave us appetite for more. As we moved on, we discussed the ups and downs of life. In the evening we encamped for the night early, to give time for the heavy wagons to get out of our way. We found a nice, grassy spot near the road, and, as the sun was descending, the shade of a large wild cherry tree presented a lovely place to rest; and, like Jonas under his miraculous ivy, we did so. A strange confidence took possession of my mind, and I said to Col. Baker:

" We shall soon get relief."

"Oh, no!" said he, "that reckless Brinkworth went too far, and is captured by the Confederates."

"Well," said I, "we will soon see."

I felt certain that the boy would return. The colonel had no confidence in the seemingly idle proposition. He took off his coat, and placed it on the grass for a pillow, saying as he did so: "I will sleep off the hunger." I said nothing more. In about twenty minutes our brave Brinkworth came galloping on his old horse, as he did in the morning, and the poor animal was loaded with purchases made by the adventurous youth. He had two chickens, a sack of biscuits, and a sack of apples. No time was lost in getting these things ready, and a first-class repast — a real picnic — was very soon laid out on the green grass. We ate all we wished, and carefully took up the fragments for future needs — as the apostles were instructed to do by our Saviour, after the multiplication of the loaves and fishes. That night some fat cattle and some commissary stores reached the camp. Good supplies of fresh meat and other provisions were furnished to the soldiers, while the officers purchased what they stood in need of. Col. Baker and I did not fail to profit by the experience of the past few days. We laid in a good supply of necessaries for the remainder of the journey to Newport News. After we arrived there, it took considerable time to get ships ready and to load them with the freight belonging to our brigade. This gave us time to refresh ourselves after the long, dusty march. On the road we could have no Mass, no public services of any kind. I managed to say my office daily during the three years spent in active campaigns, excepting a few days when it was absolutely impossible. I said it on horseback during short intervals, when meals were being prepared, and even at night, after sick calls and other duties had been attended to. We had no lamps, no gas, no electric lights; but I always had a few candles with me, and by using a bayonet for a candle-stick, thrusting the point into the ground, managed pretty well.

CHAPTER XVI.

FEAT OF "JACK GASSON"—THE BATTLE OF ANTIETAM.

EN passant, I must tell an anecdote of Capt. John J. Gasson, or "Jack Gasson," as he was familiarly called by his companion officers. He was the first *aide-de-camp* of Gen. Meagher. Gen. Meagher was not with us at the time, and I suppose "Jack," being his first *aide*, thought it eminently proper that he should do something desperate to show his courage and to save the nation. We read in the history of Rome that "an earthquake opened a great gulf in the forum, and the augurs declared that it would never close till the most precious things in Rome were thrown into it. Marcus Curtius arrayed himself in complete armor, mounted his horse, and leaped into the chasm, declaring that nothing was truly more precious than patriotism and military virtue." "The gulf," say the historians, "closed immediately upon him, and he was seen no more." While we were encamped on the banks of the York River, "Jack," in presence of the entire camp, mounted his horse, and, putting spurs

to the animal, dashed down the bank, which was
almost perpendicular and nearly one hundred feet in
height. Horse and rider tumbled over each other
till the bottom was reached, and, strange to say,
neither was killed. He must certainly have had it in
his mind that no Roman could out-do " Jack Gasson,"
a wild Irishman. He was perfectly fearless. " What
man can dare, I dare," was his motto. No wonder
the Confederates would cry out when they beheld
the green flag: " Here comes that d—— green flag
again." They knew the undaunted courage of the
race, and had tested the same more than once. Withal,
these . very men were religious, and like children in
church.

We had some leisure time before starting on the
transports for our destination, and I announced that
several days had passed without Mass. At once the
good men went to work building an altar. That
evening many went to confession. I celebrated Mass
next morning at a very early hour, and those who
were ready received Holy Communion. We then
took shipping at Newport News for Aquia Creek,
under orders to report to Gen. Burnside at Falmouth,
on the Rappahannock River, opposite Fredericksburg.
After landing at Aquia Creek, we went by rail to
Falmouth, where we remained only a short time. At
this time, Pope, with a large army, was conducting a
campaign which resulted in disaster to the Federal
troops. Great confusion existed, and we were ordered
back to Alexandria, our old camping ground which

we left in 1862. We had scarcely time to have food prepared, when orders came to march to Arlington Heights, opposite Washington, thence on to support Gen. Pope, camping at Tenallytown. Major-Gen. McClellan was now, by necessity, put in command, not only of his own troops from the Peninsula, but also of all those left after the battles fought under Gen. Pope. Lee determined to carry the war into Maryland, and made plans to capture Harper's Ferry. This strong position was most disgracefully surrendered by Col. Miles, who commanded there, giving up 47 cannons, 7,500 small arms, 40,000 rounds of ammunition, 50 rounds of canister-shot, six days' rations for 12,000 men, and 11,583 men and officers, on September 15, 1862. We had made forced marches through Maryland from Tenallytown, and, on our way, passed through Frederic, Md. Father Ouellet, S. J., and myself stopped at the Jesuits' residence in that city, where we got, what the boys called, "a square meal," then passed on hurriedly, with many kind wishes and hearty prayers from our hospitable hosts. Most of us knew nothing of the disaster about to take place at Harper's Ferry. Our brave Gen. McClellan overtook the Confederates at South Mountain, on September 14, 1862, and badly worsted them. It became our turn to lead the army next day. We were in advance of all, and, as we dashed along, following the retreating Confederate forces, we saw, on every side, men and horses, dead and dying. I dismounted occasionally, and

when I found men still living, did what I could for
them. If Catholics, I heard their confessions, and
if Protestants, baptized them, as individual cases
required. . Following up a routed and retreating
army is very exciting. The men seemed to be wild
in their pursuit of the Confederates. Finally we
came up to Antietam. This stream empties, not
very far from where we were, into the Potomac
River. Here Lee took a stand. On September
16, 1862, no great fighting was done, except a
fearful cannon duel. Next morning, September
17, the battle opened. The Confederates outnum-
bered McClellan's force, and, besides, they had
the choice of position. Our brigade received orders
to go in " double quick," that is, on a full run.
I gave rein to my horse and let him go at full
gallop till I reached the front of the brigade, and,
passing along the line, told the men to make an Act
of Contrition. As they were coming toward me,
" double quick," I had time only to wheel my horse
for an instant toward them and gave my poor men a
hasty absolution, and rode on with Gen. Meagher
into the battle. In twenty or thirty minutes after
this absolution, 506 of these very men lay on the field,
either dead or seriously wounded. Gen. Meagher's
horse, a beautiful bright bay, was shot under him,
and also the horse of the notorious Jack Gasson. I
shall never forget how wicked the whiz of the enemy's
bullets seemed as we advanced into that battle. As
soon as my men began to fall, I dismounted and

began to hear their confessions on the spot. It was then I felt the danger even more than when dashing into battle. Every instant bullets whizzed past my head, any one of which, if it had struck me, would have been sufficient to leave me dead on the spot, with many of my brave soldiers, as the bullets came from the Confederates at very close range. All the wounded of our brigade, numbering hundreds, were carried to a large straw-stack, which had to answer for a hospital. Here they had dry straw at least; but during the day, as all could not get into the shadow of the stack, the hot sun made it very uncomfortable for them. Here I saw one poor man with a bullet in his forehead, and his brains protruding from the hole made by the ball. Strange to say, he lived three days, but was speechless and deaf, and had lost his senses entirely. I attended another, a well-built man, in the full vigor of manhood, and about thirty years of age. A ball had passed directly through his body. He lived but two days, and died in great agony.

McClellan defeated the Confederates, who sustained a terrible loss, and then marched on and took possession of Harper's Ferry. I remained behind several days with the wounded. The next day after the battle I had a small hut erected near the straw-stack, celebrated Mass, and gave Holy Communion to all who were prepared. In doing so, I was obliged to carry it to them, as they lay here and there on the straw, unable to move — stepping over some, and walking around others. Those ready to receive were

8

pointed out by a good soldier, or each made a sign for himself. Those who died were buried on the field, and the wounded were removed to the city, where they could be more easily cared for. A glance over this battle-field—that will ever occupy a prominent page in the history of our nation—shows that the battle was a terrible one in more than one sense. First, 500 pieces of artillery were engaged, and, counting both sides, about one hundred and seventy thousand men. Had the Confederates been success-ful—as they would have been if opposed by a less skilful general than McClellan—it is hard to say what would have been the result. The field presented a sickening sight the day after the battle—on September 18, 1862. Meagher's brigade did its duty as a military body, and received the highest commendation from Gen. McClellan—and from many historians since. Gen. McClellan, in a long report of its charge and other action during the battle, says, among many other words of praise: "The Irish Brigade sustained its well-earned reputation."

Having passed several days in doing all that I could for the wounded men, finding my services no longer required, I moved on to join my command at Harper's Ferry. Father Dillon was not with me at this battle—he had been sick, and was absent on a sick leave,—but joined us at Harper's Ferry. A new regiment, the gallant One Hundred and Sixteenth Pennsylvania (to our great joy) was added to our brigade. With this regiment came a chaplain fresh for active service, and in excellent spirits. He was all new. He had a new horse, new trappings, new ideas. He was anxious to try his horse, to accustom himself to horseback riding, so that on future marches he would be at home in the saddle. Consequently, he proposed to take a ride to Chambersburg, about twenty-two miles from where we were encamped. Fathers Costello, D. D. (pastor of Harper's Ferry), Dillon, Ouellet, S. J., and the writer, started early in the morning, as we must return the same day. The new chaplain dashed off in front of us, and was very brave. We were veterans, already inured to the business, and knew how to save ourselves. We returned at seven the same evening, having made forty-four miles. Next morning, our new chaplain was very sore, and he seemed to be convinced that his saddle was made of iron, with the hard side up, and that his horse did not run easy. A conviction also grew on him that riding forty-four miles in one day, to try a new horse, a new saddle, and a new rider, did not accord with the ideas he had formed from reading about "prancing steeds, richly caparisoned war horses." He kept his bed for three weeks, while the horse rested and grew fat, and he arose an older and wiser, if not a sounder man. Dr. Costello had some experience in riding; but he, too, although he did not acknowledge it, was pretty sore after the ride. Fathers Ouellet, Dillon, and the writer, were as fresh the morning after, as when we started; in fact, we could have repeated, without the least inconvenience, the same journey that day, with fresh horses.

CHAPTER XVII.

THE CAMP AT HARPER'S FERRY—BANQUET, RECONNAISSANCE, ETC.

OUR camp was a charming one, located on Bolivar Heights, the grounds very clean and kept in perfect order. The country around us was delightful in the variety of its scenery. Harper's Ferry is justly celebrated for its romantic beauty. It is situated at the confluence of the Shenandoah and Potomac, the Potomac being the boundary between Maryland and Virginia. Here both streams cut their way through the Blue Ridge, or, rather, the mountain of rock seems to have split in two and receded, and now stands off in dignified silence to let the roaring waters pass. The outline of the mountains is very bold; huge rocks, hundreds of feet in height, hanging with a most threatening aspect over the roads at the edge of the water. The junction of the Shenandoah and the Potomac divides the Blue Ridge in such a way that the mountain is fashioned into very fantastic shapes, forming lofty peaks and craggy walls of rock that rival the mountains of Switzerland in rugged grandeur. Here the bugler

delighted us by sounding clear notes which rever-
berated through the gulches of the mountains for
miles and brought back echoes the most perfect we
had ever heard. It was simply charming. While
we listened, late in the calm evening, seated around
our camp fires, a pathetic feeling crept over us, each
dwelling on his own thoughts, which, for the time,
were all the company he desired. First came flashing through our minds the poor dead companions we
had left behind in their cold graves at Antietam.
Then, as the scene of the late terrible conflict faded
from our minds, while still under the fascinating
charm of the clear bugle notes, we found ourselves
wandering back, year by year, to our very childhood,
playing once more with our dear sisters and brothers
under the shadow of the paternal roof. All the
vicissitudes of life passed in review before our minds,
and occasionally, as the bugle tones died softly in the
distant hollows of the mountains, we naturally dwelt
on the unknown but sublime scenes of the future.
Finally, conversation inspired by such feelings had
more than an ordinary interest. Only late into the
night, by an unspoken, common consent, we retired,
with hearts full of emotion, and brains somewhat
tired from too much thinking, as we " turned in,"
each on his favorite plank, to dream of " home and
mother." Some had no mother on earth to dream
about; but, piercing the clouds and vaults of heaven,
could contemplate the most glowing of all scenes,
since there, for all, was " home and mother." Very

vividly do these reflections and dreams recur to me. They left a deep impression on my mind. Harper's Ferry is between fifty and sixty miles above Washington on the Potomac, and before the war the place had a population of two or three thousand. It was also the seat of an important arsenal and armory. John Brown made himself famous by the capture of these works, with a view to liberating the slaves of the South, and was hanged December 2, 1861. As we were in easy communication with Washington, many persons came to visit relatives in the army. Among our visitors were distinguished ladies, the wives of our officers. There I had the pleasure of meeting the wife of Gen. Thomas Francis Meagher, a lady of marked character and possessed of more than an ordinary degree of refinement and excellent social virtues. She was a devout convert to the Catholic Church, and was highly respected by the army officers, many of whom had known her and her family in New York long before the war. Here, also, for the first time, I met the venerable Dr. Brownson. Finally, the President, Abraham Lincoln, came and reviewed the entire army. The camp was like a city, where nearly everyone knew his neighbor, and each must be introduced to visiting friends and partake of the good things brought in abundance. At Gen. Meagher's headquarters a sumptuous banquet was given, at which many famous officers, with their wives, were present. Among them was the gallant Gen. Hancock. Our esteemed Division Commander,

Gen. Richardson, of Michigan, was not there. We had left him in a country house near Antietam, where he had received his mortal wound. Dr. Costello, Fathers Dillon, Ouellet, McKey, and the writer were present, and on this occasion we made up in part for the privations of the past. The following Sunday, Dr. Costello, pastor of Harper's Ferry, invited as many as his church could accommodate, and we assisted at Mass. After Mass the same party, as on the previous Thursday at Gen. Meagher's banquet, partook of a bountiful dinner with the pastor. So the time passed, very pleasantly and agreeably, and the much-needed rest served to recruit the strength expended in the long marches of the campaign we had passed through, not to speak of the racking excitement of the battles with their bloody scenes of death.

It may be noted here that we left the Peninsula on August 17, 1862, and were constantly in motion till we reached Harper's Ferry, September 23. Counting marches and countermarches, we had passed over six hundred miles when we arrived at our camp on Bolivar Heights, after the battle of Antietam. The reader may see from this how badly the jaded troops were in need of rest. In the early part of October, 1862, our brigade was ordered out on a reconnaissance. We started early in the morning, passed around the foot of the mountain, and marched through a beautiful valley. The weather was then cool enough to be pleasant. The valley was rolling, and every now and then we reached elevated ground, enabling us to overlook a landscape, than which I never saw finer. The fields were fresh and green, and the persimmon trees were loaded with their tempting fruit. The pine trees were in groups, and as we looked from the hill-tops we could see these grouped trees exactly resembling islands in a vast body of water. On we went until four in the evening, when we halted near a place called Charleston, and waited for further orders. There, on the slope of a beautiful hill dotted with trees, the men took dinner. The evening before our departure from camp my orderly put into my saddle-bags a chicken which he had bought and cooked for me. But nothing else did he put in—not even salt, or bread. Riding all day, in the bracing air, had given me an excellent appetite. I let my horse eat grass, and having found the chicken, from which nothing had been cut except one "hind leg," I proceeded to make the most of the situation. I ate the chicken, and when I reached camp at eleven that night I got some bread. The axiom, *fames est optimum condimentum*—"hunger is the best sauce," was put to a practical test. I greatly relished the chicken, although I had nothing to eat with it. We spent a few weeks profitably at Harper's Ferry. Reconnaissances, followed by skirmishes, were kept up in various directions. These, it seems, were designed, and were necessary to find out the movements, strength, and ultimate designs of the Confederates. More than four weeks passed in this way. About this time Father James Dillon was transferred to the command under Gen. Corcoran, and located for some time at Suffolk, Va. Father McKey remained with us until we reached the Rappahannock, when he resigned — being forced to do so by sickness. The hardships of the march from Harper's Ferry completely prostrated him. This left only two priests, where there had been four for a short time. The remaining two were Father Ouellet, S. J., and the writer.

CHAPTER XVIII.

AN ARMY EXECUTION.

ONE day, shortly before noon, one of my men came to my tent, and said to me: "Father, there is to be an execution this afternoon."

"How do you know?" I asked.

"I was over to see a friend in the next brigade, and met an orderly coming from headquarters, who told me all about it," he replied.

It is a strange fact that men in the ranks frequently had more news than any of us. Those carrying orders, called orderlies, might, perhaps, be afraid to communicate news to officers, while they would tell, in confidence, companion soldiers what they knew, or what they had heard this or that general say.

I asked the soldier: "Where is the man who is to be executed?"

"He is under guard, at division headquarters."

The soldier who told me was God's angel. I felt from that moment a great desire to see the condemned man. It was raining; but, no matter, I started. I was soon wet through, and my feet were very wet; but, not stopping to think of this, I went directly to the general, asked about the man — who he was, and what he was.

"Indeed," said the general, "all I know about him is that he deserted to the enemy, was tried by court-martial, and he is sentenced to be shot."

But he courteously volunteered to send one of his staff officers with me, who would secure the interview I desired with the poor man. After a short time, I was presented to the condemned soldier, whom I found to be a young man of German descent — born in this country. I asked him if any minister attended him.

"Yes," said he, "but he is gone to dinner."

I decided to do nothing final in the absence of the minister, since he was attending by official request. In the meantime, I questioned the young man (who was not more than nineteen) about religious matters, and found him very ignorant on those points. In fact, he had never given much attention to religion, and even his parents — as I afterward learned — were equally careless. But, as he was about to die, matters looked serious to him — though he did not seem to realize fully the situation. I asked him if he had ever been baptized, and he answered no. His parents had told him that he might choose for himself, when he saw fit. He had never joined any particular Church; but his parents were, as near as he could tell, members of the Methodist Episcopal Church. When I found him so ignorant of Christian teaching, I took a wide range, and asked him if he believed in God.

"Oh, yes," he said.

"Do you believe in Christ, and that He died to redeem the world?"

"Yes."

"Do you believe in the Holy Trinity?"—and a number of similar general questions.

I feared that by not understanding my questions, if put too deep, he would say that he did not believe some vital point. Finally, I said to him: "If you knew that Christ wished you to be a Christian, and to be baptized a Catholic, would you comply with His wish?"

"Yes," said he, "I have not much time to live now, and want to do all I can to please God."

At this time the minister came along, and as one of the guards saw him at a distance, he said: "Boots is coming!"

I asked the guard whom he intended to designate by that name

He said: "It's the minister that 'tends this man."

"Well," said I, "do you not consider it a mark of disrespect to call your minister by such a name?"

"Oh, no; they all do it."

I had never met the minister before, and when he came in, I told him who I was, and why I came; namely, to see if anything I could do would be acceptable in the case. He did not say much, but talked a little about faith. Then, turning to the

young man, whose name was Adam, he said: "Adam,
do you believe you will be saved?"

" Y-e-s," said Adam, falteringly.

"I sincerely hope you will; I do most sincerely
hope you will," said the minister.

This was the lesson he taught the young man,
and the only one; namely, to believe. During his
remarks, I was revolving in my mind what was best
to be done. I ventured to state that I had learned
from the young man that he had not been baptized.
The minister was a very tall gentleman, had very
long legs, and wore correspondingly long boots.
This circumstance made the boots look conspicuous,
because, though the gentleman was tall, he had
a short body. Hence the irreverent called him
"Boots." He had a squeaky voice, and in reply to my
allusion to baptism, said, in his peculiar hard tone:
"Well, there is not much time now;" and again,
turning to Adam, asked: "Adam, do you believe
you will be saved?"

" Y-e-a-s," said Adam.

" I hope it will be so; I do, I do," said the minister.

"Now," said I, "as we have but little time, I think
we should act promptly about this question. Not
only do Catholics believe baptism necessary, but
most other Christians do likewise."

"Well," said he, in a still higher key than before,
"I do not know what your Church teaches, but our
Church teaches that all that is necessary is to be
baptized in the Holy Ghost. I will go and see the

general, and learn what time the execution is to take place."

While he was gone, I determined what to say to him on his return. In a few minutes he entered, announcing that the hour was fixed for one o'clock p. m., sharp.

"Then," I said, "we have but half an hour, as it is half-past twelve o'clock now—and I made this proposition: "If baptism will do the young man no good, in your estimation, it will certainly do him no harm; therefore, if you have no objection, I will baptize him."

He could not refuse. Having no time to risk, I sent for some water immediately, and baptized the young man. I said to him: "Now, you are a Christian; offer your life to God in union with the sufferings of Christ on the cross," and a few other exhortations. For the first time I noticed a genuine softening in his disposition, as the light of faith, secured to him by the sacrament, seemed to show in his countenance. He had only a few moments to live, and when the squad of armed men came to escort him to death, he went out as coolly as if he were going to dinner. Eight or ten thousand troops were drawn up in a hollow square, with one end of the square vacant. The condemned man was placed at that end. A squad of twelve men, with muskets loaded by one of the sergeants, came forward. According to rule, the sergeant puts no ball in one of the guns, and no one of the soldiers knows whether his gun has a ball in it or not. The twelve soldiers, under the command of an officer, stood in front of the condemned man. The sentence was read and the provost-marshal drew a cap over the man's eyes. Then the officer gave the stern commands: "Get ready, aim, fire!" Eleven bullets struck the young man; still he was not dead. The provost-marshal was obliged to use his own revolver, to put him out of pain. Scenes like this jarred my nerves much more than a battle. And now, when more than a quarter of a century has passed since this took place, it causes a shuddering sensation to think of it; still more to write all the circumstances of such a dreadful spectacle.

CHAPTER XIX.

THE IRISH BRIGADE AT FREDERICKSBURG.

IT may be understood that, for the sake of order and interest, I follow, in my narrative, our line of march in an unbroken and consecutive manner. I also give the exact dates for each principal occurrence. In the last chapter, however, I anticipated a little by referring to the march from Harper's Ferry to the Rappahannock River. Let us now go back and start from Harper's Ferry. On November 1, we had our last solemn service there, and on November 2, 1862, general orders came, and all the troops were put in motion. We passed out of the camp at Harper's Ferry, took the east side of the Blue Ridge, and marched toward Warrenton. The weather was exceedingly fine, and the valley through which we passed was a veritable prairie. Nothing of importance occurred on our way during the first few days. The two great generals, McClellan and Lee, seemed to be watching each other's movements, and learning each other's designs by sending out skirmishing expeditions. On November 2, a sharp fight took place at Snicker's Gap. The same occurred at

Ashby's Gap on the 3d. Thoroughfare Gap was occupied on the 3d by Gen. Sigel. It is well known that military men attach great importance to such positions—passes or gaps through mountains. On November 5, while at Warrenton, Va., an order came from Washington relieving Gen. McClellan and placing in his stead Gen. Burnside. This created great excitement and the deepest possible regret on the part of officers and men. Many of the officers resigned on the spot. The generals waited on McClellan and expressed their esteem for him in the most flattering terms. Finally, he obeyed, like a true soldier, and passed the command over to Burnside, saying simply as he did so: "Well, Burnside, I turn the command over to you." He passed through the troops who were in lines on either side of the road, and as he went by, the wildest excitement prevailed. Salutes were fired and he was heartily cheered. When he boarded the train which was to take him to Washington, the soldiers uncoupled the car, rolled it back, and seemed determined not to let him go. He spoke to them and restored order by telling them that they must always obey lawful authority. Poor Burnside deserves credit for accepting the command under compulsion, declaring and confessing his inability to replace McClellan.

When we started from Harper's Ferry, as usual, we knew nothing about our destination. At Warrenton, Burnside, doubtless by advice from Washington, changed the plans made by McClellan. We were

9

marched on and on till we found ourselves back on
the north bank of the Rappahannock, where we
stopped for a short time before going to Maryland,
prior to the battles of South Mountain and Antietam.
And, late in November, we were back again. The
Irish Brigade was ordered over the river by Gen.
Sumner to explore the situation, and, finding a battery in position, captured two of the guns and drew
them away by hand in short order. Gen. Hancock
said: "Gen. Meagher, I never saw anything so
splendid."

Before going farther, I would say a word on our
position. We camped at Falmouth, on the north
bank of the Rappahannock, opposite Fredericksburg.
The ground here is elevated. Looking across the
river, we saw the city, and immediately behind the
city the hills rising in terraces, in the form of a semi-
circle, as if made by nature for a most impregnable
position. It was now getting late in the season, and
we set about fixing our habitation for the winter —
thinking, of course, that we were there to stay. We
settled down in earnest; built log huts, roofed them
with tents, and built chimneys of sticks and mud—for
there was plenty of mud. Streets, walks, and other
conveniences were constructed. Father Ouellet, S. J.,
and I appointed regular times for Mass, sermons,
and other religious duties. In the meantime, the
Confederates massed on the hills behind the city, on
the south of the Rappahannock, built breastworks,
and got all their heavy artillery in the best possible

positions. To complete their work they had over three weeks. On December 10, the gallant Seventh Michigan — under a withering fire from the opposite side — constructed a ponton-bridge, gaining thereby the admiration of the entire army. This one daring deed was enough to give national glory to the troops of Michigan. One of my men, hearing the rumor, came to me, and said: "Father, they are going to lead us over in front of those guns which we have seen them placing, unhindered, for the past three weeks."

I answered him: "Do not trouble yourself; your generals know better than that."

But, to our great surprise, the poor soldier was right. On December 12, we were ordered to move; marched to the banks of the river, and the men rested on their arms all that night, ready to move at a moment's notice in the morning. During the day it snowed, and the ground was covered. I got on a small brush-heap, made by one of the men, to keep myself out of the mud and soft, wet snow. There, in the open air — in company with my poor men — I spent the night. They did not know what a fearful fate awaited them next day. On the morning of December 13, we crossed the ponton-bridges. Cheers were heard as we were going on, and some said: "It may be our last cry." We were formed into line of battle, and ordered up in front, with absolutely no protection for our ranks. As we advanced, our men simply melted away before the grape and canister, and the tens of thousands of muskets, well protected behind the carefully constructed breastworks. Gen. Meagher advised every soldier of the brigade to put a sprig of box-wood in his cap, so that he could be identified as a member of the brigade should he fall. These men were found dead near the cannon's mouth, on Mary's Heights. A correspondent of the London *Times*, observing the battle from the hilltop, said: "Never, at Fontenoy, Albuera, or Waterloo, was a more undaunted courage displayed by the sons of Erin than during those six frantic dashes which they directed against the almost impregnable position of the foe."

But the place into which Meagher's brigade was sent was simply a slaughter-pen. I have heard many blame Meagher for taking his brigade into this pen; but such persons do not know what they criticise. Gen. Meagher and his brigade simply obeyed the orders of superior officers, and went in at the time and place assigned them. Had Gen. Meagher disobeyed such legitimate orders, he would have been liable to be cashiered, and thus have disgraced himself and his race for all future time. Needless to say, our brigade was cut to pieces. Many were seriously wounded, and recovered later on, but for the time we had only the remnant of a brigade. I saw one of the officers, Lieut. O'Brien, of the Eighty-eighth, shot in the neck, the ball coming out near the jugular vein. When he tried to eat a piece of ginger-bread it partly came out through the hole made by the ball. Strange to say, he recovered. This fact is recorded for the benefit of medical science. Just as the remnant of our brigade came out of action, Capt. Sullivan and I were talking in a street of Fredericksburg, and congratulating each other that a few escaped even without a wound. He left me to pass across the street, and as he reached the center — ten feet from where we had been talking — a cannon ball came down the street and struck him about four inches above the knee, and cut away his leg. I heard his confession at once, as I knew he could not live. He was carried to the rear, and all that could be done by the faithful surgeons was done; but he died that night. This was the experience of hundreds.

CHAPTER XX.

THE battle of Fredericksburg took place, as we have seen, on Saturday, December 13. That night Gen. Burnside withdrew and recrossed the Rappahannock. This left most of our wounded on the bloody battlefield where they fell, and where they lay all night with undressed wounds and no food or drink. Col. St. Clair Mulholland, since brevetted Major-General, was one of the number. Next day, Sunday, both armies were engaged in collecting the wounded and burying the dead. After returning from the battlefield we found a temporary shelter on the north side of the river, where we spent some time in caring for such of the wounded as had been saved from the battlefield; then we tried to rest a few hours. When I said Mass in the morning, I had a very small congregation compared with former ones. After Mass the day was given to visiting the wounded, who were transferred as soon as possible to the rear, where the Sanitary Commission did good, noble, charitable work, attending to the wants of the suffering, feeding them luxuriously and binding up their wounds. All of us were sad, very sad. After a few days we were settled down in the same quarters which we had occupied before going into the battle of Fredericksburg. Now, for certain, we thought we were in winter quarters to stay. To our surprise, we were soon called to enter another campaign. The mud was so deep that the impossibility of moving an army at that season was soon demonstrated. After the heavy rains, cannons went down so deep, it was said, that "the spots were marked where they had disappeared, so that they could be dug out in dry weather." Other tales, illustrating the situation, were told. One of them I remember: "A man was going along on the edge of a forest, when, looking out into the so-called road where troops had passed, he saw a hat in a great mud-hole. He reached out for it, and discovered a head under it. 'Why, what are you doing there?' he cried out. The man in the mud answered: 'I am looking for my horse; he is somewhere below.'"

We spent the winter in that very camp. Gen. Meagher went to New York to recruit the brigade. While he was there a solemn Requiem Mass was celebrated for those of the brigade who fell during the campaign of 1862, and especially for those slaughtered at Fredericksburg. The Mass was celebrated in St. Patrick's Cathedral, and Rev. Father Ouellet, S. J., who had resigned the service, was the celebrant. During the winter, the regular routine work of camp life occupied the soldiers. Mass was celebrated daily, confessions heard, and the sick administered to. One day an orderly came for me to go about six miles, to attend an officer of a Michigan regiment. His name was Lieut. John O'Callighan. Frequently I was called in this way to distant parts of the army, where there were no Catholic chaplains, and my life, in this respect, much resembled that of a priest in charge of a parish. Later on, after a rain, frost covered the ground with ice. Gen. Meagher, having returned from New York, spent some of his time riding around among the soldiers' camps, accompanied by his staff. While returning one day from one of these rides, our brave Capt. "Jack" Gasson thought it proper to do something to break the monotony. So, dashing off in his usual style, his horse slipped, fell, and threw "Jack" violently on the hard, frozen ground—where he lay senseless. Gen. Meagher sent for me, and I hastened to see "Jack," as the officer who came for me assured me that "Jack" was finished at last. When I reached him, "Jack" had so far recovered as to give evident signs that he was not going to die just then. He had received no vital injury, but his collar-bone was broken, and he had several painful wounds. My great surprise was to find him lamenting, not his wounds nor the danger of life, but that he had fallen on level ground. If it had been going over a stone wall or down a precipice fifty or a hundred feet, there would have been some glory in it; but to be broken up, and perhaps killed, on level ground was ignominy he could not endure. How would such an unworthy action sound in history? What would his New York and European friends say? He thought they would drop his name from the roll of chivalric knighthood forever!

Here we close the year 1862. During this year, the Army of the Potomac had passed through all the well-known battles of the Peninsula — South Mountain and Antietam, in Maryland, not to mention many, many skirmishes — winding up with the memorable battle of Fredericksburg. To do this, the army had moved over not less than fourteen hundred miles, and the poor men had to carry with them a load equal to at least fifty-seven pounds. History records deeds accomplished during 1862 which were features of warfare unknown in this or past generations.

CHAPTER XXI.

OUR winter quarters at Falmouth resembled a large town. Visitors, friends, and relatives of the officers and soldiers, came from New York, New Jersey, Philadelphia, Boston, and elsewhere. A constant coming and going was kept up. Happily, we were also so situated that we could get all the necessaries of life. Those of our number who had been wounded at the battle of Fredericksburg returned as soon as they were able. They came not willingly, but in one sense, readily and cheerfully. They wished to see and chat with their old comrades over the late battle scenes, to find out how many were killed, how many were wounded, and how many still stood in the ranks of the brigade. Occasionally, a squad came and brought much news from home and messages from relatives to those in camp. They thoroughly canvassed the past history of the war, and future prospects. In a word, our camp-fires were places of great interest for three months. Besides the wounded, now perfectly recovered, many fresh recruits came into our ranks, and swelled our number considerably. It

(138)

was very amusing to watch this raw material listen—
with open-mouthed astonishment—to the war stories
told by their veteran companions, who, strange to
say, were not always satisfied with telling the naked
truth, which was certainly harrowing and startling
enough, but did not scruple to heighten the coloring
to satiate the morbid desire of their new companions,
who wished to learn all about real war-life.

Several days previous to St. Patrick's Day preparations were made for its worthy celebration; for
St. Patrick's Day, with the Irish race, is one of
enthusiastic devotion. For on this day is honored
the "Apostle of Ireland," who brought the light of
the Gospel to the whole nation, and turned a pagan
country into one thoroughly Christian. The words of
the prophet may be applied here most appropriately:
"The people that walked in darkness have seen
great light; to them that dwell in the region of the
shadow of death, light is risen." No nation on the
face of the earth has shown greater appreciation
of such a great blessing. Consequently, St. Patrick
is honored as the instrument in the hands of God
in conferring this inestimable favor. He is honored
as a saint, and gratitude to him is unbounded, since
his mission was so blessed that it lifted the entire
nation to the highest standard of Christian virtue,
so as to deserve for it in justice the title of "The
Island of Saints." Looked on as a Christian nation,
it is no wonder that St. Patrick's Day became a kind
of national holiday, and a day of general rejoicing.

It is not easy for strangers to understand why we
show such great love and veneration for St. Patrick,
without taking into consideration the above circumstances. Hence, although not an ecclesiastical holiday, on which no servile work may be done, still the
day is commemorated by the Irish race wherever its
sons and daughters are to be found. Gen. Meagher,
surrounded by a very intelligent body of officers and
men, "brave and true," made elaborate plans for the
celebration of this day, March, 1863. They recognized it first, and above all, as a day of devotion and
thanksgiving to God for the gift of faith and means
of salvation. The primary object in the programme
was a "Military Mass"—of which I have given an idea
in chapter XIV. Gen. Meagher had a consultation
with me as to what I would require, and gave me a
large detail of men, under a commissioned officer,
to construct a rustic church. The church we built
in the following manner: Posts, about fifteen feet
long, were cut in the pine forest, and planted in the
ground two feet apart. Along the tops of these were
fastened beams, on which the rafters rested. This
was the skeleton. Then the upright poles, two feet
apart, were interwoven, basket-like, with green pine
branches, and in the same way the roof was formed.
Such a roof would of course not keep out rain; but,
fortunately, none fell that day. It kept out the
sunbeams effectually, however, and the inside was
very cool and pleasant. For seats, crotchets were
planted in the ground, and standing up about eighteen

inches. Large poles were laid in the crotchets, and on these sat the officers and men — much the same as men sometimes perch on a rail fence. For the general officers and distinguished guests there were placed, in front, all the camp stools that could be found in that portion of the army. An altar was also constructed and tastefully decorated with evergreens. When the whole was finished it presented a really delightful picture, and was in fine contrast with the surrounding white tents, the green and white making a pleasing effect. A beautiful vestment of water-colored silk, richly embroidered with gold, was presented to me by the officers and men of the brigade and was worn for the first time on this occasion. It is worthy of remark that this vestment, first used over a quarter of a century ago, is kept on exhibition by Prof. James F. Edwards, in the "Bishop's Memorial Hall," at Notre Dame University. At eight o'clock, after breakfast, the most distinguished guests arrived, and the brigade having formed ranks under orders, men and officers marched to the rustic church. The day previous I had secured other priests to assist me, and at my request, good Father O'Hagan, S. J., of the Excelsior Brigade, preached, and I celebrated the solemn service of the day. Gen. Meagher, who was well instructed in his religion, directed the military bands when and how to play during the Mass. Gen. Hooker, commander-in-chief, and many other distinguished officers were present. After Mass, Gen. Meagher, accompanied by his staff, brought Mrs. Col. Van Schaick and other ladies to visit our rustic church, which was quite a curiosity, and also to inspect the beautiful vestment which looked so grand in camp. The contrast with its surroundings seemed to make it ten times finer than it would have appeared elsewhere. I mention Mrs. Van Schaick in a special way, because she was the wife of a nobleman from Europe, who entered the army simply for the experience to be gained in practical warfare. She was a practical Catholic, a brave woman, and could ride almost as well as her gallant husband. Thus the day's celebration was devoutly opened, as it should be; and perhaps few congregations on that day assisted at divine service with greater piety, many saying to themselves, "It may be"—as it really was for many —"the last St. Patrick's Day we shall live to see."

After the morning's religious devotions came the sports. A general invitation had been sent to all the officers of the Army of the Potomac, and all that could come did so. Maj.-Gen. Hooker, then commander-in-chief of the army, was present with his staff. It was estimated at the time that fully twenty thousand participated in, or at least witnessed, the sports of the day. The novel and daring nature of the celebration "took" with all the soldiers. It was, indeed, so brilliant and creditable that I heard distinguished soldiers claim that their grandmothers or grandfathers were Irish. Ever after the fame of Bull Run, no soldier was ashamed to be an Irishman

in the Army of the Potomac, and, especially on this
occasion, when everything connected with the celebration was so soldierly—we might say chivalrous.
Well-described, the scene would outshine the grandest
pageants related of the most gallant knights of
Ivanhoe. Many festive celebrations had I seen before,
but this surpassed my wildest fancy. The very exciting race most graphically depicted in " Ben Hur"
between the hero, Ben Hur, and his rival, Messala,
would seem tame in comparison. On those plains in
Virginia, you might find, not one, but hundreds of
the character of Ben Hur, educated, handsome,
fashioned after the noblest type of manhood, spirited
and brave as any knight that ever stood in armor.
They were equally ready to dash into the smoke of
battle and up to the cannon's mouth, or ride a steeple-
chase, such as was noticed in chapter VIII. of this
narrative. This feat is full of hazard and perils of the
most startling nature. A great stand, built for the
occasion, was occupied by the judges of the various
feats. Of course the major-generals were there too.
Many soldiers and line officers were under and
around the stage, and when Gen. Meagher rode
round, as director of the whole movement, he cried
out, as he neared the stage, which possibly might
not have been too strong:

"Stand from under! If that stage gives way, you
will be crushed by four tons of major-generals."

Those who were to enter the steeple-chase assembled in the uniforms prescribed, and no one rode

except commissioned officers. Over the vast plain
could be seen the thousands who assembled to witness
the day's doings, riding backward and forward, dashing over fences, fallen trees, streams, and ditches.
When you met them, you could see fire flash from
their eyes, exhibiting the wild impatience of the
ancient Greeks waiting for the gates to open on the
Olympian games. Conspicuous among the riders, I
noticed Col. Van Schaick and his accomplished wife.
Other ladies, also, rode with their husbands, with
grace and creditable skill; but, as Col. Van Schaick
came into view in full gallop, his horse springing over
every obstacle, Mrs. Van Schaick, well-mounted, came
at the side of her husband with a clever fearlessness
which proved that, though not competing, she deserved
a prize among the first. While admiring the husband and wife, one could easily discern that both
had had much experience in that kind of exercise.
Finally, the sports commenced, and they far surpassed the expectations of the multitude. This kind
of pastime became very popular in the army ever
after. Under the extensive bower, constructed of
pine branches, at headquarters, lunch was served at
one o'clock. Ham sandwiches, lemonade and other
delicacies were prepared there, and probably not less
than fifteen hundred partook of the generous hospitality of Gen. Meagher and the Irish Brigade.
Our famous Capt. Jack Gasson was in his glory all
that day. What an appropriate hero he would have
made for a novel on knight-errantry! Although he

was spoken of in a familiar way as " Capt. Jack," he was a high-toned gentleman and a gallant soldier. He was courteous enough to attend a king. The participants in the various sports of the day covered themselves with glory and drew the admiration of the entire Army of the Potomac.

10

CHAPTER XXII.

COLLECTION MADE IN THE BRIGADE FOR THE POOR IN IRELAND.

IT will be remembered by many that in the spring of 1863 the papers were filled with reports of the suffering poor in Ireland. We had passed the winter in comparative comfort—we had all the substantial food we wanted, no very hard marching, and no fighting. We saw the papers very regularly, even if we had to pay a high price for them. Every day we were expecting orders to march; to open a new campaign, which, of course, meant a new series of hardships, privations, and battles. Before starting, we resolved to do some act of charity, that the Lord might remember us in our own days of distress. A collection was proposed for the poor in Ireland. As soon as it was announced, one Sunday at divine service, the officers and men showed their love for their brethren " down in the land of bondage," and the following article, copied from the New York *Freeman's Journal*, of May, 1863, shows the result. Many of those who contributed have passed to their reward; but our Lord remembers their act of charity even to this day. The names of all, as far as possible, were given and are once more presented in print as a reminiscence of the war. Perhaps some of the sons and daughters of these brave men may rejoice to read the names of their fathers in connection with this act of charity.

RELIEF FOR THE POOR OF IRELAND.

CAMP OF THE IRISH BRIGADE, NEAR FALMOUTH, VA.,
MAY 25, 1863.

To His Grace the Most Rev. Archbishop of New York:

YOUR GRACE:—I take the liberty of inclosing to you the sum of $1,240.50, being a contribution of a portion of the officers and men of two regiments of this brigade and the Ninety-fourth N. Y. V., to the fund now being raised for the relief of the suffering poor in Ireland.

In thus intruding on your kindness, and requesting you to be the medium of transmitting to the proper authorities this handsome contribution from the gallant men of the brigade, I need scarcely remind Your Grace that the amount would have been far greater had not our ranks been so terribly thinned by death, wounds, and sickness consequent on the arduous campaign of the past fourteen months. Still, with that noble charity and love of country, which has, and I hope ever will, characterize the Irish emigrant in America, the remaining few of the Irish Brigade have spontaneously, and without any concert of action, come forward to contribute their mite to the general subscription, and that, too, when I have reason to know that over $35,000 were, after last pay day, sent to their wives and children in New York, Boston, Philadelphia, and other parts of the country.

When I reflect on the hardships and dangers of a soldier's life, the temptations to extravagance which beset his path, and the hardening effect of constant exposure to the perils of the field of battle, I can not help congratulating myself (as their chaplain) and their countrymen at home and abroad on the spirit of generosity and true piety which is exhibited among the men of this brigade.

I may mention, in conclusion, that the Sixty-ninth Regiment of the brigade are following the good example of the other regiments, and in a very short time I expect to have the pleasure of intruding again on Your Grace's kindness, by forwarding that regiment's contribution also. Had the subscription been set on foot at the proper time, I have no doubt that this regiment would have contributed an amount commensurate with its well-recognized gallantry. I also understand that one company of the Twenty-eighth Massachusetts Regiment of Volunteers has forwarded its contribution to Boston.

Annexed is the list of contributors, the publication of which, I have no hesitation in saying, will afford pleasure to the Irish people at home and abroad.

I am, Your Grace's very obedient servant,

WM. CORBY, C. S. C., chaplain with brigade.

THE IRISH BRIGADE.

LIST OF SUBSCRIBERS IN THE SIXTY-THIRD REGIMENT.

Lieut.-Col. R. C. Bently, Quartermaster James J. McCormick, $10 each.

Company B.—Capt. Gleason, Lieut. Carroll, $10 each; Sergts. P. Sheridan, W. Hally, Private P. Kenny, $5 each;——Terry, $3; Sergts. John Hayes, Owen Tumalty, J. Bergan, $2 each; Sergts. P. Hickman, E. Gallagher, M. Daily, T. Kelly, J. Dacy, $1 each.

Company C.—P. Duncan, $5 ; J. Martin, J. Granfield, M. Kelly, M. McGraw, J. O'Connor, B. Tausey, A. Linn, W. Hadigan, $1 each; P. McCharm, $2.

Company D.—Sergts. T. Duffy, J. McMichael, Privates J. Casey, J. O'Meara, J. Caldwell, P. Darley, J. Rattigan, $1 each.

Company E.—Capt. W. Quirk, $20 ; Sergts. W. Cullen, McQuade, O'Connell, Meagher, Privates Thomas Hughes, Jas. Reynolds, Timothy O'Neil, Christopher Madden, Edward

O'Brien, Michael Hanlon, $5 each; Sergts. Shehan, Thos. Hannon, $3 each; Corporal Looner, Privates John Harris, Wm. Hayes, Wm. Watson, Chas. Dodd, Henry C. Church, Thomas Ryan, $2 each.

Company I.—Capt. Thomas Touhy, Lieut. J. J. Hurley, $10 each; Lieut. John J. Sellers, Sergt. Thos. Joyce, Corporals Thos. Kelly, Pat McGeehan, John O'Brien, $5 each; Sergts. Jas. Dwyer, Patrick McCarthy, Hugh Meehan, Jas. Ganey, $1 each; Michael Moore, $3; Dennis Sullivan, John Smart, $2 each.

Company K.—Capt. John Dwyer, $10; Lieut. Matthew Hart, $12; John Cochlan, $5; Jos. J. Elliott, John Murray, $3 each; Michael Sheehan, Thos. Rutledge, Daniel Lynch, $2 each; Jas. Elliott, $1.

Sutler's Department.—James Coleman, $25; Joseph McDonough, Albert Root, Michael Roddy, $10 each; Bernard Carreher, Richard Roach, $5 each; James Smith, $2.

Recapitulation.—Field Officers, $20; Company B, $50; Company C, $15; Company D, $7; Company E, $80; Company I, $56; Company K, $40; Sutler's Department, $67; A Friend, $10. Total, $355.00.

EIGHTY-EIGHTH REGIMENT.

Col. Patrick Kelly, Surgeon Richard Powell, A Friend, $20 each.

Company A.—Capt. Gallagher, Sutler D. Renshaw, Wm. J. O'Connor, John Sparks, James Kane, Wm. O'Connor, $10 each; Wm. Foley, J. Cleary, M. Daly, J. Martin, Elias Boyer (Company F, One Hundred and Forty-eighth Pennsylvania), James Cooney (Company F, One Hundred and Twenty-fourth N.Y.V.), $5 each; J. Shandly, L. Friery, J. McNally, A. Clark, $3 each; P. Dean, J. Farrel, J. Kennedy, J. McBridge, M. McDonald, F. Lenehan, Joseph O'Harra, P. Quinlan, Jas. O'Connor (Company H, Ninth N. Y. S. M.), $2 each; T. Crystal, J. Ledwich, P. Meehan, H. Smith, T. Reilly, $1 each.

Company B.—Michael Reynolds, $10; Geo. Geoghan, John Webster, Patrick O'Neil, John Keegan, Richard Tinnen, Martin Concannon, $5 each; Patrick Sexton, Thomas Reilly, Patrick Croghan, John Carver, H. Polster, John Fitzgibbon, $2 each; Austin Everson, Geo. Funk, John McDonnell, $1 each.

150   MEMOIRS OF CHAPLAIN LIFE.

Company C.—Capt. Dennis F. Burke, $20; Sergts. Benedict J. Driscoll, John Desmond, Private Charles Joyce, $5 each; Sergts. James Fox, Richard E. Harrison, Corporal Mark Ternan, Privates Jas. Toban, Michael Larkin, Bernard McNally, Daniel Leary, James White, John Wallace, A Friend, $1 each; John Brady, 50 cents; John Cade, Thos. Tuomy, $3 each; Michael Linehan, $4; Wm. J. Walsh, $2.

Company D.—Ross McDonald, Edward Johnson, Thos. Sheridan, D. Alton, $2 each; John McGowan, Patrick Tracy, Patrick O'Brien, Henry Blake, Hugh Burns, Daniel Lenighan, Lawrence McAuliffe, $1 each; Dennis Kelly, $3.

Company E.—Capt. Thos. McN. O'Brien, $20; Sergt. George Ford, Private Thos. Lynch, $5 each; Sergt. John Morton, Private Michael Hyde, $2 each; Sergt. Herr, Corporal Jas. Greene, Privates Alexander McKenna, Michael Hayden, John Noonan, Wm. Flanigan, Bernard Woods, Matthew English, James Smitz, $1 each; Sergt. Jos. Hyland, $3.

Company F.—Sergts. Jas. Carr, Patrick Hagan, Privates Jas. Flaherty, Wm. Henry, Cornelius O'Brien, Jas. Rolland, $2 each; Sergt. Patrick McNamara, Privates Pierce Butler, Michael Geary, Timothy McGlynn, $3 each; Sergt. Jas. Shea, $2; Privates Jos. Dwyer, John Ahearn, John McFadden, $1 each.

Company G. — Capt. Michael Egan, $10 ; Sergt. Thos. Smith, $5; Sergts. Lawrence Buckly, Jas. Birmingham, Corporals Wm. Coyle, John Gallaghan, John Walsh, $2 each; Sergts. Thomas Roach, Wm. O'Neil, Thos. Cahill, Francis Kirnan, Hugh McCormick, Joseph Lardener, John Monahan, Martin Fallon, $1 each; John Kilcoyne, $3.

Company H.—Capt. Maurice W. Wall, Assistant Acting Adjutant-General, $20; Hospital Steward Richard Dowdall, $10; Sergts. John Meighan, Robert W. Gordon, $5 each; Sergts. Jas. Sweeny, Wm. Burke, $3 each; Corporal Geo. Hamilton, Patrick Connolly, Patrick Drew, John Small, $2 each; Jas. Nevin, Jas. McCarthy, Patrick McKenna, John O'Donnell, John Groves, John McConnell, Hugh Leahy, Joseph Daily, $1 each.

Company I.—Lieut. Patrick Ryder, $20; Sergts. M. McGrane, D. Leonard, T. McDonald, Corporal T. Berry, Privates J. Curyan, Wm. Rodgers, Patrick Smith, Sutler's Clerks

William Hastings, Chas. Salmon, John Cusick, John Canton, Aneas Walker, $5 each; Sergt. T. Murray, $10; J. O'Connor, J. Marion, $3 each; P. Condon, N. Carroll, M. Hogan, M. Hoey, J. Keifer, John Kane, M. Lynn, J. McGowan, D. O'Keefe, P. Ryan, M. Sullivan, Joseph Scott, Samuel Mitchel, $1 each; Wm. Keating, Thos. Radford, M. Graham, John Ferry, $2 each; Jas. Roe, $13.

Company K.—Lieut. Thos. O'Brien, $20; Lieut. John Madigan, John Shea, $10 each; Sergts. Southwell, Patrick Healy, Corporals Timothy Doheny, Owen Hughes, $5 each ; Sergts. Hugh Curry, Corporals John Dalton, Cornelius Ahearn, Privates Jas. Dillon, Joseph Devereux, John Foley, Wm. J. Brown, Jas. Maher, Wm. Maher, Patrick Shehan, Garrett Roach, Patrick Murray, Alex. McCain, Peter Kellegher, John Hardyman, $2 each; Edward Burke, Owen Reilly, Patrick Murphy, Wm. F. Tighe, Jeremiah Crowley, Owen Philbon, Michael Carroll, John Farmer, Patrick Eagan, Thos. Trainor, $1 each; Company C, Twenty-eighth Massachusetts, per Capt. Hatton, in command of company, $31.

Recapitulation. — Field Officers, $60; Company A, $128; Company B, $55; Company C, $57.50; Company D, $18; Company E, $46; Company F, $47; Company G, $37; Company H, $62; Company I, $130; Company K, $100 ; Twenty-eighth Massachusetts, Company C, $31. Total, $771.50.

CHAPTER XXIII.

INCIDENTS AND REFLECTIONS.

TIME is passing rapidly now, and as the warm weather, green grass, and budding trees show that spring is at our doors, we look forward to another campaign and a general engagement. Both armies have spent the winter in recruiting, and the great generals on both sides have matured their plans to crush each other and to "end the war in a few weeks!"

April 27, 1863, found us all in motion. General orders showed that our time of peace and tranquillity was over. Now you see us leave the old "camping ground," our log huts, our rustic city and our rustic church. Behind us the remnants of what was a camp. Empty quarters of officers and men, and rude chimneys standing out like ghosts—not even a dog or a cat left behind to show that human beings lived a whole winter on the left bank of the Rappahannock River. Our brigade formed a part of the army which was sent up the river. We left camp at noon, marched until midnight, then rested in the woods the remainder of the night. Next morning, at daybreak, the march was resumed and we reached the United States Ford on the night of the second day's march. Ponton-bridges were ready and we crossed by the light of the moon. Some of our wags cautioned their companions, late recruits, to walk in the center of the bridge, alleging that the Rappahannock at this point, near the junction of the Rapidan, was full of alligators of enormous size—so large, indeed, that one of them required two or three men for a breakfast! It was amusing to observe the innocent men watch the running stream, expecting every moment to see a monster rise to the surface and dart for his prey on the bridge. But, apart from fancied dangers from these monsters, there were real perils enough ahead of us. Some people regard soldiers as reckless, hardened men, but there is a bright side to this question. The Christian soldier does not fail to recognize a Providence always above him, and in time of expected peril evinces the real, genuine piety—that which he learned at his mother's knee and which he imbibed with his mother's milk. On this occasion, as on many others in my experience, these soldiers asked themselves: "What will to-morrow bring about?" As a rule, a soldier does not wish to parade his piety, and often, through human respect, he prefers to be considered as possessing a sort of bravado; but under all this, men of faith, in times of serious peril, think of the great future and pray for help and protection.

In the army desperate cases occasionally occur, which are very embarrassing, and at times the most severe measures are taken on the spur of the moment, by the officers responsible for discipline. On one occasion I saw an excited crowd of soldiers around an officer, the major of the regiment. One of the soldiers had mutinied, and was fast gaining strength among his companions. The major could do nothing with him, and the scene was growing more and more exciting. How it would terminate was hard to foresee, and the authority of a superior officer was in very serious jeopardy. As the excitement grew, the circle grew also, and it was difficult to reach the major or the soldier in mutiny. Finally, news of the affair reached the colonel, who had been in the regular army before the war. He mounted his horse, put spurs to him, and rushed through and over the crowd with a drawn sabre in his hand, and, when he reached the soldier, cut him down. In an instant the soldier lay bleeding and senseless on the ground. A shudder passed through his companions, who immediately slunk away. The colonel rode off, satisfied that for a time at least he had put a stop to disobedience. This action is hard to contemplate, and many would cry out that it was inhuman. Military men, however, adduce strong reasons for such severe measures, especially when in an active campaign and in front of a national enemy. Such scenes as this are not frequent, because the majority of men go into army life determined to obey and to do their duty. It is not surprising, however, where there are so many thousands, that some among them, having very

quick tempers, fly off and defy authority. Among
officers and veterans it is an axiom to obey first, and
if there be a supposed injustice, to speak of it afterward; not, however, before showing absolute obedi-
ence to the order given, be it right or wrong. On
another occasion I saw a man receive from his captain
a ball in the eye. The man had defied his captain's
authority, and the captain drew a revolver and put a
ball in his head. Fortunately, it did not kill him.
The ball glanced outward and did not strike a vital
point. Here I may note what remarkably erratic
courses bullets take in certain cases. I remember
seeing a colonel, the colonel of the Sixty-first New
York Infantry, I think it was, shot in the stomach,
and the ball was cut out near the spine. He was
attended by a surgeon, a most excellent one, Dr.
Frank Reynolds, of my regiment. The colonel said
to Dr. Reynolds:

" How about this case?"

" Well, I say it is certainly serious," said the doctor.

" I know that," said the colonel, " but how long
may I live?"

The doctor replied: " Usually men do not live more
than three days."

To this there are many extraordinary exceptions.
When Gen. Shields was a United States officer in the
Mexican War, a ball passed through his body, and a
Mexican surgeon passed a fine silk handkerchief
through the opening, following the course of the
bullet, and by so doing removed the clotted blood,

and the general recovered and was able to fight in the Union ranks in '62-'65. But, to return to our story, about six weeks later my brave Dr. Reynolds was in Washington, and the doctor, who was quite a wag, met there the same colonel on the street and in good health.

"Are you the colonel of the Sixty-first, and not dead?" asked the doctor.

"Yes," replied the colonel, "I am the same and not dead, as you see. I never felt better in my life."

"Well," said the doctor, "you ought to have died to save the honor of my profession."

The ball had struck one of the brass buttons on the colonel's coat, and glancing, passed through the skin, went just under it round the body, and was cut out, as I have said, near the spine. To all appearances it seemed that the ball had passed straight through the body, and in that case death was most certain to follow in a few days at farthest. This colonel, no doubt, had kind, saintly friends at home, who never forgot to pray for him. His case was one of the many thousands of narrow escapes which bore the marks of divine protection—to all appearances miraculous. Oh, how precious are the prayers of loving, devoted hearts under such circumstances! How inspiring the thought of God's providence in sending a guardian angel to spread his holy wings over us in hours of dread peril—perils, too, at times which we ourselves do not perceive or realize.

On Saturday, May 2, 1863, we were located at

Scott's Mill, guarding a ford across the river at that point, only a few miles from Chancellorsville. This was regarded as a most important point, and "to be held, cost what it would." In this position we could hear the booming of cannon and bursting of shells, and, as we were now becoming veterans, we knew what might be expected next day. Very early next morning, Sunday, I prepared to celebrate Mass on the slope of a hill facing the brigade. In this locality, even in May the grass was quite green, the trees had a new spring dress, and the little birds, not knowing what the cannon and commotion portended, sang away as if to celebrate a festival. A rustic altar, constructed the night previous with a few boards which we had found in the vicinity of the mill, stood under a spreading beech tree, and looked very picturesque. As I have said, Mass was commenced very early. Shortly afterward, the battle commenced, too; but I continued and finished. "God bless and protect my men!" was all the sermon preached that morning. I had scarcely finished Mass when we were ordered to advance. My faithful hostler had my horses ready, and as soon as I could pack the vestments—a task which I could perform in about seven minutes—I started with my command to celebrate a bloody Sunday. Our men were in good spirits, however, and after our short morning service each felt that all that could be done under the circumstances had been done, and, quite resigned to fate, we marched into a battle that turned out to be one of considerable magnitude.

CHAPTER XXIV.

BATTLE OF CHANCELLORSVILLE.

AT sunrise, Sunday morning, May 3, 1863, the battle opened with terrific cannonading. Simultaneously commenced the bursting of shells and the harsh, crashing sound of musketry, reminding one of a dreadful storm, the coming of mighty, angry winds, driving the dark and threatening clouds, sweeping everything material in their path, the rolling reverberations of great thunder-bolts that seem to give fitting expression to the thoughts of an offended God. The Eleventh Corps was outflanked, and, being taken by surprise, fell back in great confusion. I saw the entire command—composed of infantry, cavalry, and artillery—coming pell-mell toward our location, from the right wing, where they broke. Our brigade was ordered to form line and stop the fugitives at the point of the bayonet. A panic has a strange effect on men, precisely as when it enters a herd of cattle, when, as I have often seen, they will run through fire to escape real or imaginary danger. The men were formed into line once more, and the cannon caissons, loaded with haversacks, were wheeled into position; but in the disorder many were killed and wounded. Our brigade passed other troops, and marched under orders to a front position and was lustily cheered. This was invariably the case, and was the best proof of the popularity and respect in which it was held by fellow-soldiers in the Army of the Potomac. Every now and then you could see our men drop one by one to the ground, wounded or killed. At this point the Fifth Maine Battery, which had been doing effective work — handled as it was by expert and brave men — was left without men to continue the firing, nearly every one being killed or wounded, and would soon have fallen into the hands of the Confederates and been turned against us, had not the brigade rushed in, under a galling fire, and, with the loss of many excellent and gallant men, drawn the battery by hand from the position amid the renewed cheers of other brigades that witnessed the intrepid deed. The wounded were, many of them, placed in the Chancellorsville mansion. Here I went with my surgeons. This large building also furnished quarters for Gen. Hooker, commander-in-chief. The Confederates got exact range of the building, and in a short time the location became "very hot." As Gen. Hooker stood on the porch, a cannon-ball struck the pillar against which he was leaning at the time, and the violent concussion so stunned him that he fell to the floor. I saw another ball strike one of the large brick chimneys and send the bricks flying through the air with terrific force. Still another came and struck a poor soldier who was quenching his thirst at the well near the building. We were unwilling to leave the wounded, and while we were in a dilemma as to what was best to do, another ball came and struck the fore-leg of a beautiful bay horse belonging to an officer on Gen. Hooker's staff. It smashed the entire leg from the breast to the hoof. The poor horse jerked back, broke the halter-strap, fell on his back, then recovered himself, arose and hobbled away on three legs, dangling the hoof of the fourth leg, which was held suspended by a strip of skin. This strip of skin, about two inches wide, and the hoof were all that remained of the fore-leg. Blood flowed profusely and streaked the ground wherever he passed. He was soon shot and put out of pain. I hardly remember a sight that touched my heart so keenly during the entire battle. The innocent animal had no part in the fight, but he was a silent victim.

During this battle the gallant "Stonewall" Jackson, so noted in the Confederate army, while disposing his troops on the plank road that passes in front of the Chancellorsville mansion, was shot by his own men. They did not know that their general was outside the lines, and they fired briskly at what they supposed was a body of Union troops. He was not killed outright, but expired shortly afterward, on May 10, 1863. He received his wounds less than half a mile from the Union lines west of Chancellorsville. I mention the incident, because the news of his being fatally wounded caused considerable

commotion in Union circles at the time, and also
because it forms quite an important event in the history of this battle. My good orderly ventured up after
awhile, seeing that the Confederates had the exact
range of the spot, and said: "Father, you will stay
here till you are killed and your horses too!" I
told him to take the horses to the rear. He did, and
did not stop until he had crossed the Rappahannock
River and was seven miles from the front. He got
out of range! Of course, it was the great regard he
had for the safety of the horses that induced him to
go so far. After a time the surgeons moved to the
left into a forest; but many of the wounded were left,
of necessity, in the Chancellorsville mansion, and,
horrible to say, were burned, the place having caught
fire. Shortly after, it fell in between the two lines of
the contending forces.

While in the woods the surgeons had a man on a
rude table that had been constructed from planks
found at Chancellorsville, and while they were getting ready to amputate a limb, a cannon-ball swept
the man off the table, smashing him to pieces, and
left the terrified surgeons on either side of the table
almost paralyzed with consternation. It seemed as
if a mysterious edict of God followed some men,
while others passed through the entire war without
receiving even a dangerous wound. To illustrate
this, let me mention a few cases that came under my
notice. It often occurred to me that God wished to
punish us for past sins of pride and disregard of His

11

benefits, and that a certain number had to die. I know of a captain who was wounded, and by a strange accident, in falling down the side of a small hill, fell on the point of his own sword, the hilt of which stuck firmly in the ground, and the blade passed through his body. I saw some soldiers on the march chase a rabbit, and a beautiful drummer boy, only fifteen years of age, ran in front of one of the soldiers, who was about to shoot at the rabbit, and the shot passed through the boy, who dropped dead. A soldier of our brigade was out one night on picket duty. While "fooling" with his musket in play, one of his companions asked him if he had any fear of picket duty where sharpshooters pick off their victims. "No," said he, "I have been through too many battles to feel fear on picket duty." He had scarcely finished the sentence when his gun accidentally went off and the ball passed through his head. He never spoke again. Another of our brigade, a teamster, undertook to pass over a small mountain stream which an athlete could jump over, and it was not deeper than, perhaps, three or four feet. He was riding one of his mules. The mule stumbled and fell on his rider, who was drowned then and there. The mule had become tangled in some way in the harness and could not get up. A young man whose time had expired was honorably mustered out of the service after three years of hard fighting and all the privations and hardships of campaign life. His heart was full of joy at the prospect of receiving once more the embraces of loving parents and kind sisters. Just before starting he desired to see a loved companion, and he ventured once more to the front. Just as he reached the breastworks a sharpshooter put a ball through his head. He never spoke another word. I could tell so many cases of this kind where death came when least expected, and often entirely off the battlefield; but I must now return to my narrative.

The battle went against us. Everything was done for the wounded, both temporally and spiritually, that circumstances would allow. Night covered the scene with a very dark mantle. Thousands that day had gone to meet their God—some well prepared, others, perhaps, in sin; but let us hope that their terrible sufferings and their blood piously offered to God in union with the sufferings of our Saviour secured their pardon. Many of the wounded, besides those in the Chancellorsville mansion, were burned as they lay helpless in the burning forest that night. At length I was nearly exhausted with fatigue and hunger. On one of the horses which I had ordered to be taken to the rear by my faithful orderly—who wished to preserve the lives of the horses at any hazard—was the small and only supply of provisions of which I was master. I borrowed Col. Kelly's horse and rode for miles, but I could find no trace of horse or man. Finally I crossed the river, and after going a few miles farther in the rain that was now pouring down, and sinking deep at times into the mud-holes made by the passage of artillery, I found my heroic orderly and the horses quite safe.

Here I procured something to eat and then spent the night in the woods in company with several officers, the horses, and my brave orderly. I had no fear while he was with me, for I knew that he had a knack of saving life. Many of our wounded men were left in the hands of the Confederates and the balance were sent to the rear, where they were well cared for. Those who were strong enough to bear transportation were sent to Washington, and many of them were nursed by the Sisters of the Holy Cross, who had been sent from Notre Dame, Indiana, for that purpose. The good Sisters of Charity, who resided in Washington, had also more than they could do, but day after day all these devoted Sisters worked for the wounded, letting everything else go for the time. God bless these good nurses! Many lives were saved by their skilful care.

CHAPTER XXV.

OUR RETURN TO CAMP FALMOUTH.

MAY 5, 1863, found us recrossing the Rappahannock River and wending our way back to the old camp at Falmouth on the left bank of the stream. Thus, for the third time, we found ourselves located there, and there we remained during the remainder of the month. While on our way to our old camp we went zigzag through the country. One evening we halted, and in some way the soldiers secured for me the "fly" of a tent. This is just like the roof of an ordinary house with no gable ends. It rested on a pole some four feet from the ridge of the roof. Some of our men who had been rambling about the country after we had bivouacked, found a good Catholic family, poor but honest and devout. From this family they received kindness not looked for, and they became interested in them, especially when they saw a young child, about two years old, in danger of death. Immediately it occurred to the men to bring me to baptize the child. The family had not seen a priest in two years. When my men came and told me the circumstances I started at once on foot, guided by my zealous friends. After a long and very rough walk we reached the cabin. The good people were rejoiced to have the chaplain of the Irish Brigade visit them and perform a ceremony which they ardently desired at that critical moment. We conversed with the good people, who told us of many trials and hardships passed through during the war, which had turned Virginia, more than any other State, into one great battlefield of blood, devastation, and misery. They were on the verge of starvation. As a rule, all the men able to carry guns were in the army, and only the old and the weak, women and children were found at home. These were helpless victims, without temporal or spiritual consolation. Each of us gave them a few dollars, and the sum total surely kept them from want for a part of the spring and summer. I admired the poor soldier who earned his $13 per month by long marches, exposures to perils and death, on and off the battlefield, who was so generous when there was need for real charity. While at the house, suddenly we noticed the coming of a great storm, and we started for camp on " double-quick." It became very dark in an incredibly short time, and the rain came down in torrents. The harder it rained, the harder we ran. The ground over which we had to pass was exceedingly rough. It was an old field, left uncultivated, since its last crop, two or three years previous, had been partly taken from it by the brawny colored sons of toil. The result was many tumbles for us. I could not help laughing at the awkward plunges some of my companions made, but, finally, my own turn came. My toe struck a small, sharp elevation of ground, resembling, in shape and size, a pineapple, and down I came on the edge of an old fence-rail, barking my knee and shin badly and tearing my trousers from the knee down. At last, drenched and looking as sorry as wet hens, we reached our camp. I went directly to the improvised "tent fly" to find my blanket fixed for a kind of bed, folded in such a way as to catch all the rain pouring from the roof, just as if placed for a trough to carry the water from the eaves. This was done by my skilful (?) attendant— in all kindness, it is true, but with no forethought whatever.

Under such conditions of army life we consoled ourselves by saying that even this condition of things was better a thousand times than the fate which had befallen many of our companions on the battlefield a few days previous, and those poor fellows, helpless from serious wounds, who were caught in Chancellorsville in the burning buildings and in the burning forest. I pushed a bayonet into the ground near the center of my humble roof, where the rain was not falling, lighted a candle and placed it in that portion of the bayonet that fits on the musket. Then, half reclining on one arm near the feeble light, read my office for the day. Having finished my prayers as best I could, and consoling myself with the thought of having secured, by Baptism, the salvation of a

tender soul, redeemed by the precious Blood of our
Lord, and of being instrumental in bringing at last
some consolation to a destitute family, I slept in my
wet clothes and wet blanket for a few hours until
the bugle called us for more marching. On campaigns like this we had not with us many changes of
clothing, and the first thing I had to do in the morning was to mend my trousers. I managed to carry
with me a needle and thread, and at the mending I
went. The stitches were about three to an inch, and,
for me, I thought that was not bad. We went on
very well the next day, and arrived, as I have mentioned, at Camp Falmouth. This was the shortest
campaign we made. We accomplished little—sent
a few souls to heaven, exceedingly rejoiced, it may
be, to be out of this wicked world—and our only
consolation was that, as far as human weakness goes,
we had all tried to do our duty to our fellow-man
in his time of need, either of soul or body. Now
we were in camp, and we were very blue. During
the previous December our troops were simply
slaughtered at the battle of Fredericksburg—that
field was plainly visible from Camp Falmouth—
and now, in the spring, we had been in another battle
scarcely less disastrous. No help for it now; it was
useless to sigh over the past, though many orphans
might weep and mothers and wives bewail at home.
The great nation groans at the loss of her brave
sons in a fratricidal, cruel war. Nevertheless, we
must settle down to business once more. We must

hold regular services, for the holy Sacraments bring
consolation to pious, repenting souls, when all
earthly comfort fails to do so.   President Abraham
Lincoln visited our camp on May 7, and had a long
conference with Gen. Hooker and other generals.
They held, in fact, a regular council of war, and in
short order new plans for future campaigns were
matured.   The next chapter will open an account of
a new departure, both for the Union and the Confederate armies.

CHAPTER XXVI.

IN CAMP AND ON THE MARCH.

A FEW weeks in camp passed rapidly. We were reconstructed, and early in June, 1863, the Army of the Potomac was once more in motion. Lee had his army headed north, bound to carry the conflict out of Virginia into Pennsylvania. The range of mountains passing through Virginia, running northeast, divides West Virginia from Virginia proper. This "Blue Ridge" range figured prominently in our campaigns. Along this range and beyond, on the west side, the Confederate troops passed, while our army kept on the east side and crowded the Confederates as much as possible away from Washington. In almost parallel lines, both armies moved on. Just when and where a general engagement might occur, was not known. At intervals the cavalry of either side encountered each other, and desperate struggles were the result. The infantry and the flying artillery were also brought into action occasionally, but no general engagement occurred during the month of June. Our march from the banks of the historic Rappahannock, this time, turned out to be one of the

(170)

longest which we had yet undertaken. Counting the zigzag route our Second Corps had taken to Gettysburg, Pennsylvania, it was between two and three hundred miles in length. But we were all glad to get away from the destructive scenes of our two late campaigns. The poor soldiers, who had to carry about sixty pounds daily under the burning sun of a more southern climate than they were accustomed to, found the continued marching of from sixteen to eighteen miles per day very severe. Many of them dropped dead from sunstroke. Every day brought us farther and farther from the Rappahannock, south of which lay, in their last sleep, between twenty-five and thirty thousand of our dear companions. Sad reflections were made by our officers and men, many of whom left behind in silent graves relatives who were to ·be seen no more in this life, while all had to mourn cherished comrades who had fought side by side with them on many a bloody plain. The march, however, was a relief, as we entered on new scenes, although the general line of direction did not differ greatly from former marches, and since this was the third time that we had marched through Virginia, we had become familiar with the general features of the country.

Nothing very unusual occurred during the march until we reached a beautiful plain at the foot of a very high hill, or a "young mountain," as the soldiers called it. The top of this hill was covered with splendid rocks, interspersed with trees and

shrubs. As it was Saturday night, I determined to
celebrate Mass next morning on the top of this little
mountain. The idea was eagerly and enthusiastically
received by my men, and they gave all the help
necessary. Before leaving the place we erected a
cross on the spot where the Mass had been celebrated.
This was over a quarter of a century ago, and possibly
that cross stands there still. During the entire march
Mass was celebrated as often as circumstances would
permit; but perhaps this was one of the most romantic
ever celebrated in Virginia, even in the early missions
among the Indians. Like high Olympus or Mount
Horeb, here there was natural sublimity and grandeur
in the holy Sacrifice on the mountain top.

As I come now in the line of march to Frederick,
Maryland, a scene occurs to me which took place
there. I am not entirely certain of the exact spot,
but I am sure that it was near Frederick. A spy from
the Confederate army was caught. He had in his
possession a complete account of our troops, our
trains, and our route. He was tried and he confessed;
moreover, he said that if he had not been caught, in
twenty-four hours from that time he would have
had possession of all our army train. He was suspended from a tree and left there, and while the
army passed I saw him hanging by the neck. It was
rumored at the time that some one had suggested
to send him to Washington and let the authorities deal
with him there. If the rumor is true, Gen. Hancock
swore: " No! If you send him to Washington they will

promote him." There was really so much kindness
shown in Washington, even to culprits, that the
generals in the field decided that strict severity was
necessary somewhere, to keep up discipline. Passing
through Maryland it was really admirable to see how
careful our men were of private property. No fields,
gardens, or private houses were at all injured. The
men had been warned that, being in a loyal State,
they had no right to molest or destroy private
property. This told on the conscience of each man.
Besides this, Gen. Hancock had issued a severe
general order to our corps, adding a serious penalty
should anyone be found in works of depredation.
One evening he rode through the camp to see if his
orders were in full force. At a distance he saw a
sheep running, and it seemed that some men were
chasing the animal, thinking, notwithstanding the
order, that a little mutton for a change would be a
feast. The general put spurs to his horse, and when
he reached the spot he swore at the supposed culprits:
"Blank, blank, you blank, blank, scoundrels! Did
you not hear my orders? Send out the man that killed
that sheep! I saw the animal drop! Do not try to
evade, or I will have the whole company punished."
No move was made, and the general was very much
displeased. He renewed the threat of punishment
in still more vigorous language, and while he was
in the midst of his speech the sheep jumped out of
the brush and ran off. The general, as he wheeled
his horse round to return to his quarters, said: " I

take it all back. I am glad you have not transgressed my orders." The fact is, the sheep, no doubt, was chased but not killed. The animal was about exhausted at the time and dropped in the brush, but when it had rested for a time it was all right. To be truly candid, however, I am of opinion that that sheep did not die a natural death! Gen. Hancock was a great and a brave soldier, much respected by our corps, which he commanded. He was a polished gentleman and had a keen sense of propriety. Addicted merely through force of habit to the use of profane language, when excited, he would invariably stop short when he discovered the presence of a clergyman. This occasion was no exception, which showed his sense of propriety, as it is particularly impolite to speak in the presence of any professional man in a way that is offensive or distasteful to that profession. In other words, the general showed a respect for religion in respecting its ministers. The following anecdote illustrates the force of habit in swearing; but in this case the reflection on the bishop is heavy: "An English Episcopalian bishop said to a lord in Parliament: 'Do not curse so; it is wicked.' 'Well,' said the lord, 'I curse considerably and you pray considerably, but neither of us mean anything, you know.'"

CHAPTER XXVII.

ON June 28, 1863, we halted at Frederick city, fifty to sixty miles from Baltimore. Frederick is quite an old town of about 9,000 inhabitants. The people might be called "old-fashioned." Quiet, easy-going, kind-hearted, and great lovers of old friends and old customs. This is the reputation they have. Here is located a State institution or college, founded in 1797. Here also is located a flourishing novitiate of the Jesuit society. Not far off, to the north, in the same county, is the venerable Mount St. Mary's College, the *alma mater* of many Catholic bishops and priests. In going to Gettysburg we left Mount St. Mary's to the right, passing in our line of march about a mile or two from the grounds. In the vicinity of Frederick we found the country very beautiful. The fields were like gardens in the highest state of cultivation. The fences were neat and well built. The buildings were not grand, but they had about them an air of comfort, and they looked like real homes. I never entered a house during our long march of between two and three hundred miles from

(175)

Fredericksburg, Virginia, to Gettysburg, Pennsylvania. Early on the morning of June 29 our corps started from Frederick toward Gettysburg, and we did not halt for the night until about eleven p. m., having made the longest march made by infantry of any department during the war. This achievement is what is claimed. Our men carried, as I have said elsewhere, about sixty pounds, including musket, cartridges, provisions, shelter-tent, and blanket. We marched thirty-four miles. Considering the load that the men had to carry, it was a marvellous feat, and it was what Cæsar would call a "forced march." Being more or less veterans at this time, we knew what it meant. We knew that there was desperate work ahead and that our services would be soon required. We halted in a ploughed field. A gentle rain was falling, but no matter, we must rest. Beside a tree, that seemed to me in the dark to be an apple tree, I couched, under no tent, no canopy, except the canopy of heaven. I folded my blanket about me and was soon fast asleep. When one is very hungry and very sleepy, it is hard to decide which of the two, food or sleep, nature craves most. I would put sleep first. This has been my experience. I must note here that when we left our old camp Falmouth, opposite Fredericksburg, we were under Gen. Hooker. While on the march, on June 28, he was superseded by Maj.-Gen. Meade. During the long march on the following day, I heard the men make many curious remarks about the skill of various generals. Besides this, they

talked on numerous subjects, from philosophy to
"hard-tack" and pork! Late in the evening some of
them became exceedingly tired and declared that they
could not, and would not, go any farther. "Oh, come
on!" others cried; "Little Mac is surely in command."
Where they got this idea I could not tell, but it was,
in fact, a general rumor, which I heard repeated again
and again, that he was in command and that he was
following up with an incredibly large force. Later
on we heard that this report was purposely started to
give more confidence to the rank and file. Be that
as it may, the rumor seemed to have a good effect on
the men. It was surprising to see them holding out
to the very last. No stragglers were found on the
road behind — a very unusual thing on a long march.
In the army during the war it was not uncommon to
see men drop from weakness, like jaded horses, give
out and fall helpless to the ground. Besides the
cases of utter exhaustion, men would sometimes "give
up," when very much fatigued, lag behind and seek
rides in the ambulances, or perhaps stop by the roadside and sleep till the morning, and then leisurely
follow the advance. These were called "stragglers,"
and if the battle was over when they arrived, they
could sit by the camp fires and tell more about it
than those who were in the fight. Late in the evening the marching of a tired army is a sight. As a
rule, not a voice is heard. Fatigue and drowsiness,
added to a rather weak and faint feeling, indispose
men to converse, and by silent consent each one

discontinues conversation. The click of a large spur, the occasional rattle of a sword, and other mechanical movements are the only sounds heard above the slow, steady tramp of the line and the heavy tread of the few horses that carry mounted officers. Even these mounted officers frequently dismount and walk to avoid being overpowered by sleep and to save themselves from falling from the horses. Many, many times I had to do so. How men live through all this is a mystery. But a kind Providence pressed many of us onward and preserved us, and for this, I am not ashamed to say here, few of us are truly grateful, few of us render the thanks which God has a right to expect. One of the ten lepers came to thank Jesus. "Were not ten made clean? and where are the nine?" Only one was found thankful! Here He complains of our want of gratitude.

CHAPTER XXVIII.

GETTYSBURG.

OUR march is not yet at an end! July 1, 1863, one o'clock, p. m., found us at Tanytown, Pa., where our corps was massed and where Gen. Meade established his headquarters. Suddenly a courier came up at break-neck speed, his horse panting and covered with foam. He announced that fighting was going on at Gettysburg. The Confederates, with a very superior force, encountered our cavalry and the First and Eleventh Infantry Corps, and the Union troops were driven back in confusion. Gen. Meade dispatched Gen. Hancock, the commander of our corps, to the scene of strife with orders to take full charge of the field—cavalry, infantry, and artillery. Accompanied by his excellent staff, Hancock dashed off and was soon on the ground restoring order, examining the grounds, and forming plans for a general engagement next day. Gen. Meade sanctioned Hancock's plans, and ordered his adjutant-general, Gen. Seth Williams, to send all the troops to the front. This was on the afternoon of July 1, and at once we resumed our march. We had about thirteen

(179)

miles to go. Next morning, July 2, a memorable day, Hancock posted us on Cemetery Ridge. Opposite and about a mile from us, on Seminary Ridge, we could see distinctly the lines of the Confederates. Much of the day passed in the disposition of troops on either side. The two great contending forces watched each other keenly with beating hearts and anxious expectation of what result might follow the pending struggle. Generals are in a "brown study," staff officers and orderlies are dashing along the lines from left to right and from right to left, carrying orders. On the flanks the cavalry and light artillery are on a sharp look-out, and all are astir. One can hardly imagine the stupendous task it is to dispose a large army of tens of thousands of men and hundreds of cannon to advantage. Each cannon has usually six horses, and the caissons containing the ammunition, balls, and shells are drawn in the same manner. Consider what a line and a body all this makes; and how much time and study is required to bring all into position, and to make such a combination as will give reasonable hope of success. In doing this we spent most of July 2, until about four o'clock, p. m. And now, the two great armies are confronting each other. Lee had eighty to a hundred thousand men and over two hundred cannon. Meade had even more men, and over three hundred cannon, but he could not use them all at once on account of the broken nature of the country. Gettysburg, the county seat of Adams County, is a small town of about 8,000 inhabitants and is located in a basin or valley. We can scarcely imagine the trepidation of these poor people—men, women, and children—in their defenseless, quiet homes, surrounded by such armies as were there from the first to the fourth of July, 1863. Many fervent prayers were said and holy vows pronounced, no doubt, especially on the nights of the first and second. The proportions of the pending crash seemed so great, as the armies eyed each other, that even veterans who had often "smelled powder" quailed at the thought of the final conflict. At about four o'clock the Confederates commenced firing, and one hundred and twenty cannon from their side belched forth from their fiery throats missiles of death into our lines. The Third Corps were pressed back, and at this critical moment I proposed to give a general absolution to our men, as they had had absolutely no chance to practise their religious duties during the past two or three weeks, being constantly on the march. Here I will quote the account of Maj.-Gen. St. Clair Mulholland, then a colonel in the Irish Brigade, a Christian gentleman and as brave a soldier as any in the Army of the Potomac, to which his wounds and his army record will testify:

"Now (as the Third Corps is being pressed back), help is called for, and Hancock tells Caldwell to have his men ready. 'Fall in!' and the men run to their places. 'Take arms!' and the four brigades of Zook, Cross, Brook, and Kelly are ready for the fray. There are yet a few minutes to spare before starting, and the time is occupied by one of the most impressive religious ceremonies I have ever witnessed. The Irish Brigade, which had been commanded formerly by Gen. Thomas Francis Meagher, and whose green flag had been unfurled in every battle in which the Army of the Potomac had been engaged from the first Bull Run to Appomattox, and was now commanded by Col. Patrick Kelly of the Eighty-eighth New York, formed a part of this division. The brigade stood in column of regiments, closed in mass. As a large majority of its members were Catholics, the Chaplain of the brigade, Rev. William Corby, proposed to give a general absolution to all the men before going into the fight. While this is customary in the armies of Catholic countries in Europe, it was perhaps the first time it was ever witnessed on this continent, unless, indeed, the grim old warrior, Ponce de Leon, as he tramped through the Everglades of Florida in search of the Fountain of Youth, or De Soto, on his march to the Mississippi, indulged this act of devotion. Father Corby stood on a large rock in front of the brigade. Addressing the men, he explained what he was about to do, saying that each one could receive the benefit of the absolution by making a sincere Act of Contrition and firmly resolving to embrace the first opportunity of confessing his sins, urging them to do their duty, and reminding them of the high and sacred nature of their trust as soldiers and the noble object for which they fought. . . . . The brigade was standing at

ABSOLUTION UNDER FIRE.

Given by Father Corby, of Notre Dame University, Ind., to the troops in the battle of Gettysburg.
July 2, 1863. He was then Chaplain in the famous Irish Brigade of New York.

'Order arms!' As he closed his address, every man, Catholic and non-Catholic, fell on his knees with his head bowed down. Then, stretching his right hand toward the brigade, Father Corby pronounced the words of the absolution:

'*Dominus noster Jesus Christus vos absolvat, et ego, auctoritate ipsius, vos absolvo ab omni vinculo, excommunicationis interdicti, in quantum possum et vos indigetis deinde ego absolvo vos, a pecatis vestris, in nomini Patris, et Filii, et Spiritus Sancti, Amen.*'

"The scene was more than impressive; it was awe-inspiring. Near by stood a brilliant throng of officers who had gathered to witness this very unusual occurrence, and while there was profound silence in the ranks of the Second Corps, yet over to the left, out by the peach orchard and Little Round Top, where Weed and Vincent and Hazlitt were dying, the roar of the battle rose and swelled and re-echoed through the woods, making music more sublime than ever sounded through cathedral aisle. The act seemed to be in harmony with the surroundings. I do not think there was a man in the brigade who did not offer up a heart-felt prayer. For some, it was their last; they knelt there in their grave clothes. In less than half an hour many of them were numbered with the dead of July 2. Who can doubt that their prayers were good? What was wanting in the eloquence of the priest to move them to repentance was supplied in the incidents of the fight. That heart would be incorrigible, indeed, that the scream of a Whitworth bolt, added to Father Corby's touching appeal, would not move to contrition."

In performing this ceremony I faced the army. My eye covered thousands of officers and men. I noticed that *all*, Catholic and non-Catholic, officers and private soldiers showed a profound respect, wishing at this fatal crisis to receive every benefit of divine grace that could be imparted through the instrumentality of the Church ministry. Even Maj.-Gen. Hancock removed his hat, and, as far as compatible with the situation, bowed in reverential devotion. That general absolution was intended for all — *in quantum possum* — not only for our brigade, but for all, North or South, who were susceptible of it and who were about to appear before their Judge. Let us hope that many thousands of souls, purified by hardships, fasting, prayer, and blood, met a favorable sentence on the ever memorable battlefield of Gettysburg. The battle lasted three days and was the greatest of the war. A comparison between the battles of Gettysburg and Waterloo has frequently been made by various writers; the greater of the two is, very likely, that at Gettysburg.

During a visit to the Gettysburg battlefield, about a year ago, in 1889, Maj.-Gen. Mulholland told me that a soldier of his regiment knelt near him while the general absolution was being given and prayed with more fervor than the General had ever before witnessed. Twenty minutes later that poor soldier was a corpse!

The Irish Brigade had very many advantages over other organizations, as it was at no time during the war without a chaplain; but I was the only one at the battle of Gettysburg. Often in camp and sometimes on the march we held very impressive religious services, but the one at Gettysburg was more public, and was witnessed by many who had not, perhaps, seen the others. The surroundings there, too, made a vast difference, for really the situation reminded one of the day of judgment, when shall be seen "men withering away for fear and expectation of what shall come upon the whole world," so great were the whirlwinds of war then in motion.

About a week after the battle, while on the march, a captain, a non-Catholic, rode up to me, and after an introduction by a friend, said: " Chaplain, I would like to know more about your religion. I was present on that awful day, July 2, when you ' made a prayer,' and while I have often witnessed ministers make prayers I never witnessed one so powerful as the one you made that day in front of Hancock's corps just as the ball opened with one hundred and twenty guns blazing at us." Just then I found use for my handkerchief to hide a smile which stole to my countenance caused by the, to me, peculiar phraseology in which the good captain expressed his mind. I could not but admire his candid, outspoken manner, though, and I gave him an invitation to call on me in camp, when I would take pleasure in giving him all the information in my power. One good result

of the Civil War was the removing of a great amount
of prejudice. When men stand in common danger,
a fraternal feeling springs up between them and
generates a Christian, charitable sentiment that often
leads to most excellent results.

CHAPTER XXIX.

GETTYSBURG — THE TWENTY-FIFTH ANNIVERSARY.

THROUGHOUT this narrative I have followed my subject chronologically. Here, by way of parenthesis, I feel impelled to write a chapter on the celebration of the twenty-fifth anniversary of the Battle of Gettysburg, which celebration took place in July, 1888. It will not be out of place here in connection with the account of the battle itself. Plans on an extensive scale had been prepared for a national celebration of this anniversary. The surviving veterans of the Irish Brigade sent me a pressing invitation to attend with them; considering, as they expressed it, that "such a meeting would be incomplete without the chaplain who had been their companion in prosperity and adversity since the very first campaign made by the brigade." I accepted, and am glad I did so. I witnessed there one of the grandest and most interesting sights of my life. The emotions that filled my breast when I met the surviving officers and men once more on the field that drank in the blood of so many of our dead companions may be more easily imagined than described. I shall never

(187)

forget that meeting. It was estimated that fully fifty thousand were present—embracing North and South, East and West. Some came from California to be present, others from far distant Alaska, and thousands from the Gulf States swelled the waves of moving, surging humanity. Officers and men, women and children, came from every quarter. The old soldiers, from North and South, wished to visit once more, before their death, the spot of such thrilling interest; the spot that formed the greatest and fullest chapter of war history; the spot that received the blood of many times ten thousand heroes; the spot that still gives war incidents which thrill the blood of a generation then unborn, and which will continue to do so for many generations in the future. There is now a growing interest circling around Gettysburg battlefield, more than any other, in the school-boy of to-day that is really marvellous. Not only did the old soldier wish to revisit, in peace, this historic spot where he had fought, and possibly bled and left a limb, but he also desired his wife, taken to his bosom perhaps since the war, his sons and daughters, many of whom were also born since the war, to see the place which not only the nation but nations, had talked about so much. Yea, he desired even his friends and relatives to enjoy with him the reminiscences of July 1, 2, and 3, 1863. The meeting did not consist of an idle gathering. There were programmes for each day and each part of the day. The dedication of monuments was a prominent feature. Brass bands led the way to some particular locality where a monument had been erected by a military brigade or division to commemorate the identical place where such organization fought twenty-five years before. Here great numbers clustered around a stage or platform, from which some distinguished general or selected orator addressed the multitude. Besides, the old field was covered with tents, numbering probably ten thousand. Many, after every tent and every house in the town was filled, slept on the ground. No matter, camp life again! I learned that from twelve to twenty trains on one railway alone, bringing thousands more, were blocked on the route, so great was the flood of humanity constantly pouring into Gettysburg for this celebration. The sight was in great contrast with the scene enacted there twenty-five years previous. Then it was war, now peace; then we heard the roar of cannon and the groans of the dying; now we hear the rich stentorian voice of the enthusiastic, patriotic orator, the inspiring strains of martial music and the merry laugh of youth and beauty, whose hearts long to distinguish their lives by great heroic deeds worthy a nation now so exalted among all the nations of the earth—a free nation handed down to us by our illustrious forefathers to be kept intact and united till the end of time; a nation born of the patriotic, liberty-loving heroes over a century ago and now cemented in the blood of their children's children, never again to be disrupted by political strife or ungovernable passion. Much time was agreeably spent in looking over the battle grounds, which are very extensive.

The government purchased the locality and mapped out the whole area fought over during the battle. Twenty-five years' skill and industry have wrought a great change in the place. At the time of the battle it was: "Wheatfield," "Peach Orchard," "Seminary Ridge," "Cemetery Hill," "Bloody Angle," "Devil's Den," etc. Now it is: "Battle Avenue," "Culp's Hill Avenue," "Hancock Avenue," "Reynold's Avenue," "Sickles' Avenue," "Howard Avenue," "Cemetery Gate," etc. I must note here that the national cemetery at Gettysburg is a credit to our country. There are soldiers buried there, unclaimed by relatives, to the number of nearly four thousand. In various other national cemeteries in the United States (many of which I have visited—notably the one in Louisiana, near New Orleans, where there are twelve thousand graves) there are buried three hundred and twenty-five thousand one hundred and forty-three patriots. All these cemeteries are kept in an artistic style that rivals our handsomest city parks. This is done at the expense of the general government, and each cemetery receives daily the personal supervision of the officer in charge and such care that the most fastidious can find no fault, while it delights every man of good sense to see such respect shown our fallen heroes. My remarks are much longer than I had intended, but the deep interest I feel in the subject must be my apology to any reader who may find them uninteresting. I will now devote another short chapter to the actual doings of the Irish Brigade at Gettysburg in July, 1888.

CHAPTER XXX.

ANNIVERSARY EXERCISES—GETTYSBURG.

FOLLOWING our plan in all former celebrations, we opened our celebration of July 2 (the exact anniversary day of our deadly struggle there as a brigade) with a "Military Mass." Father Ouellet* was with us again on this occasion and sang the Mass. The choir came from New York, while the members of the local choir did their best to make everything pass off creditably. Among the singers present from New York, I remember Mrs. Florence Rice Knox, who possesses a rich, smooth, and powerful voice, full of pathos; Miss Ritta E. Bronson, whose voice was very sweet and pleasing, and Prof. Edward O'Mahony, who held his own pretty well, considering the charms of the voices around him: Mrs. Knox, Miss Bronson, and the splendid chorus too numerous to mention, even if I could remember their names. I must not forget to mention the organist, one of no

---

* The Rev. Thomas Ouellet, S. J., was chaplain with me in the brigade from November, 1861, till April, 1862, when he resigned. He re-enlisted February 15, 1864, and continued until the end of the war in 1865. Between these dates he acted as hospital chaplain at Newbern, North Carolina.

ordinary ability, Miss Grace Haverty, daughter of
our former quartermaster. Here I wish to mention
also the great service rendered us by the pastor of
Gettysburg, who, by the way, became pastor the year
after the battle, continued twenty-four years in the
same position, and is still there. His name is the
Rev. Joseph A. Ball. While not yet ordained priest,
and being in vacation, he walked eighty miles to the
battlefield when it was covered with the fresh horrors
of war. He had but two dollars on which to make
this trip. While repairing the steeple of his church
twenty-four years after the battle, his carpenter found
a bullet in the timber which had been fired from the
South. I am now in possession of said bullet. I
was urged to address the multitude at the Anniversary Mass service. Imagine one who ought to be a
"grim old warrior" standing before his "companions
in arms" addressing them after a separation that
dated to March 20, 1865, nearly a quarter of a
century! At first I got on reasonably well, until,
looking over those assembled, the surviving members
of our illustrious and numerous band as it appeared
at Alexandria, Va., in the fall of '61, I happened to
make this statement, "Here is what is left of us;
where are the others?" when I filled up very unexpectedly and could not speak for several minutes. I
had struck a very tender chord. The celebrant,
although eleven years older than I, wept like a child,
and the brave old warriors before me who had stood
the shock of many battles also wept. We were on the

spot where many of the "others" had fallen; heroes
whom we had helped to carry out of our ranks. The
place, the circumstances, the remembrances, the old
friendships renewed, contributed to emotions that
perhaps may not be well understood except by the
participants.

I was credibly informed that among the dozens of
orators—most of whom were generals—who spoke
at the various dedications of monuments, many were
so choked with emotion as to be obliged for a time
to stop speaking. This is a new proof of what we
often notice in history—that the bravest of generals
have tender hearts. It may seem paradoxical; nevertheless, it is true. Well, the grand "Military Mass"
being over, an hour or so was passed in talking over
old times. Then we proceeded to the dedication of
the monument erected to the memory of the Irish
Brigade, a beautiful structure, the shaft terminating
in the form of a Latin cross. This was solemnly
blessed and the particulars of the following programme were strictly carried out.

PROGRAMME

OF MEMORIAL CEREMONIES, JULY 2, 1888,

of the survivors of the

IRISH BRIGADE.

———

In dedicating and presenting to the Gettysburg Battlefield
Association, on behalf of the State of New York,

A MONUMENT

To the Memory of the Members of the New York Commands
of the Brigade, who fought on many well-stricken
fields for the preservation of the
Union and in the

CAUSE OF UNIVERSAL LIBERTY.

———

1. The President, Capt. Toal, introduces Gen. Nugent as
   presiding officer.
2. Gen. Nugent introduces Chaplains.
3. Religious Services and Address by Rev. W. Corby.
4. Address by Chairman.
5. Letters from Distinguished Absentees.
6. Song by Florence Rice Knox and Miss Ritta E. Bronson.
7. Chairman introduces Orator of the Day.
8. Gen. Burke delivers Oration.
9. Poem by William Collins.
10. Benediction by Brigade Chaplains of the Cross, *De Pro-
    fundis* and *Miserere* chanted for the dead by the choir
11. Presentation to Gettysburg Monument Association, by
    Col. James D. Brady.
12. Response by the Gettysburg Monument Association.
13. Song by Prof. Edward O'Mahony—" How Sleep the Brave
    Who Sink to Rest."
14. Poem by William Geoghegan.
15. "Star-Spangled Banner."
16. Benediction.

Master of Ceremonies.—President of the I. B. V. A., Capt. John T. Toal, Sixty-ninth N. Y.

Special Aids.—Vice-President, Dennis Sullivan, Sixty-third N. Y.; Ca₁ t. John R. Nugent, Sixty-ninth N. Y.; Dr. William O'Meagher, Sixty-ninth N. Y.; Capt. W. L. D. O'Grady, Eighty-eighth N. Y.

Chairman and Senior Officer.—Brig.-Gen. Robert Nugent, U. S. A.

Chaplains.—Very Rev. William Corby, C. S. C.; Rev. Thomas Ouellet, S. J.

Orators.—Brig.-Gen. Denis F. Burke, U. S. V.; Col. James D. Brady, Sixty-third N. Y.

Choir and Glee Club.—Mrs. Florence Rice Knox, Miss Ritta E. Bronson, Prof. Edward O'Mahony, with chorus.

Poets.—William Collins, William Geoghegan.

Sculptor.—Hon. Maurice J. Power.

Quartermaster.—Lieut.-Col. James Quinlan, Eighty-eighth N. Y.

Commissary.—Maj. P. M. Haverty, Eighty-eighth N. Y.

Officer of the Day.—Capt. Chas. M. Grainger, Eighty-eighth N. Y.

Officer of the Guard.—Lieut. David Burke, Sixty-ninth N. Y.

Special Aids.—John Londregan, Sixty-ninth N. Y.; Lieut. John Dillon, Sixty-third N. Y.; Alexander McIlhargy, Sixty-ninth N. Y.; Michael Corcoran, Eighty-eighth N. Y.; William Moran, Sixty-third N. Y.; Patrick Lucy, Sixty-third N. Y.; John Smith, Sixty-ninth N. Y.

Color Guard.—William Parrington, Sixty-ninth N. Y.; Joseph Devereux, Eighty-eighth N. Y.; Con. Ahearn, Eighty-eighth N. Y.; James Dwyer, Sixty-third N. Y.; William F. Maher, Fourteenth Battery.

Reception Committee.—Lieut.-Col. James Smith, Sixty-ninth N. Y.; Maj. Dwyer, Sixty-third N. Y.; Lieut.-Col. J. D. Mulhall, Sixty-ninth N. Y.; Alexander Jeffreys, Fifteenth Battery; Lieut. E. M. Knox, Fifteenth Battery; Walter Bogan, Fourteenth Battery; Capt. P. J. Healy, Eighty-eighth N. Y.; Peter F. Rafferty, Sixty-ninth N. Y.; Lieut. John Murphy, Sixty-ninth N. Y.; Lieut. John O'Connell, Sixty-ninth N. Y.

IN MEMORY OF THE FALLEN DEAD OF THE IRISH BRIGADE.

Whose Monument was Unveiled on the Battlefield of Gettysburg, July 2, 1888.

BY WILLIAM COLLINS.

I.

Peace spreads her wings of snowy white
    O'er Gettysburg to-day ;
No sound is heard of coming fight,
    No marshaling for the fray ;
War's grim battalions dream no more
    At morn the foe to greet ;
The long, long, fitful strife is o'er,
    And we as comrades meet.

II.

We meet in love, and, hand in hand,
    Above our brothers' graves,
We pledge true fealty to the land
    O'er which our banner waves;
But while its folds in glory swell
    And proudly flaunt the air
We think of those who fought and fell
    To keep it floating there!

III.

Of those who in their manhood died
    To blot out Slavery's stain,
And rear aloft in all its pride
    Fair Freedom's flag again!
'Tis ours to raise this cross on high
    Above the Irish dead,
Who showed mankind the way to die,
    When Truth and Freedom led.

IV.

They came from a land where Freedom was only known by
    fame;
Where Slavery's spell, like a breath of Hell, had banned and
    barred her name;
Where the brave man moaned in fetters, and the patriot wept
    in thrall,
And red with the blood of martyrs the despot ruled o'er all!
But when on Freedom's soil they stood and saw her banner
    soar,
And heard the foeman's mustering shout re-echo on our shore,
They leaped, as leaps the lightning's flash athwart the storm-
    tossed sky,
For that old flag with bosoms bare, to triumph or to die!

V.

This soil is the grave of heroes—it is not common mold!
Each foot is dyed and sanctified with the blood of the brave
    and bold;
And an incense rises from their graves to light us on to fame,
And mingles in each patriot soul and sets his heart aflame,
And nerves the veriest slave that e'er shrank from a tyrant
    foe
To leap to life with armed hand, and give him blow for blow—
To strike the despot to the death though bulwarked round in
    steel,
And right, with fierce and desperate strength, the wrongs that
    brave men feel!

VI.

Here, on the field of Gettysburg, where treason's banner flew:
Where rushed in wrath the Southern gray to smite the North-
    ern blue;
Where'er that blue, by valor nerved, in serried ranks was
    seen
There flashed between it and the foe the daring Irish Green!

And never yet, on any land, rushed forth to Freedom's aid
A braver or more dauntless band than Ireland's brave Brigade.
Pause on their graves!　'Tis holy dust ye tread upon to-day—
The dust of Freedom's martyred dead, whose souls have passed
　　away!

VII.

No more the ringing bugle blast
　　Shall fright the trembling air;
No more the squadrons hurrying fast
To meet the charge—perchance their last—
　　Amid the battle's glare;
Their pride, their strength—all, all are past.
　　In peace they slumber there,
And comrades true beside them lie,
　　Who oft, on field and flood,
Fought in the strife for Liberty
　　And sealed their faith in blood;
But never yet beat hearts as proud
　　As those which Ireland gave.
Night's sable mantle was their shroud,
　　The battlefield their grave!

VIII.

But though from earth have passed away
　　Their spirits bold and true,
And tombed in cold and senseless clay
The hearts that bounded warm and gay
In war's wild wassail—every fray
　　Where men could dare and do—
Their deeds will shine in Freedom's ray,
　　While tyrants stand appalled;
Their name and fame shall last for aye,
And brighter burn from day to day
Till the sun sinks into eternity,
　　And the Judgment Roll is called!

THE IRISH BRIGADE AT GETTYSBURG.

Respectfully Dedicated to the Surviving Veterans of that Famous Corps.

BY WILLIAM GEOGHEGAN.

I.

O comrades, step with reverent tread
    Toward this historic mound ;
The soil that soaks the brave man's blood
    Is always holy ground.
Here five and twenty years ago
    An Irish phalanx stood,
And here they swelled the battle tide
    With generous Celtic blood.

II.

Thro' many a fierce, ensanguined fight
    Two banners o'er them flew—
The emblems of the land they left
    And the land they came unto ;
No stain e'er fell on either's folds —
    No foeman e'er could say
He'd plucked a tassel from those staffs
    Or snatched a shred away.

III.

Though rent and splintered, flags and staffs —
    With foemen face to face—
Above the vanguard's fire-swept line
    Those flags maintained their place,
And out of Stonewall Jackson's lips
    The wrathful sentence drew:
" There goes that damned green flag again
    Beside the Yankee blue ! "

IV.

On Fair Oaks field, on Marye's heights,
    Thro' Fredericksburg's dread days,
Well, well, the Southland's veterans knew
    Those blended banners' blaze.
Where'er the fight was desperate
    And spears struck fire from spears,
Those flags flashed out above the lines
    Of the Irish Brigadiers.

V.

The war drum's throb and bugle sound
    Ye loved to hear is o'er—
The damp, cold earth is heaped above
    Your hearts forevermore;
But memory of your gallant deeds
    Enlivens, stirs, and thrills,
Like echoes of a clarion call
    Around Killarney's hills.*

———

"ONE LINE OF EMMET'S EPITAPH HAS BEEN WRITTEN!"

———

"Tenting on the Old Camp Ground" was then rendered.
The recollections of five and twenty years ago and the pathos
of the voices, especially that of Mrs. Rice Knox, left few dry
eyes "on the Old Camp Ground." An excellent reed organ,
brought all the way from New York, was skilfully presided
over by Miss Grace Haverty. It stood near the rock from
which general absolution had been given to the army, July 2,
1863. In an almost similar way, three days were spent in dedicating numberless monuments that dot the entire battlefield
of July 1, 2, and 3, 1863.

———

* The echoes of a bugle or horn blast reverberate among the Kil-
larney hills long after the original sound producing them has died
entirely away.

CHAPTER XXXI.

WE now return to take up the thread of our narrative, which we dropped at the end of the battle of Gettysburg to tell the story of the celebration of the twenty-fifth anniversary of that battle.

Gettysburg battle once over, the army followed up Lee, and as he retreated toward the Rappahannock River we also moved in the same direction. July 1 found the Army of the Potomac fighting at Gettysburg, after a zigzag march of between two and three hundred miles from the banks of the Rappahannock to the battlefield. Now, after the battle (having spent some time in burying the dead), we began to march again and were obliged to retrace our steps to the place from which we had started in June. I will not ask the reader to follow this counter march, but will simply relate a few incidents which occurred on the way. During our return we had occasional spats with the Confederates. One morning, after marching all night, we received orders at break of day to halt and prepare some coffee. Just as the small fires

began to send their tiny columns of smoke toward
the sky the sun peeped out, as it were, to see what
was going on. Acting-Brigadier Kelly, commander of
our brigade, and myself had just halted under a large
wild cherry tree, when, to our consternation, a cannon
ball crashed through its branches over our heads!
This ball was followed by another and another. We
had no notice whatever of the Confederates being so
near us, and it was a complete surprise. Had not our
men been veterans, and brave ones too, we might have
witnessed a genuine panic. One of our officers
remarked that it was an insult to call so early, "even
before breakfast." It did seem very impolite, but no
time was lost. Our men grasped their arms. Pettit
wheeled his battery into position, with his usual skill,
"got the drop on them," and soon put a stop to the
intrusion. In this conflict I lost my horse, but, fortunately, I had another at my disposal. The loss
caused me very great inconvenience, however, as I
lost also a small altar stone and some other necessary
articles which I always carried with me for the Holy
Mass. Needless to say, we also lost our coffee. The
Confederates withdrew, but only to seek a better
chance to annoy us later in the day. We started to
gain "vantage ground," and they did the same.
There was considerable timber and brush in that
locality, and the ground was so uneven that we could
not see the enemy nor could he see us. As we came
to a clear spot along a railway that passed our moving
column, I noticed almost in front, but somewhat to

the left of us, a line of soldiers at the edge of a wood.
I remarked to one of our officers: " Why are those
troops out there? I supposed we were in the lead!"
"Oh," said he, "there are no troops there—can not
be." "Well," said I, "there *are*, and if you will
mount my horse you can see them." I dismounted,
and the lieutenant, who was on foot, stepped into the
stirrup and at a glance saw the troops, who, by this
time, were a little closer; and he saw, too, that they
were Confederates who were trying to outflank us
and gain the "vantage ground" first. We dispatched
word immediately by an orderly to the commander,
who ordered a "halt! front face! march!" Then "halt!
ground arms!" The commander took advantage of
the bed of the railway. It passed through an elevation,
making a cut that was perhaps two or three feet deep.
In this cut—an excellent breastwork—the Union
troops rested on their arms and waited for the Confederates to come up. Had I not seen the Confederates,
mounted as I was on a horse fully sixteen hands high,
we might have been cut to pieces. Each army, or
portion of an army, watched the other and manœuvred
for quite awhile. As we could do nothing, two doctors
and myself proposed to retire and get some coffee, and
to find a place for the wounded in case there should
be a battle, as by this time it was getting late in the
afternoon. We selected a place which we thought
would be suitable, with ambulances and hospital men
ready and awaiting results. The young man who
attended me had been very much demoralized by the

experience of the morning surprise, and he had lost
our coffee and provisions. We made a fire, however,
and procured a few ears of corn from the supply
brought for the horses, cooking it in the fire, which
half burned and half roasted it. This we were eating as best we could, when a scout suddenly rushed
in and told us that we were cut off from our troops
by the Confederate cavalry. It was getting ·dark
and we hurried away. The doctors mounted and I
did the same. They were gallant young surgeons.
One rode on either side of me and several men were
mounted and followed after us. To an excited
lieutenant who had charge of the ambulance I looked
very much like a general. Riding up in front of
our calvalcade and tipping his hat to me, he said:
" General, where shall I direct the ambulances?"
I did not undeceive him but replied, in a tone of
authority: " Have them driven to Fairfax!" I knew
that so far the command was correct, and the
lieutenant did as I told him. We marched the night
through, having had nothing to eat all day except the
parched corn. At four o'clock next morning, having
passed over a small river, the Occoquon, I think, and
finding ourselves safely out of the trap, we halted,
tied our horses to some small trees, and, though it was
raining gently, slept on the ground until seven.
Then started again, and, coming to a small log cabin,
entered and asked for something to eat. The poor
people seemed to be alarmed and said they had nothing.
" Oh," we said, " we do not wish to deprive you, and

we are willing to pay." Then they took courage
and gave us some fat pork, corn bread, and a kind of
coffee, made, I think, out of burned peas. But it
was warm. There were three of us, the two doctors
and myself. We gave our hosts five dollars, and they
were delighted, and so were we. Hunger made that
breakfast the most delicious we had in six months.
We continued our journey, and when we reached
Fairfax, again near to our troops, we saw a tent where
a sutler was selling cakes and canned meats. One of
my companions went in to make our purchases while
I stayed outside with the other. After marching all
night and sleeping in the rain, I had quite lost the
appearance of a general, for which I had been mis-
taken on the evening previous. While standing outside the sutler's tent, covered with mud, horse-hair,
and oak-leaves, my hair and beard, unkempt and
uncombed for three days, flying in the wind, a man on
horseback dashed up to the same tent, dismounted with
considerable nonchalance, and with scarcely a glance
at me, peremptorily ordered me to hold his horse.
Suiting the action to his words, he extended his bridle-
rein toward me. It was customary in those days to
hand a boy or an idle loafer ten or twenty-five cents
for holding an officer's horse for a short time. The
occurrence was somewhat stunning. " How hath my
greatness fallen in one night! " I soliloquized. "Last
night I was taken for a general; this morning I am
taken for a loafer waiting to earn ten or twenty-five
cents." The man who had commanded me to hold

his horse was not an officer, as far as I could ascertain. He looked like one who was earnest in his duty. Just as he was extending the bridle-rein to me, the doctor, who had been making the purchases in the tent, came out, and, lifting his right hand to his hat very politely, by way of salute, said: "General (keeping up the joke), I have a good supply for to-day." The stranger who owned the horse looked sharply at me, with terror in his face, and quickly darted out of sight. He seemed confounded at the thought of having asked a general to hold his horse.

A few days' marching brought us within five miles of Warrenton, where we encamped. Here we had a chance to wash, comb our hair and beards, and feel like white men once more. I could not say Mass the whole week, as I had not the means. On Saturday, however, it happened that information came to me that there was a Catholic Church in Warrenton. I started at once, and found a small church. There were not many Catholics at any time in the town, and I learned that the church had been erected by the Semmes' family, aided by one or two other rich families. Mrs. Semmes was at this time a widow. I found her to be a very dignified, intelligent lady. She had a large family of brilliant daughters. Many of the daughters and female relatives had married officers in the army and navy; but, if I mistake not, most of the male portion were engaged in the war in the Confederate cause. Mrs. Semmes herself had strong secession proclivities. She had charge of the church, and gave me a small altar stone and also baked some altar breads for me, and, although she thought I was on the "wrong side," as she expressed it, we parted good friends, united in holy Faith which no war can disrupt, and against which even "the gates of hell can not prevail." I have ever since cherished an esteem for the family, and have had the pleasure of meeting several members, notably Mrs. Fitzgerald, a most accomplished lady and one of the best harpists I have ever heard. Also, Mrs. Dr. Clarke, an equally refined and accomplished lady, well known, especially, in the best Catholic society in New York City. Next day, Sunday, to my great joy and to the joy of all our men, I celebrated Holy Mass on the "Tented Plain," *coram* "*Militibus in armis.*" Thus we sanctified another spot in Virginia on our march, as we had done hundreds of times before, and which we continued to do until we reached the *end* on the banks of the Appomattox River near Petersburg. The children of Israel were conducted by a pillar of fire in the night and a cloud in the day; so, in our darkest hours and during our longest marches, the Holy Sacrifice made us feel that we had God with us to guide and assist us to live well, and, if need were, to die well.

CHAPTER XXXII.

AN OFFICER'S PREPARATION FOR EXECUTION.

FOR obvious reasons real names can not be given in the following account. In July, 1863, there were in our camp two officers, both captains, whose tents were next each other, separated by only a few feet. The canvas walls did not obstruct the sound of the voice. In one of the tents was Capt. Peter (let us call him) and in the other Capt. Paul. One day Capt. Peter heard the conversation going on in Capt. Paul's tent. It was about himself and of a disparaging nature. Capt. Peter felt his blood boil, but he went out of his tent so that he might not hear any more of the talk. After awhile he returned to his tent, sat down all alone, and began to read. Again he heard the conversation about himself, and growing still worse, in proportion, probably, as more wine had been taken. Capt. Peter could stand it no longer. He got up to remonstrate, and, with no serious intention, just as he was passing out of his tent took up a revolver that lay on a stand near the door, and walked over to the front of his neighbor's tent. He turned back a portion of the canvas that formed the closing, and demanded, in a stern voice:

" Captain, do you mean what you have been saying about me? "

" Yes," came the defiant reply, " and more."

Having the revolver in his hand, he shot Capt. Paul. That moment his regret was so great he wished the arm that did the shooting had dropped from his body in time to save the life of his fellow-officer. But his regret was too late. He was court-martialed and sentenced to be shot. He did not belong to my command, but he sent for me and told me the entire circumstances as given above. Then he said to me: " Father, do what you can for me. I have but a short time to live—only a few days." I put him on retreat and spent all the time I could with him ; and oh, how fervently the poor man prayed! He ate almost nothing, wept bitterly over the sins of his past life, asked God thousands of times, day and night, to pardon him and all his enemies; begged for mercy, also, for the poor soul he had sent prematurely to eternity; and, finally, he made a confession with heartfelt sorrow. I kept before his mind the infinite mercy of God, the sufferings of Christ on the cross, and other reflections of a similar nature. I spent most of the night previous to the day set for his execution in his tent, and was seriously affected by his groans and lamentations over past transgressions. Next morning I brought him Holy Communion. He received most devoutly, and, after making a pious thanksgiving, told me that he had prayed all night— had not slept one hour. Finally the time came, and

14

a squad of men, with fixed bayonets, were at hand to lead him out. Just then an officer came dashing forward and cried: "Halt! A dispatch received! Pardon granted!" The prisoner was in the act of moving out in sad silence to meet his death when this announcement fell on his ears. The reaction was too much for him—he dropped into a seat and fainted. He had nerved himself to meet death, and, very unexpectedly, he was free. This narrative, although touching by the nature of the subject, is still far short of the reality. One must witness such scenes to realize them to the full extent. It occurred to me at the time, and frequently since, that his earnest preparation for death would form an excellent model for all of us. It was one full of faith and self-conviction, accompanied with deep humility and true contrition. In August I received from his accomplished wife the following letter, which I copy *verbatim*, written in answer to the one I had written to her breaking the news of her husband's fate, and offering all the consolation I could under the circumstances:

"X——, KY., Aug. ——, 1863.

"THE REV. WILLIAM CORBY:

"I have received yours of July 30, and feel deeply indebted and *truly grateful* to you for the kindness you manifested toward my husband in the hour of his great trial. The consolations of religion are always sweet—always soothing to the soul of the believer; but when called upon to sever earthly ties, to bid farewell to earthly scenes, when our days and *hours* are numbered, oh! how precious then is the assurance of a Lover's undying love; His promise of pardon and life everlasting to all

who believe in Him   How welcome, then, is the Minister of
God, to point the way to that glorious rest prepared for the
children of God in heaven!   Be assured, then, of my heartfelt
thanks for your kindness.   My earnest prayer is that you may
long continue in your labor of love; that, like St. Paul, you will
have fought a good fight, and there will be, therefore, laid up
for you a ' Crown of Life.'

" Very respectfully,

" JANE ———."

Other priests in the army had, possibly, incomparably more chances than I to bring consolation to
the afflicted, to minister to the needy the rites of the
church, and to extend a helping hand, not only to the
sick, wounded, and dying soldiers, but also to send
authentic accounts to the anxious and weeping relatives at home, which must have been to them a balm
to aid in healing and curing their bleeding hearts.
Amid the long marches, during deprivations of food
and shelter, those chaplains felt their mission was
not absolutely and entirely a fruitless one.   In my
limited experience I can say that the answers to hundreds of letters, written at the request of distressed,
sick, wounded, and dying soldiers, were teeming with
sentiments of sincere gratitude.   But who can tell
what a boon it was for the poor departing soul to have
a chance, far from all churches, far from home; yea!
perhaps in the depths of a dismal, mountainous land,
covered with wild forests, to receive the sacraments
of Holy Church! The good soldiers were not unmind-
ful of such advantages, and, consequently, would
sacrifice all comfort and make almost any sacrifice to
accommodate the priest whom the Church, in her

maternal care for souls, placed over them to minister to their spiritual wants.

We continued our routine of marching and counter-marching until we finally entered a campaign called " Mine Run." But from this Gen. Meade was obliged to fall back about November, 12, 1863. Some cavalry and artillery fighting followed up our corps, the 2d. We met some loss and some of us had " very close calls." However, we captured a battery of six guns and seven hundred and fifty prisoners. Another move was made in December across the Rapidan, but no general engagement took place. This closed the year 1863, and our troops went into winter quarters on the north banks of the Rapidan River, which empties into the Rappahan-nock about fifteen or twenty miles up the river from Fredericksburg, Va.

CHAPTER XXXIII.

THE time for which most of the men of the Army of the Potomac had enlisted had now nearly expired. A general move was made to induce the veterans to re-enlist "for the war." The members of the Irish Brigade were among the very first to do so. In December, 1863, the Government gave us free transportation to New York for ourselves, horses, and servants. We reached New York City January 2, 1864, and lived in the city a portion of that winter. A grand banquet was tendered us in Irving Hall, where Gen. Meagher made one of his typical, eloquent speeches. He was followed by many others. The hall was a commodious one and highly decorated. American shields were placed around on the walls, and the names of all the battles in which the brigade had taken part, from that of Yorktown to that of Gettysburg, were written on them. The old flags, full of bullet holes, were suspended amid the new ones lately presented by friends in New York. So the hall presented an appearance well suited to the occasion. The galleries were full of ladies, many

(213)

and most of them, were related, so to speak, to the brigade. It was noticed that most of them were dressed in black. We naturally asked ourselves the questions: Was there a mother there who had not lost a son? Was there a daughter there who had not lost a loving father? Was there a sister there who had not lost a noble, promising brother? And for what? In what cause? In the cause of Union and Liberty! A boon the sons of Erin could appreciate, since, under the hand of tyranny and oppression, many of their forefathers had died of starvation and want. Even at that very time cries of suffering came across the billows of the Atlantic, telling how precious was the liberty they were enjoying in the land of their adoption and under whose flag they had marched and fought; and, even if many had died, better die in a good cause than starve to death under the iron heel of despotism; and these sentiments were often expressed during our sojourn in New York. The men visited their homes, and found themselves once more in the embrace of their loving families.

The number of our men, however, was not large. Battles and sickness had served to thin our ranks; nevertheless, those who were at home were real heroes and were idolized as such by the people. Their friends " trotted them out," to use a homely phrase, as one would show off curiosities in a museum. The veterans, too, were full of war stories without drawing on their imagination to manufacture them. Simple oral narrations of what occurred in the camp,

on the march, in the battle, with a description of
the life they led, their sleeping places, their food,
the kind of water they had to drink and use in making their coffee, were all more impressive than any
written page, from the very fact that such accounts
were known to be real. The soldiers did almost nothing but talk, and the people and friends looked on in
silent admiration. Thus passed the time, while on
Sundays they had the pleasure of once again going
to their parish churches to be refreshed by the sweet
music of the choirs and organs and the eloquence of
their beloved pastors, whom, thank God, they lived to
see once more.

The officers, however, were, on the other hand,
very busy. One of the objects of our visit " on
furlough " to New York was to recruit the decimated
ranks of our brigade, and by an extraordinary
effort wonders were accomplished. Lest, perhaps,
too much luxury in city life might unfit us for the
hardships of war, we received timely notice to
return to camp. During January and February,
especially, much had been done to fill up the brigade,
and, as we made ready to return to camp, we found
many new companions anxious to learn of us—who
were now regarded as authorities, having been so
long in the field and having passed through so many
battles—all about the life of a soldier in " active service." Our situation was enviable, and we felt our
dignity too. Many of our officers remained behind
to complete the work of recruiting, and as fast as

they could they sent on large numbers of recruits, so that the spring of 1864 found us back in camp Brandy Station, on the north bank of the Rapidan, from which we started for New York, with our ranks so thoroughly replenished that we were nearly as numerous as in the beginning, September, 1863. Here we spent the spring-time, with nothing to do except to keep up the routine work of camp life in winter quarters. I was very much pleased to learn that my old companion, the Rev. Thomas Ouellet, S. J., who resigned on April 25, 1862, had re-enlisted as chaplain, with commission dated February 15, 1864.   Father Ouellet was a good little man and a very genial companion.   The men and officers were delighted to see him back.   He was very popular when with us before, and during his absence of nearly two years we had learned to appreciate his value, and his reception was really a cordial one.   We "put our heads together," as the saying goes, to plan out the spiritual work for the coming campaign, which we knew must take place as soon as the weather and the roads would permit.   In the interval, we spent our time in giving every opportunity to our men to practise their religious duties, and took care to draw in the raw recruits by giving them to understand that once the campaign opened, as we knew by experience, there might be a general engagement at any time, and when least expected.   Prudence, therefore, suggested that preparation for the worst should be made in advance.   I met one good man who was rather slow in following this advice. He was familiarly known as "Jack." In fact, I never found out his family name. He thought there was time enough, and remarked to me, in a vein of good humor:

"Father, will you not be with us on the march?"

"Certainly," I replied.

"Then," said he, "I will get a touch just before the battle."

"Oh, you will? May be," said I, "you may get killed before the regular 'fighting' begins."

"And do you tell me so? How is that?" said he.

"Do you not know that a sharpshooter from behind a tree, or even from the top of a tree nearly a mile away from you, can send a ball that is sufficient to send you into eternity? Besides, a cannon-ball or shell, sent from a big gun that is several miles off, may, and often does, send a dozen or more to their last home."

"O holy Moses! Father, are you in earnest, or are you only joking with me? How can they see so far?"

"I am in earnest. The sharpshooters have telescopes that run along the barrels of their guns. Ask any of the veterans."

"Well, Father, I will take your advice and be around to see you this evening after the 'taps.' I have been wild enough in my early days, and it is time now to turn over a new leaf." He kept his word, and was ever after faithful to his religious obligation. There was considerable life in the Army of the Potomac during the spring months of March and April, 1864. Many of the officers had visits from their wives. Friends and relatives came to the camp, and many festivities of a harmless nature served to keep up the good spirits of the troops until a general move would be commenced. There was a large hall built for army purposes of common lumber in our camp. This was at the disposal of the Commanding General, Coldwell, and on Friday he kindly sent word to me that I might have the use of it for services for the Irish Brigade on the following Sunday, which happened to be the first Sunday of March, 1864. I gladly accepted the offer, and went to work to prepare my little sermon for the occasion with more than ordinary care, knowing that many of mixed creeds would be present. In this I was not disappointed. Gen. Coldwell, though not a Catholic, as far as I know, and all his staff, composed of brilliant young officers, attended in a body. What other officers and men attended not belonging to our brigade, I could not tell. At all events, the great hall was more than crowded. The officers were seated in front, and back to the door and away out on the grounds the men of the brigade, and others, in devotional reverence, clustered to hear Mass and to listen to an instruction, such as it was. This "Military Mass" was celebrated by my friend, Father Ouellet, S. J., and seemed to be a service characterized by special fervor and piety. The brigade felt very much complimented at the spontaneous and kind offer of our good Gen. Coldwell, whom we always regarded with great respect for his excellent soldierly and gentlemanly qualities. Besides, the honor conferred by the presence of these officers was highly appreciated. Many of the non-Catholics who attended pronounced the service the most inspiring and religious in form, which they had witnessed since entering the army.

CHAPTER XXXIV

THE EXECUTION OF A SOLDIER.

IN camp the officers have time to attend to many
duties which have been necessarily postponed
on account of marching, fighting, or reconnaissances
incompatible with such duties. So, when in camp, all
cases for military offences were tried, and old decisions
disposed of. Early in April, 1864, the case of a
soldier named Thomas R. Dawson, not of my brigade
but of the Nineteenth Massachusetts Regiment, then
in the Second Corps, came up. He had been court-
martialed and condemned to die—to "hang by the
neck until dead." He sent for me, and before I began
to do anything for him he told me his story, in a
simple, candid way, that left no doubt in my mind as
to the truth of what he said. Still, the sentence had
been passed and he must die. The facts as given to me
were as follows: He with two other soldiers wandered
from camp, and, coming to a house, they found there
wine or liquor of some sort, and, needless to say,
they indulged freely. He said he became so stupid
he knew not what followed. Some men and officers on
duty, passing that way, arrested him on a charge of

rape made by an old woman of about sixty. The other two got away and escaped arrest; but he was so "full" that, unable to move, he became an easy victim. His being under the influence of liquor was not, in the eyes of the law, a sufficient excuse, for many reasons; especially because he was out of camp, and, besides, he had no business to be intoxicated. Still, taking human nature as it is, and in consideration of the other excellent qualities of Dawson, the officers of the regiment did not wish to see him die. They manifested the greatest sympathy for him. However, I began to instruct him and to aid him all I could in making a good general confession of his whole life. He entered on his religious exercises with exceeding great fervor. Meanwhile his friends were not idle. The officers of his regiment drew up a petition to the President, Abraham Lincoln, and came to me and asked me if I would be so kind as to go to Washington and present it. I urged them to form a committee among themselves for that purpose; but they insisted on my going. After I had consented, they made a new copy of the following petition:

HEADQUARTERS, NINETEENTH MASSACHUSETTS VOLUNTEERS.
CoLE's HiLL, CULPEPER Co., VA.,
April 17, 1864.
Hon. Abraham Lincoln, President of the United States:
YOUR EXCELLENCY:—We, the undersigned, humbly petition that Private Thomas R. Dawson, Company H, Nineteenth

Massachusetts Volunteer Infantry, now in charge of the provost-guard, Second Division, Second Army Corps, under sentence of death, may be pardoned and returned to duty in his regiment. Previous to the commission of the violent act for which he has been condemned, he was an excellent soldier, intelligent and obedient. Since his trial, he has been on one occasion, while sick, an inmate of the Regimental Hospital without a guard, and had every opportunity to effect his escape had he desired to do so. His course at that time is very creditable to him. He served during the Crimean War in the ranks of the British Army and obtained the Victoria Medal and Cross of Honor, bestowed only upon the bravest and most daring soldiers of that splendid force. As in duty bound, we will ever pray,   Your obedient, humble servants:

EDWARD RICE, *Major Commanding, Nineteenth Mass. Vols.*
ELESHA A. HIAAKS, *Captain,*   "   "   "
JOHN I. B. ADAMS, *1st Lieut.,*   "   "   "
THOMAS F. WINTHROP, *1st Lieut. and Reg. Q. M.,*   "   "
I. P. PRATT, *Assist. Surgeon,*   "   "   "
JOHN B. THOMPSON, *1st Lieut.,*   "   "   "
JOHN C. FERRIS, *1st Lieut.,*   "   "   "
CHARLES SIDNEY PALMER, *1st Lieut.,*   "   "   "
EPHREM ABBOTT HALL, JR., *1st Lieut.,*   "   "   "

I certify to the above; all the officers *present* with the regiment.

WILLIAM M. CURTIS,
First Lieut. and Adjutant of the 19th Mass. Vols.

This will be presented by W. Corby, Chaplain, Irish Brigade, Second Army Corps.

I made no delay; got a pass to Washington, and boarded the train at 9 a. m.; but, although the distance was not perhaps sixty miles, I did not reach Washington until about twelve that night. The army train was composed of box cars and flat cars, freights, and these were crowded with sick soldiers

and wounded men, who were too weak to be sent
sooner since the last battles and raids. The poor sick
and wounded suffered terribly on this tedious trip,
necessarily prolonged on account of the frequent
stops we were obliged to make in order to let other
trains, bringing provisions to the front, have the
right of way. I counted my own hunger and fatigue
as nothing in comparison, although I had had nothing
to eat from the time I left until I reached Washington, at midnight. The length of time on the way
gave me a better opportunity to think over my plans
and speeches, so as to insure a show of success in my
important mission to the President.

Next day I brushed up, and, being comparatively
young, I felt like a fresh, blushing lieutenant as I
neared the " White House." I met the guard, sent
up my card, and received an immediate response to
enter. I did so, and made known the object of my
visit in a few clear terms. The good President was
inclined to be positive; said it was a " hard case,"
promised to take the matter into consideration,
and, across the back of the petition, which was
folded in the long form usual with military papers,
wrote: " See for the 25th of April." This was
intended for a note to remind him of the time set for
the execution. Feeling that my case was about gone
I put in a few more pleadings. The President then
asked what had I to say in extenuation of the crime.
I answered that I could not say anything on that
score, since the man had been tried by court-martial

and had been found guilty; but I added that good reasons had been set forth in the petition for mercy and pardon. I showed that an actual injustice had been done, according to military standards, in keeping the man so long—some months—under sentence; the suspense he had undergone must be considered as unnecessary cruelty. Still the President was not inclined to grant the pardon, and said that suspense was more or less inevitable, on account of the movements of the army. But, finally, I touched a tender chord. All who knew President Lincoln knew that he was a very tender-hearted man. I said, almost in despair of my case: "Well, Mr. President, since I have seen from the start that it was out of the question to plead the innocence of this man, or to say anything in mitigation of his crime, I have confined myself to pleading for his pardon; but, since Your Excellency sees fit not to grant it, I must leave his life in your hands." This was too much! His tender heart recoiled when he realized that a man's life depended upon his mercy. As I started across the "green room" to take my departure he turned in his chair, and, throwing one of his long legs over the other, said: "Chaplain, see here! I will pardon him if Gen. Meade will, and I will put that on the petition." Then, under the note "See for the 25th of April," he wrote:

Execution set for the 25th

If Gen. Meade will in writing says he thinks this man ought to be pardoned, it shall be done,

A. Lincoln

April 19, 1864

I felt proud of my success, and thought often of the importance of the document which I carried back to the " front " and delivered to the officers who had drawn up the petition.   It showed that my mission was not an entire failure.   Still, I felt that Gen. Meade would not take it on himself to put in writing his assent to the man's pardon.   I wanted the officers to go to Meade in a body, but they were shy of such duty, and begged me to do so.   I did, but with little hope of success.   I called on Gen. Meade, then commander-in-chief of the Army of the Potomac, and, producing the document with the name of the President, I told the general the whole story in a few words. He looked at the paper a few moments, and then said:

" Father, I know that your mission is one of charity; but sometimes charity to a few means cruelty to many.   If our discipline had been severe, or cruel, if you will, in the beginning, we would not have so many causes for execution now.   Besides, the President has the final acts of that court-martial in his possession, and he should have given the final and positive decision.   I will *not* act."

"Then the man must die," said I.

" You may see the President again."

"There is not enough time left.   The execution is set for the 25th, the day after to-morrow."

" Well," said he, "you may telegraph; I will give you the use of the military wires."

"No," said I, "the case seems to me to be now between you and the President.   I have done all I could."

The fact of the matter is, at that time the generals in the field, or some of them at least, thought that the kind-hearted President was too good in pardoning so many, and some blame was attached to him on this account. Now, the general-in-chief could not see his way clear to do what had been found fault with in the President. I returned with a heavy heart and told the officers of the failure. They still urged me to telegraph, and I went and consulted our good friend, Gen. Hancock, commander of our corps. He advised me to telegraph. "You can do so from my headquarters," he said, and he wrote an order to the operator for me. I telegraphed, but I was told afterward that, in all probability, the message never reached the President. The secretary of war, very likely, put the dispatch in the fire, for I never received an answer. All this time our poor sufferer was between hope and despair. He made, however, a good preparation for death. God gave him the special grace of what seemed "perfect contrition"; for, like Mary Magdalen washing the feet of Christ with her tears, he also bedewed the ground with tears of sorrow and sincere repentance. Shortly before the hour of execution the officer of the provost-guard sent to me for permission, or, rather, asked if I would allow the condemned soldier some whisky to brace him up. I promptly replied: "No! his faith will brace him up. I want my penitent to die sober; to die with a clear mind and with a heart prefixed by true contrition and the holy sacraments."

The troops were drawn up and massed in front of the scaffold. I accompanied my penitent, encouraging him to make a generous sacrifice of his life for Him who did not hesitate to die for our redemption. He felt confident that he had done all he could; had confessed contritely, received Holy Communion devoutly, and trusted the rest to God's mercy. He walked with a firm step. He had permission to speak, and he said: "You may break my neck, but you can not break the seal of manhood." He seemed to be roused to say more, but, fearing he might become excited, I suggested that he ought to stop there, and he did. The black cap was adjusted over his eyes, the rope placed about his neck, the signal was given, and he dropped into eternity, April 25, 1864. By his death, encountered with Christian sentiments and united with the merits of Christ, he wiped out the sins of his past life. Had he been pardoned he might not in the end have died in as excellent dispositions.

CHAPTER XXXV.

THE BATTLE OF THE WILDERNESS.

THE spring campaign opened May 4, 1864. Gen. Meade still continued commander-in-chief of the Army of the Potomac. Grant, who was confirmed by the United·States Senate as lieutenant-general and commander-in-chief of all the troops, on the 2d of March, 1864, made his headquarters with us in the Army of the Potomac and had much to say about our movements. He ordered Meade to advance across the Rapidan on the above date. The "ball" opened on the 5th, and until about the 20th of June we were almost continually under fire, not being out of range during the whole of that time. Counting reserves, the Army of the Potomac had 160,000 men. The Irish Brigade, having recruited, as stated elsewhere, during the winter, went on this campaign in strong force. We abandoned our winter quarters and started out on one of the most severe campaigns of the war, fighting and marching almost continually. Our brigade, with the rest of the army, started across the Rapidan early in the day, and after marching, halting, and marching again, we stopped

(229)

in the night on an open plain. All we knew was that we were to stay there *pro tem.* Good Father Ouellet and myself stretched out on one army blanket and put another over us. I placed my soft military hat over my face to keep out the damp night air. Our heads, as we discovered in the morning, were only about ten feet from a country road and on this some troops passed before *reveille* floated on the morning breeze.

Some soldier, while passing, saw my hat and evidently made up his mind that it was a better one than his own. Of course, he did not know who I was or what I was, and cared less. If it had been Gen. Grant, the circumstance would not disturb his equilibrium or annoy his conscience more or less on that account. So, softly lifting my hat from my face, he replaced it with his own. Soldiers sleep soundly after marching fifteen or twenty hours. It was so in my case, and I did not feel or perceive the loss of my hat until *reveille*, when we arose. Father Ouellet and I noticed at once the strange hat, and it did not require much study to understand the situation. My hat was new, and consequently clean; the hat which I found in its place must have been in use two or three years. It was originally a soft hat, but at this period of its existence it had become quite hard, with grease and dirt soaked and ground into every fiber, and it looked as though it had been covered with black wax more or less polished. The lining had been torn out a year or two previous, and the bell of the hat had assumed the form of a cone or pine-apple! Just entering on a desperate campaign as we were, I could not go back nearly a hundred miles to get a new hat, and to find the stolen hat would have been as finding a crow-bar in mid-ocean. There was no alternative; I must wear that very dirty, greasy, and unseemly hat or go bareheaded. The thought of it spoiled my morning meditation. In due time I mounted my horse and started on the march. As I rode out among the officers and men, even my own troops did not know me. Many of them thought some "dead beat" had stolen my horse, since the horse was well known in the Second Corps. Here and there I was recognized and had to enter into an explanation of the hat business. This was great fun for many, but not for me. However, we had not very far to go till we came in contact with the Confederates, May 5. This was the beginning of the famous "Battle of the Wilderness," the first under Grant in the Army of the Potomac. It was a terrible battle, in which many of our poor men fell, and was continued all the next day with increased fury. On the 7th, Lee fell back to Spottsylvania Court House, and on the 8th, Sunday, Father Ouellet and I managed to say Mass while both armies were making preparations to renew the bloody strife. The soldiers who had been seriously wounded waited with anxiety for the Holy Communion, which was given them early, their confessions having been heard the previous evening. On the 9th, there was considerable skirmishing. Having attended all our wounded as best we could, and being on the point of starting under orders to cross the Potomac River, I made one more round, and up to the left I found Daniel Lynch, a private soldier of a most obliging disposition, and for a long time detailed to assist in the quartermaster's department. Poor Lynch was a good-natured fellow, had many friends and no enemies; but in the discharge of his duties he made many blunders for want of system and education, and on this account he was returned to the ranks again to carry a musket. He was a brave, dutiful soldier, and when I found him he knew me perfectly. His mind was clear, but he had in his body eight bullets. I prepared him for death, and, dropping a parting tear, was obliged to leave him to his fate in the Wilderness of Virginia. Out of his goodness and kindness of heart he had rendered me many services in '62-3. I remember on one occasion we secured some beans, which, with a limited quantity of pork, would be for us a genuine feast, as at that time we had no provisions. Instructed to cook them, he started to a farm-house to get water, but could find no pail to get water from the deep well, so he tied the black pot to a pole and let the pot down into the well. The beans were in the pot. The string broke and pot, beans, and all were lost. After waiting for a long time for something to eat the captain in charge sent for "Dan," as he was familiarly called, and as he came up he showed signs of trepidation.

The captain roared at him: "Dan, where are those beans?"

The reply came slowly, for Dan had an impediment in his speech: "The p-p-p-p-ot's in the w-well."

"But the beans! Where are the beans?"

"T-the b-b-beans w-w-was in t-the po-p-pot!"

Then, poor Dan fled before the anger of a hungry, infuriated captain, and the prayers that followed the poor fellow on that occasion were not holy. Dan, however, did not mind these little exhibitions. He became used to them, and was just as cheerful an hour afterward, just as willing to do a kind service, as if nothing had occurred to disturb the peaceful mind of a modern "Tribe" camped on the banks of the "River Po."

CHAPTER XXXVI.

ON the 10th of May the battle began. The fire of musketry and cannon opened all along the line, and smoke rolled up into great clouds. The fierceness of the conflict showed a fury born of desperation on both sides. Wild dashes were made by our men and lines were captured, to be in turn lost and captured again. The battle proved, finally, to be the most sanguinary of the entire campaign. Our men fell in every direction, and this gave abundant occupation for the priests who were there. Father Ouellet and myself had all (and more than) we could do in attending to those who were mortally wounded, while we must be in readiness, at a moment's notice, to administer the last rites of the Church to the new victims of the engagement. That evening, as we moved up with the advancing troops, the battle at a late hour finally ceased, and we reconnoitered to see where we could locate for the night. Near a spot where many of our wounded were being collected, we found a small island, a stream of clear water having divided and passed on either side. The little

stream passing round us was not more than four feet
wide and about three feet deep. The island was
perhaps fifty feet long and thirty feet wide. It was
covered with beautiful evergreens, mostly pines, that
furnished excellent shade in the heat of the day,
should we happen to stay there a few days to enjoy
it. The ground was clean and covered with the
"pine-needles" that fell from the trees and lay quite
dry on the ground. These pine-needles we used to
call "Virginia feathers." We flattered ourselves that
we had found a veritable paradise on a small scale,
where we could spend at least a part of the night in
sweet repose. Congratulating ourselves on our find,
we determined to hold this little fort as long as we
could, as our headquarters, while ministering to the
wounded, of whom there were by this time a large
number. All this being determined, Father Ouellet,
who carried a lantern, and I started out to see what
new cases might need our ministerial services. We
spent a good portion of the night on this service, and,
returning exhausted by fatigue, lay down to rest and
slept very soundly. In the morning we were both
literally covered with wood-ticks. These vermin
infested that spot and turned our paradise into a land
"cursed to bring forth evil things." These wood-
ticks are of a livid color, a species of "Acarus."
They bury their heads and shoulders, so to speak,
in the skin, and as they feed on your blood their heads
swell inside the skin and their bodies swell outside.
The body assumes the size and shape of a large

pea, and, to remove them, you must break the body and leave the head bedded in your flesh. Father Ouellet and I had to go through this morning exercise by way of making our toilet. During the day we suffered terribly. The heads of those pests were still in deep and caused a burning sensation that was anything but comfortable. That night we secured a quantity of salt and washed in water impregnated with the salt. This helped us some, but for many days we endured great pain. When perspiring, the raw wounds filled with the perspiration and smarted so as to throw us into a fever, and we passed whole nights in sleepless agony. It may seem strange to introduce this theme in the midst of such fierce conflicts, but this is precisely my reason for doing so. Hundreds, thousands, I may say, have written up those conflicts and painted them in the bloodiest colors. Whereas few, if any, have entered at length into the details of other trials and sufferings incurred by the poor soldier while serving his country. What I relate is personal experience; but I hope, by the relation of such, to give my readers—if I should have any—a notion of war life not entirely made up of the "blood and thunder" of the battlefield. This will also help to depict what hundreds of thousands endured during the war. At the end of this tenth day Gen. Grant formulated his famous dispatch to Secretary Stanton. After passing his opinion on the result of the six days' fighting, he said: "I propose to fight it out on this line if it takes all summer." On the 11th we had no fighting of any account, and had more time, consequently, to look after the wounded and dying soldiers. On the 12th, our Second Corps, of which the Irish Brigade formed a part from the beginning, made a charge and captured three thousand men and forty guns. As we started early that morning to accomplish the strategic movement, we passed over some ground contested by the pickets and skirmishers on the day previous, and, in the woods, on the slope of a hill and even along the roadside, we passed many dead soldiers not yet buried. I found one Confederate who was mortally wounded, but who still had full consciousness. He had not been baptized, and after some instruction, at his request, I baptized him and hastened on to attend, if necessary, any others that might need help. The battle of this day continued till late and ended a fearful struggle of eight days, during which time the Union army lost, in killed and wounded and missing, 29,350 men—a large army in itself; while the Confederates lost, perhaps, even more. Heavy rains set in, and no serious or important move occurred till about the 17th of May. That morning our troops were ordered to advance, and more carnage was looked for. Very early that morning the colonel of the Twenty-eighth Massachusetts, a regiment which formed a part of our brigade, called on me and told me that he *felt* that he should get his "discharge" that day. He was a very brave officer, and up to this time had no serious misgivings, although he had not missed a battle of any note from the beginning. But this morning, having made his confession, he gave me a slip of paper, on which he had marked down what he wanted me to do—namely, to turn over to the quartermaster a horse he had purchased in Washington a short time before, and on this horse was afterward discovered the brand "U. S."—showing that it was the property of the Government. He had been deceived, but still did not wish to keep what he found out the man in Washington could not in honesty sell. Other items were to be attended to, and then he handed me the following letter, which has, by a mere accident, remained in my possession ever since. It was addressed to his wife, and ran as follows:

"MAY 17, 1864.

"MY DEAR ELLEN:—I am well. No fighting yesterday; but we expect some to-day. Put your trust and confidence in God. Ask His blessing. Kiss my poor little children for me. You must not give up in despair—all will yet be well. My regiment has suffered much in officers and men. I am in good health and spirits. I am content. I fear nothing, thank Heaven, but my sins. Do not let your spirits sink; we will meet again. I will write you soon again; but we are going to move just now. Good-by, good-by; and that a kind and just God may look to you and your children is my fervent prayer.

"RICHARD."

The letter was written with a lead-pencil, and the address of his wife was legibly written on the back of the folded paper, but not put into an envelope. He requested me to send it to his wife in case he got killed, as he expected. One can see from the tone of the letter that he had a strong presentiment then and there of his death; for, although trying to console and keep up the spirits of his beloved wife, he could not conceal his sentiments; as, for instance, where he says: "Kiss my poor little children for me"; and, again, when he says: "We will meet again," he had evidently in his mind the world to come. Sure enough, he received his death-wound very soon after; but in the mercy of God he was not killed outright. He lived, I was told, to be transported to Washington, where his loving, faithful, and weeping wife and children met him and embraced him before he departed for the unknown future. I can not tell just why, but among all the other terrible and touching scenes of this campaign up to the date of the above letter, not one made such a deep impression on me. Even now, after about a quarter of a century, while penning these lines, tears of sympathy fill my eyes. Of course, I never sent the letter to his wife; because, first, I was not to do so unless he got killed; and, secondly, under the circumstances, he reached Washington before the letter could possibly get there except taken by hand on the cars. Although we did not lose many on the 17th, on the next day we lost in killed and wounded one thousand two hundred, and on the 19th about fourteen hundred.

It would be tedious for the reader to follow the march in all its ramifications during this campaign, so I will simply summarize, in as brief space as possible, up to the 20th of June. As we have seen,

this campaign opened on May 4, when we crossed
the Rapidan and headed for Richmond. From that
time on, we marched, fought great battles and small
ones, and engaged in many fierce skirmishes in
which considerable loss took place. We encountered
untold hardships from heat, dust, hunger, and thirst.
Many of our horses died from thirst or were overcome by the heat. Men, too, dropped in the road
and expired. This was kept up from the 4th of May
till the 20th of June. In the interval, we crossed
the old rivers made so familiar to us during our campaign under McClellan, in '62; namely, the Potomac,
North Anna, Pamunky, Chickahominy, James, and
others, and landed in front of Petersburg, Virginia.
In this campaign, out of 160,000 we lost 100,000 men
in less than two months! This will give the reader
some idea of the hardships of those who survived,
following the hardships of war step by step in this
campaign. In all that time, although not fighting every day, we were only at very short intervals
out of bullet-range of the Confederate rifles, and the
poor men—covered with perspiration, dust, and vermin
—could not even wash, part of the time, for want of
water; besides, marching, fighting, digging rifle-pits,
etc., kept them engaged so constantly as to prevent
them. Father Ouellet and myself followed also the
fortunes of war, and with our dauntless brigade
marched by day and by night just as our troops had
to do. Piety was put to a severe test in this campaign; still, when a halt was sufficiently long, we

said Mass, and encouraged our men by exhortations as best we could. When one of them was found dying from sickness or mortal wounds, the priest was of substantial service; and from the carnage and hardships of this dreadful campaign one may easily see that the opportunities to assist dying soldiers were not wanting every day in the week. "Fighting it out on this line" was expensive in men and money. But it satisfied the cry: "On to Richmond!"

CHAPTER XXXVII.

OUR LIFE AT THE "FRONT."

IN front of Petersburg there were some very scientific works of defense built by the Confederates, under the skilful direction of generals in the Confederate service. They were so constructed that when troops captured an outer line another line would command the flank of the capturing party, and the troops in possession of the second line could get in an enfilading fire. This is a most destructive fire, and for persons not familiar with military terms, I would say, it is simply shooting, not across the line, but *lengthwise*—just as a hunter desires to shoot birds perched on a rail along the line of a fence.

This reminds me of a story told by a hunter, given to exaggeration, and will illustrate my point. He stated that on one occasion his shot gave out, but he had plenty of powder; and seeing a long line of wild pigeons perched on a board fence, he put in his ram-rod on top of a heavy charge of gunpowder and fired, and strung on the ram-rod ninety-nine of the birds! His friends asked him why he did not say a hundred? "Do you think," said he, "I would tell a lie for one bird? No, sir!"

FATHERS CORBY AND OUELLET UNDER FIRE.

After these works fell into the possession of the Union troops, Father Ouellet and I went to inspect them in some of our free time. Having done so, we ventured out still farther in front of our troops, and as we rode along we came to the top of the high hill or bank from which we could look down into the valley of the Appomattox River, on the banks of which Petersburg is built. We were "taking in" the scenery, and trying to discover, if possible, the position of the Confederate army. Finally, beyond the plain and far off on the side of an elevation of ground we noticed something very indistinctly stirring up a dust. The dust seemed to be about the size of smoke made by the discharge of a cannon. We watched the dust made there and the progress it was making, but had no fears or apprehensions whatever. We had neglected to take our field-glasses with us, not thinking we would have any use for them, so our observations were not very satisfactory to us, and at such a great distance we could see only very indistinctly. But, evidently, officers in the vicinity of the dust had not forgotten their field-glasses; for, in less time than it takes to write it, after we observed the first sign of dust, they discharged a cannon which sent a ball at us with a screeching whiz that was really wicked in the extreme. Father Ouellet was seated on his white horse and I on a large chestnut horse. The Confederates had our range, and it was probably the white horse that first drew their attention; thinking, likely, that we were officers inspecting their works, to which they wished to put a stop at all events. Father Ouellet wheeled his horse round without delay, and while doing so, and instantly after the first, came a second shell and struck the bank just in front of us, nearly on an exact line. Father Ouellet, while putting spurs to his horse, was making quick tracks, but I had a semi-view of his face, turned partly toward me, as he cried out: "Did you see that?" The expression of consternation on his face made me laugh outright; for, although I felt that the danger was serious, he, as a Frenchman, was quicker than I and took in the situation more perfectly the first instant. The first ball passed over our heads and the second one was a little too low, but if they had had the exact range the first time, ourselves and our horses would have been blown into fragments! We retreated, however, in good order, and there was no casualty! In this place our lines were advanced by degrees till we were close to the Confederate lines; so much so that balls fired by sharpshooters frequently passed through our ranks, and on one occasion, when Father Ouellet's tent and mine were side by side, a ball passed through his tent near where he was saying his office. It became so hot for us, after a while, that many of the troops, Father Ouellet and myself included, built bomb-proof huts by excavating in the hillside and covering the top with logs split in two, flat side down. This was a precaution taken not only as a security against stray rifle bullets, but also against cannon-balls or shells.

Our front line was so close to the Confederate breast-works that it was not possible to fire cannon with any effect in a direct line, so mortars were used. These sent their shells at a high angle of about forty-five degrees or more, and, having reached the highest point, dropped into the Confederate lines. The Con-federates, in turn, sent some of these "messengers of death" into our lines in the same way. Hence the necessity of bomb-proof huts. We often spent a part of the night watching the bombs passing up and then descending. The course of the bomb or shell could be easily followed by the eye at night, as the burning fuse attached to it was distinctly visible. The second day that I was located in this place, while standing near my tent talking to an officer, one of those dangerous things passed over our heads and killed a horse tied to a post a few yards away. This locality was not only uncomfortable to our troops on account of the proximity of the Confederate guns, but also on account of the burning sand and lack of shade, excepting what we had in our little huts, underground and only fit for wood-chucks. How-ever, there we remained, like "patience on a rock monument," or, imitating the example of Micawber, "waiting for something to turn up."

CHAPTER XXXVIII.

EXECUTION AT CITY POINT—MOTHER'S LETTER.

ON July 12, 1864, I received the following communication from Gen. Meade:

"HEADQUARTERS ARMY OF THE POTOMAC,
"July 12, 1864.

"Rev. W. Corby, Irish Brigade, Second Corps:

"REV'D SIR:—There are two men to be executed on the 15th inst., one of whom, especially, is very anxious to secure the services of a priest. If you will be pleased to attend him, the provost-marshal at headquarters will be instructed to furnish you all facilities necessary to discharge the functions of your sacred office. By order of "MAJ.-GEN. MEADE,

"S. S. WILLIAMS, "Com'd'g Army of Potomac.

"Acting Adj't-General."

I ordered my horse at once, and, accompanied by the aide-de-camp and orderly who were sent with the message, I was conducted to headquarters. The acting provost-marshal was informed of my arrival, and instructed to see that I received all the necessary information and means to prepare the condemned. On being introduced to the provost-marshal, the name seeming strangely familiar, " Richard F. O'Beirne," I asked him if he were not from Detroit, Mich. He said, "yes," and looked inquiringly at me.

(246)

I told him that I was also from the same place, and a
son of Daniel Corby. "O! Father Corby, how are
you?" he cried, grasping my hand. "I have heard
your name frequently mentioned here in the army,
but I had no idea that you were from Detroit and a
son of Daniel Corby, whom I know so well!" This
officer, then acting provost-marshal, had not met me
nor I him since we were small boys, about fifteen
years of age. He was a very exemplary youth,
served in the cathedral in Detroit as censer-bearer
for many years, and stood in great favor with the
Right Reverend Bishop and the clergy in the city.
After we had talked over old times a few minutes, the
question of attending the poor condemned soldier
came up. Provost O'Beirne gave me a tent and had
my horse cared for, and I went immediately to the
place where my future penitent was under guard. I
found a man who was quite young, possibly about
twenty, of an excellent frame, healthy and strong.
He had a good mind and was somewhat educated.
He was not a low, depraved person by any means,
but in time of temptation he had fallen. The crime
was much, if not entirely, the fault of his accomplice
rather than his own. I spent a few days with him
and instructed him as best I could. On the evening
of the 14th I said to my friend, the provost-marshal,
that I wished to say Mass the next morning, so as to
communicate my penitent on the morning of his
execution, and asked the marshal if he could still
serve Mass. "It has been a long time since I

performed that duty," he replied; "but with the aid of my prayer-book, no doubt I can." Everything was made ready, and next morning I said Mass, communicated my penitent under guard, and having taken some coffee which my friend had ordered for me, I spent the balance of the time with the doomed prisoner till about nine o'clock, when a general movement took place. Troops began to march, and there was a silence that made one feel the presence of death. Scarcely a word was spoken, and all one could hear was subdued orders given by an officer here and there: "Fall in!" "Right face!" "Forward!" "March!" and a few other necessary directions. Excepting the steady tramp of the soldiers and an occasional rattle of a saber, scarcely a sound disturbed the solemn tranquillity that reigned on that morning of the 15th of July, 1864. The troops finally closed "en masse" in front of a large scaffold. There were, perhaps, ten thousand men present. A strong guard conducted the prisoner to the scaffold, and I rode beside him till we reached the spot. Then we dismounted and the brother of one of the victims held my horse while I attended the two men and escorted them up to the scaffold. Without very much ceremony the ropes were adjusted about their necks, and, while both continued to pray for God's mercy, a silent signal was given and both dropped dangling at the end of the ropes—dead! As I have observed before, these scenes were harder on the nervous system than the scenes witnessed in the midst of a battle, where there is rattle, dash, and excitement to nerve one up for the occasion. And the poor brother who witnessed the scene! What anguish! What a wail of grief filled his young heart! But, oh! what lamentations filled the bosom of his heart-broken mother when she beheld the corpse of her loved son, sent to her as the first news of his fate! Let her own words in the following letter, which she sent me long after the event, tell what she felt. I give it *verbatim*, omitting names:

"WESTFIELD, Dec. 22, 1864.

"DEAR FATHER IN JESUS CHRIST:—I am the unfortunate mother of X, who was executed at the headquarters of the Army of the Potomac, near City Point, Virginia, July 15. As I have learned from his own writings that you were the priest God sent to prepare him for death, may that God bless and protect you and give you a share in His heavenly kingdom when you require it, is the prayer of my heart.

"Dear Father, I wish to inform you that my son's remains came to my view two hours previous to the tidings of his death; thus unexpectedly did I see my child's remains come to me. The very day I received these tidings I was preparing to see my boy after three long years of weary servitude; but welcome be the will of God in every shape and way it may appear.

"Dear Father, my boy requested me not to forget to have frequent Masses celebrated for the good of his soul, and thus far I have had three solemn high Masses and two low Masses said. May the Almighty God give him the benefit of them. I would like to comply with all my dear child's dying requests; but in one respect I can not; that is, not to grieve for the death he had to undergo. Now he is over five months buried. I must acknowledge to you that my tears and grief are as fresh as when I first heard of it, and will be until the day of my death. I have begged of God to give me grace to forgive those who have deprived me of him, in our blessed Saviour's name, who

forgave the Jews that crucified Him, and, thank God, I have
obtained it; for I have never said any worse of them than to beg
God that my floods of tears might not injure them in either soul
or body; and I beg of God that He will give me grace to bear
the hard shock of my child's death with resignation to His
holy will; and that the holy Virgin Mary may intercede for
him, and may his soul rest in peace.

" Dear Father, I hope you will let me know if my dear child
died reconciled with leaving this world and going to meet his
God. I am always under the impression that the grief of heart
caused me troubled him more than anything else in this world
except his own soul. I also have to inform you that his movements in going toward that place of execution, and the
spectacle of his bereft and heart-broken brother looking at him
for twenty or thirty minutes, as I have been informed by him,
stand continually before my eyes. I offer all my trials and
sufferings, with the death of my son, in union with the death
and sufferings of my dear Jesus and His blessed mother, in
satisfaction for X's sins and mine.

" Dear Father, I have deferred this writing long, but I have
done it as soon as I felt able. I hope you will answer this and
send some words of consolation to my grieved heart. I must
conclude by humbly asking your blessing, and believe me to
remain,   Your obedient servant,
                                "MRS. ——,
                              "Westfield, N. Y."

I give this letter in full because in it there are full
expressions of a mother's grief, and, also, a profession of faith and solid piety that is truly edifying.
Persons of such faith do not commit suicide! They
patiently suffer their slow martyrdom till it pleases
God to send consolation or draw them to His own
kingdom with the expression: "Well done, good
and faithful servant."

Not since the war have I met my friend, O'Beirne; but a few days ago I clipped from a daily newspaper the following item regarding him:

"DEATH OF COL. RICHARD O'BEIRNE.

"HE EXPIRED WHILE ON A LEAVE OF ABSENCE ON ACCOUNT OF HIS HEALTH.

"NEW YORK, Feb. 24, '91.—Richard F. O'Beirne, colonel of the Twenty-first Infantry, United States Army, died at a New York hotel, of Bright's disease. Until November last he was in command of Fort Sheridan, near Chicago. * * * He was appointed to the full rank of colonel three weeks ago. His father was private secretary to Gen. Cass, of Detroit, during the latter's incumbency as Secretary of State, besides being a prominent judge at one time in the same city, Detroit, Michigan. So, one by one, the war companions pass off and leave behind them many sorrows in this deceitful world. 'Sic transit gloria mundi.'"

CHAPTER XXXIX.

IN July, while we were under fire at Petersburg, Col. Robert Nugent, of the Sixty-ninth, and Lieut.-Col. James E. McGee were doing excellent work in New York. They turned their whole energy to recruiting and filling up the depleted ranks of the Irish Brigade, fearfully reduced during the campaigns of '62, '63, '64. They swelled with fresh recruits our numbers beyond all expectation, and we felt proud once more of our standing as a brigade. Under the patronage of Gen. Burnside, principally, Col. Pleasants, of the Forty-eighth Pennsylvania Volunteer Infantry, excavated, with great skill and labor, a tunnel five hundred and ten feet long, stopping directly under the Confederate fort, in which were many cannon and a strong force of infantry. Then he branched to the right and left in the form of a **T**, to the right thirty feet and to the left twenty-seven. Here, under the feet of the Confederate garrison and batteries, he placed eight thousand pounds of powder. The object was to blow up the fort and thus to enable troops to penetrate the

(252)

Confederate lines. A part of our Second Corps, commanded by Gen. Hancock, marched under orders, July 26, across the Appomattox and James rivers, to Deep Bottom, toward Richmond. We marched all night. With no delay, a desperate attack was made by Hancock on the Confederate lines, capturing four guns and two hundred prisoners. This manœuvre was intended to deceive the Confederates so far that they would send troops to protect Richmond, and thus weaken the force opposite the mine. In the evening, on July 29, we were ordered back, and again marched all night under cover of darkness and halted about daylight in the vicinity of the mine on July 30, the time set for the explosion, ready to help in case of necessity. Soon the fuse was ignited, and we witnessed from some distance the destructive work of death. A great mass of earth was lifted, with a sudden electric force, carrying heavenward with it batteries, men, timber—in a word, the contents of the fort—until, reaching a certain height, it spread out like a cloud and then all came crashing down in a horrid confusion, burying alive many poor fellows who had been asleep when the mine was fired. The cavity made by this explosion was thirty feet deep, sixty feet wide, and one hundred and seventy feet long. Through this breach in the Confederate works the Union troops pushed, but by some misunderstanding confusion set in and prevented the successful accomplishment of the well-devised plan on the part of Col. Pleasants, who accomplished his work admirably well, notwithstanding the difficulties he labored under; obliged, as he was, to calculate the exact distance in the face of the Confederate guns, and, as he himself complained, furnished with an old-fashioned theodolite to make the proper triangulations. Union loss, four thousand; Confederate, fourteen hundred—sad for all. Everyone turned in to help care for the wounded, and every help for soul and body was rendered, as far as our means enabled us to do so. The next day, July 31, a letter reached me in the evening, from City Point, about eleven miles from where we were encamped. The letter had been written by a sick soldier who was in a hospital tent. I mounted my horse and started at once. Just at dusk I came to a mountain stream which had suddenly become, by recent rains, so wild a torrent that it had swept away the bridge; and as I rode up to the stream, some troops encamped on the banks warned me not to attempt to cross it as it was very dangerous. I said I must cross to minister to a sick soldier. I had a very strong and intelligent horse, a good swimmer and sure-footed. "Well," said the men, "pass over here to the left, so as to avoid any of the sunken timbers of the bridge lately swept away." I directed my horse as instructed and, fortunately, passed over in safety. "The Rubicon was passed." After fulfilling my mission, I started to return and came to this same stream about midnight. I wished to pass over in the same way I had come. My horse had remarkable instinct, and whenever I passed in certain directions, he desired, on returning, not to deviate a foot from the same line. So when we plunged into the stream, I talked to him, calling him by name, "Prince," and told him to be careful. He persisted in going a little to the right, and I said to him: "Prince! you are wrong for once," and I pulled him to the left. Presently he began to stumble over some sunken beams. Ah! then I let him have his own way. He kept to the right and after we reached the bank I could see by the light of a timely camp fire, that he had brought me out at the very spot where we had entered the stream the previous evening, under the instructions of the soldiers.

Mounted soldiers become very fond of their horses, because these faithful servants are their daily companions, and very often they spend dreary nights in each other's company, while marching; moreover, they partake of similar privations and perils. The horse soon learns to know his master, and forms a particular affection and respect for him. In 1864, when we were encamped at "Brandy Station," a major, of the Fifth Michigan, I think, was the owner of a beautiful bay horse and he lost him, or, most likely, some one took a fancy to him and borrowed him and forgot or neglected to bring him back. The major was inconsolable, and searched everywhere for his pet horse. Finally he came to a corral about six miles from his own camp. In this corral there were many horses used for military purposes. The major passed along the lines of horses, feeding, when suddenly he saw his own horse in the line, and was in turn recognized by the horse, who turned his head toward his master and whinnied affectionately, a clear sign of recognition. "*Res clamat Domino!*" The major's heart was touched, and, drawing his sword, he said in feeling and determined tones: "I would like to see a man dare prevent my taking this horse;" and, loosing him, took him back to camp in triumph, no one presuming to utter a word in opposition. It is hard to say which rejoiced most, the horse, in his way, or the master. Such incidents go to fill up the soldier's life in active campaigning.

But, to return to our sick in army-tented-hospitals. It is a lamentable fact that many died in those tents unknown and without the consolations of their religion. They were more or less careless when well, and becoming sick they either did not know where or how to get a priest; and even if they did, it may be, they became in a short time so ill as to be unconscious of the danger in which they were, and having no Catholic "chum" to attend to the matter, passed off quietly and were put in the ground. If an infantry soldier, the customary volleys are fired over his grave; if a cavalry soldier, the trumpeter sounded the thrilling notes of "taps" and "lights out." These notes are followed, in slow succession, by several more, and as the sounds drift over the distant hills and down the valleys, the sad tale told by "lights out" was—the soul is gone. This is the last bugle call for him on earth till the great day when the angel messenger from heaven will sound the dread trumpet for the general resurrection of the dead. In war or in peace, one sees the epitome of man's existence in these few words: "He lived; he died." Hence men exposed to the dangers everywhere found in soldier life should be always ready to die. And the words of the royal Prophet should be constantly on their lips: "Lord, enlighten my eyes that I may not sleep in death, lest my enemies say they have prevailed against me." The same reflection and practice is good for all men.

17

CHAPTER XL.

EXPLOSION OF A GREAT BOAT FILLED WITH ORDNANCE — SECOND EXPEDITION TO DEEP BOTTOM — HORSE DRINKS IN JAMES RIVER AND IS FRIGHTENED — BATTLE ON THE WELDON R. R. — MEN AT CARDS SHOOT AND DROP A CONFEDERATE FROM A TREE — CAPT. BROWNSON KILLED.

OUR camp near Petersburg, already referred to, was a very unpleasant one. When we first arrived in this camp we found ourselves on burning sands—no shade and no water. In July and August, under the rays of a Southern sun, the alligator flourishes; but the white man from the North finds the situation almost intolerable. I shall never forget how water was first secured for a refreshing (?) drink of coffee in that locality. Our men went into a deep, dry ravine between two sand hills, and in the very bottom they found a spot that showed signs of —mud. Here they loosened the baked clay with their bayonets, and by the aid of an old saber made a small hole, perhaps a foot and a half deep. In this hole the water showed itself, but the mud in it made it nearly as thick as "vegetable soup." They rested for

a while till the soup—the water—had settled somewhat, and then dipped out the material. It was not
inviting, but it resembled water. When men are
parched with thirst, moisture of any kind seems
refreshing. Well, they put this water in small
cans, boiled it, and furnished us—coffee! Life grew
very tiresome there, as we had simply to stay and
watch. We were perhaps twelve miles or so from
City Point, on the James River, and that locality
was our base of supplies of provisions and news-
papers. An enterprising boy would go to the landing
on the irrepressible army mule, stay at the landing
all night in a dry-goods box or under a wagon, and as
soon as the steamer came with the papers he put in
front of him his *quantum* of several hundreds and
came galloping out to the camp, crying out at the
top of his voice: "New York *Herald!*" He charged
us twenty-five cents apiece for the papers, but even
at that price we were delighted to get the news, and
he sold his papers like hot cakes. In the early part
of August, 1864, the monotony of our life was broken
by a terrific explosion of an ordnance boat on the
James River at City Point, where army supplies were
stored in great quantities, and near which a number
of troops were stationed. The explosion caused a
damage of several million dollars; killed and wounded
a large number of men, and put the balance into a
perfect panic. The troops, not knowing exactly the
cause of the unearthly report made by the explosion,
that, earthquake-like, shook the ground around them

for miles and sent forth bursting shells and other missiles of death with dreadful force, thought that forty dozen Confederate ironclads had suddenly come down the James from Richmond and let fly at them. As I was going to City Point about this time, I was appalled by the devastating effect. I saw fish, even a half mile from the river, that had been scooped up out of the water and cast forth with various sorts of rubbish by the terrible explosion. On the 13th of August we were again ordered to Deep Bottom, where the Irish Brigade took, without delay, the front line of the Confederate works. Just before going into the battle I rode my horse down into the James River to water him, letting him go down into the water alongside the ponton-bridge that crossed the river at this place. The bridge was a few feet above the spot where he was drinking. Just then a two-hundred pound ball was discharged from a parrot gun from a large war-ship which was anchored out in the river. The sudden and frightful report seemed to come up from the water. In an instant my horse made a bound like that of an antelope and landed on the top of the ponton-bridge, three or four feet above the drinking place; then, wheeling around, made for land. He went about a hundred yards before I could get him under control. I wanted to rein him back to finish his drink; but no—I really believe if he had been dying of thirst, no power could have induced him to drink again in that river, at least in that vicinity. After finishing the strategic intention of this expedition, our corps was ordered back south of the James to help the Fifth, now hard pressed on the left. At this season, the hottest part of August, we found our long march to the Weldon railroad a very hard one; besides, many of our men, marching in this great heat, under their usual load of about sixty pounds, dropped dead from sunstroke. Some, being overheated, were placed in the shade of an old fence or dusty tree; where they received the last sacraments, and were left to live or die. The priest could not stay with them, because another might fall at any minute and be entirely neglected. Finally we reached our destination, where, fortunately, we found a wooded country, and the shade was most desirable and refreshing. It was related at the time, that some of our Second Corps were sent out on picket duty, and after the first line had been deployed some of the balance on reserve determined to engage in a quiet game of cards in order to pass the time. While at the game they were somewhat startled by the whiz of a bullet, which passed uncomfortably near them. Shortly afterward another and another; but the third shot revealed whence the bullets came. They saw a Confederate sharpshooter in a tree, full thirty feet from the ground. One of the men interested in the quiet game stood up, angry at the interruption. He was from the West, where in his early days he prided himself on being able to cut off the head of a wild pigeon with his rifle. As he reached out for his gun, he said, coolly, to his companions: "That gray squirrel is pretty frisky, and I must stop his fun to stop him spoiling ours." He drew a bead on the man in the tree and fired. As the Confederate sharpshooter came crashing through the branches to the ground, the Westerner sat down and asked: "What's trumps?" He seemed as unconcerned as if he had killed a mosquito that had been annoying him. On the 22d of August we reached our destination on the extreme left, and were then ordered to destroy the Weldon railroad. On the 25th, desperate fighting had taken place at this point. In killed, wounded, and captured the Union loss was two thousand seven hundred and forty-two.

These incidents I mention to show, in as simple a form as possible, the real life we led in the army. At one time undergoing great fatigues, losing many men, both by exposure and by battle; at other times experiencing events of a sensational and thrilling interest; again seeing and hearing of occurrences so novel as to serve to enliven our ranks and even to amuse the troops and lift up their drooping spirits amid all their hardships. But behind all this was constantly present to our eyes and mind the scene of a great stream, a procession, so to speak, of human souls on their way to eternity. Many of our brigade passed off during this campaign. One, who was not exactly of our brigade, but Inspector of our Second Corps and a member of Gen. Hancock's staff, dropped in this very battle on the Weldon railroad. The one I allude to was Capt. E. P. Brownson, son of the great American philosopher, the Christian Plato, Orestes Augustus Brownson. I mention his death in particular, because, like his venerable father, he was a convert to our faith, and his conduct, even in the rough army life, gave great edification. When circumstances permitted, he was a weekly communicant, and always entered the battlefield fortified by the sacraments. To this end did the priests accompany their men on all occasions and on all the marches, ample opportunity being thus given the officers and men to go to confession at least, except in extraordinary cases, when a continued march, day and night, rendered it impossible to perform this duty. For a long time the good captain was my penitent; and when he so suddenly passed to eternity, a strange sensation filled my soul; but I had the consolation to know that he was well prepared.

At this battle we had our hands full looking after the wounded. After the smoke and thunder of battle had passed over, after all had been attended to, our thoughts were turned in another direction by the celebration of the third anniversary of the brigade.

CHAPTER XLI.

ALTHOUGH in a former chapter I gave some general notions of a "Military Mass," I will here enter more fully into details. On or about the 4th day of September, 1864, Gen. Meagher, who was on a visit with Gen. Hancock at the time, prior to his departure for the department of Gen. Sherman, to whom he had been assigned for duty, proposed an anniversary celebration for the brigade. The brigade was now three years old, having been born in September, 1861. As usual, he wished to have the anniversary commemorated in a religious manner. I mention this to the credit of the general, because he was proud of his faith, and considered no celebration dignified or worthy the name that did not begin by invoking God's blessing in the most solemn form possible. He came to me, therefore, and asked if I would be so kind as to arrange a Solemn High Mass for the occasion. I was only too glad to do him this favor, for several reasons, but, especially, because it encouraged his religious tendency, and gave an

(264)

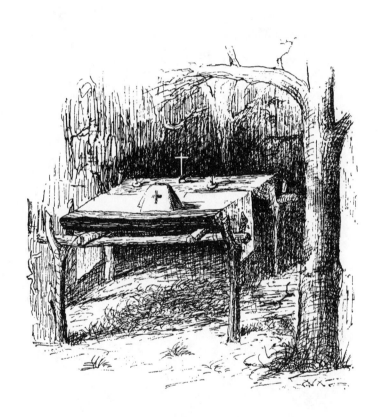

RUSTIC ALTAR.

excellent example to the soldiers in the field. Invitations were sent out to various other commanders to join us in the celebrations. These invitations were accepted by quite a number of other commands, and by the following generals, namely: Hancock, Miles, Berney, Gibbons, Mott, De Trobriand, and, of course, Meagher himself would be expected. Details of men with willing hands were directed in clearing up, beautifying the grounds, planting pine and cedar trees, and making the entire camp like fairy-grounds. A beautiful chapel tent was erected, and a grand avenue lined with evergreens led to the front entrance of the grounds and to the chapel, which was on a slight eminence. Seats were provided for the invited guests as far as possible. About nine o'clock the bugles were sounded, and the whole brigade, at this signal, began to make preparations to receive their guests. With military precision every man reported, and in a short time one could see the ranks formed in perfect order. Muskets shining, shoes polished, and all, in a word, fit to be seen on dress parade by the "Queen of the Fairies." Precisely at ten o'clock, the hour fixed for service, the guests began to arrive. First, Maj.-Gen. Hancock, surrounded by his intelligent, handsome staff-officers. Then each general abovementioned, with that exactness peculiar to army life and excellent discipline (attended in the same way), arrived just on time. As they approached, the numerous bands began to play "Hail to the Chief!" in special compliment to Maj.-Gen. Hancock, for the commander of our corps, besides being so distinguished in many ways, was notably so at the battle of Gettysburg, where he showed superior skill. Each general in that brilliant group having made his mark and record, to form very bright pages of history, received special marks of respect on that occasion. The generals were seated first, and, as each company, battalion, or regiment of invited troops arrived, place was allotted them, the members of the brigade "doing the honors," in politely seeing to the wants of the guests first, thinking of themselves last. The Rev. Thomas Ouellet, S. J., Paul E. Gillen, C. S. C., and the writer, appeared before a simple altar, dressed in modest taste, at the very moment ten o'clock was sounded by the bugle. By this time we had become experienced in such celebrations, and it is with some laudable pride that we refer to them now. Gen. Meagher, being well versed in the ceremonies of the Mass, acted as Master of Ceremonies, in as far as the music and the military duties were concerned. As soon as the priests are ready, the *Asperges me* is announced, and, instead of a grand choir, such as is heard in the royal cathedrals of Christendom, the bugles, followed by the report of numerous guns, announce the beginning. Then, under the direction of Gen. Meagher, at the *Introibo* various military bands discourse solemn music until after the *Credo*, when, again, by a sign from the Master of Ceremonies to the Officer of the Day, another discharge, a grand salute of guns, testify to *Credo in unum Deum*—I

believe in one God. The bugle follows with its
well-known notes, "tara-taran-tara," and again the
bands play. Now their music is soft, low, and sweet,
suitable to the devotion that immediately disposes
the faithful for the more sacred portion of the Mass.
The *Sanctus! sanctus! sanctus!* rouses all to a fixed
attention and is accompanied by a sudden rattle of
dozens of kettle-drums, with an occasional thundering sound from the bass drums. Shortly after this
comes that moment of moments in the offering of the
sublime mysteries. The preparatory is over, and
now you see men bow down in deep devotion as the
priest leans over the altar and takes up the Host.
Here, at a sign from the Master of Ceremonies, the
bugle notes, "tara-taran-tara," ring out over the
tented fields, and the same grand evidence of respect
and faith is given by the sound of cannon and the roll
of musketry, as the sublime words, full of power and
purpose — the supreme words of Consecration — are
pronounced. Soft music is again in order at intervals,
until the end, which is proclaimed in turn by guns,
drums, and bugles that prolong a grand *finale*. The
writer preached a short but well-prepared sermon at
the conclusion, to which Maj.-Gen. Hancock and the
other generals present listened with much attention
and respect, although many of these generals were
not Catholics. After all was over, the guests were
invited to lunch, and, notwithstanding it was Sunday,
several hours were spent at the tables, where some
very interesting speeches were made, and good wishes

expressed for the brigade. Speeches were made by
Gen. Meagher, who, in genuine oratory, was head and
shoulders above any general in the army; by Maj.-
Gen. Hancock, who spoke in the highest terms of the
bravery and devotedness of the Irish Brigade; by
Gen. Miles, who gave testimony to the same effect, as
witnessed by himself at the latest battle, and mention-
ing the details. Gens. Gibbons, Mott, and Birney
also spoke, and, finally, Gen. De Trobriand, who said
that his Irishmen claimed *him* as one of their own,
stating that his name was in reality only slightly
Frenchified from the original (*O'Brien*) which caused
prolonged merriment. This lunch and the speeches
alluded to served as a final parting with Gen. Meagher,
who then left the Army of the Potomac, joining the
army in the Southwest, where he was assigned to
duty. This celebration throws additional light on
the character of the Irish Brigade. When all the
rest of the army was more or less dormant or bewail-
ing the situation and longing for "the flesh-pots of
Egypt," the Irish Brigade was making fun and cheer
for itself and all the friends it could accommodate.
Its hospitality was limited only by its purse, and
sometimes it even borrowed or anticipated the salary
of the coming "pay-day."

REV. JOSEPH C. CARRIER, C. S. C.

Taken by Lillibrige, of Chicago, in April, 1863, as the former was on his way to
the seat of war (Vicksburg, Miss.), as Chaplain of the 6th Missouri Vols.; but
his field of action extended unofficially over the whole army of Gen. Grant,
as he was the sole Catholic Chaplain, at that time, in the whole command.

CHAPTER XLII.

AFTER the celebration mentioned in the last
chapter, a few expeditions brought us into the
fall of 1864. Nothing of great importance is now
to be recorded relative to our movements in this
portion of the army. At this time I received an
order from my ecclesiastical superior to return to
Notre Dame. The Very Rev. B. Moreau, then
Superior-General, had ordered an election of a provincial superior for this country, to preside over the
department of the United States and Canada, and to
this election I was summoned. I remained home for
several weeks, and as the Chapter or Council for
the said election was postponed, I returned to the
army and remained to give the soldiers an opportunity
of receiving the Sacraments, of making their Easter
duty, and thus preparing them to enter the spring
campaign, which put an end to the war. When I

arrived in Washington I called on Gen. Hardee, who
kindly furnished me the following pass:

> "WAR DEPARTMENT, February 22, 1865.
> " Pass Rev. William Corby, missionary, to Fortress Monroe
> and City Point, Virginia, and return, with free transportation
> on a Government transport. . . .
> " To be used but once.
> " By order of the Secretary of War.
> "JAS. A. HARDEE,
> " Colonel and Inspector-General U. S. A."

A pass of this kind was a great favor in those days
and could scarcely be obtained by any except persons connected with the army. Even within the
army limits, passes were necessary, and when I
arrived at the " front" I made application for one
and received the following:

> "HEADQUARTERS, ARMY OF POTOMAC.
> " OFFICE OF PROVOST-MARSHAL-GENERAL.
> " CITY POINT, VA., 25th Feb., 1865.
> " Chaplain Wm. Corby has permission to labor in the Second
> Corps, and to apply to Capt. Schuyler for transfer to Fifth Corps
> whenever he desires it.
> "W. V. R. PATRICK,
> " Provost-Marshal-General."

These passes I still possess, and they are to me
mementos of days full of history, full of tender feeling. They bring to mind the faces of many dear
friends, of many noble souls, and of many distinguished heroes, whose names and fame will never
fade from my memory. My good long rest gave me

REV. P. P. COONEY, C. S. C.
Chaplain 35th Ind.

fresh vigor, and I spent my time, I trust, profitably. Judging from the demonstrations they made, my return was a delight to my men. This was not confined to the Catholics. Non-Catholics, officers, and men, gave me a hearty welcome, and, disregarding hardships and privations, I felt glad to be back again at the post of duty.

The religious feature in an army is, indeed, no small matter. "Conscience doth make cowards of us all" is quite applicable in a very forcible manner in this connection. Men who are demoralized and men whose consciences trouble them make poor soldiers. Moral men—men who are free from the lower and more degrading passions—make brave, faithful, and trustworthy soldiers. Rome stood proudly mistress of the world while she held morality sacred—when a Lucretia put a stiletto into her own heart, not wishing to live after a brutal man, by no fault of hers, had violated her; when a Roman officer, Virginius, pierced the chaste bosom of his lovely young daughter rather than see her lose her virginity; when the vestal virgin was buried alive if found violating her vow of virginity; when, in a word, morality was practised and held up for admiration—during these ages the Roman soldier had no equal in the world. When these same Romans were pampered with the luxuries of every clime; when the wealth of nations poured into Rome and enabled them to indulge every appetite, every passion, then the dauntless Roman became effeminate, in the presence of the enemy a coward, and great Rome sank into oblivion. Apart, therefore, from the actual good done for religion—and this must not be underrated—the soldier is all the better as a soldier when assisted by religion. When he is gently induced to practise his duty to God and to keep alive in his heart his love of virtue, he is not made a coward by his guilty conscience; on the contrary, he is willing, if necessary, to lay down his life for justice or for his country, and to leave to posterity an example worthy of emulation. In view of this, Notre Dame sent out seven priests as chaplains, and, counting the Rev. Dr. Kilroy, who is also a child of Notre Dame, there were eight priests of the Community of the Holy Cross rendering spiritual aid to the poor soldier in the field and in the hospitals. These were the Revs. J. M. Dillon, C. S. C.; P. P. Cooney, C. S. C.; Dr. E. B. Kilroy, C. S. C.; J. C. Carrier, C. S. C.; Paul E. Gillen, C. S. C.; Joseph Leveque, C. S. C., and the writer, W. Corby, C. S. C. Many of the above went to an early grave; but while they were able they braved the dangers of the battle-field and the pestilence of the hospitals. I am not writing a history of all the Catholic priests and sisters who did noble Christian work for distressed thousands during the late war. I have neither time nor ability to do so. There is one now engaged at that task—our Rev. Father Cooney. However, I can not omit here the names of a few who spent all the time they could, consistently, with other grave duties, in the army.

VERY REV. DR. KILROY, OF NOTRE DAME.

The Rev. John Ireland, now the illustrious Archbishop of St. Paul, Minn., gave a bountiful share of his time and talent to the good work—the chaplaincy. A year of his time and brilliant talent was more than six years as compared with that of ordinary men. His great ability was exercised with the enthusiasm that has distinguished his whole career. His name was and is a power. The Rev. Lawrence S. McMahon, now the distinguished Bishop of Hartford, Conn., also performed a generous share of chaplain labor. It would require an entire volume to do justice to either of these worthy prelates, and this task I must leave to historians, to men of "facile pen." The good achieved by post-chaplains, and by priests who, though not chaplains, nevertheless exercised their holy ministry among the soldiers, is beyond computation. God alone has a complete record of their self-sacrificing devotion. For the sake of edification, however, let some one put in print the good deeds they have done. And here we may quote a paragraph concerning

"A NOBLE SOUTHERN PRIEST."

THE ONLY REPRESENTATIVE OF THE CHRISTIAN RELIGION AMONG THE 30,000 WAR PRISONERS AT ANDERSONVILLE.

[From the July number of the *Century*, which contains an article on Andersonville, the first of a series of papers on prison life during the late war.]

The writer, Dr. T. H. Mann, says of Father

18

Hamilton, a Catholic priest belonging to the diocese of Mobile:

"The only authorized representative of the Christian religion who possessed enough of it to visit the 30,000 men in the prison pen was a Roman Catholic priest, Father Hamilton, who came in quite regularly, at least every Sabbath, for several weeks. He talked kindly to us, displaying much sympathy for our condition, and administering the last rites of the Church to all the dying men who would accept, without regard to individual beliefs. He stated that strong efforts were being made to bring about an exchange by both the North and the South, and that their efforts would probably soon be successful. Upon the strength of this report we concluded to let our tunnel remain quiet for a time, thinking that if exchange failed we could have final resource to it. The exchange did fail, and a heavy thunder-shower loosened one of the timbers of which the stockade was composed, so that it settled into the shaft, discovering to the authorities our tunnel, and they quietly filled it up.

"After the war, Father Hamilton was located in Mobile, and at times officiated at various churches in other cities of the State. He died about four years ago, in Louisville, Ky., while on a visit to that city, and was buried there."

Sixty Sisters of the Order of the Holy Cross went out under the intelligent Mother Mary Angela as superioress. (Mother Angela was a cousin of the Hon. James G. Blaine.) These Sisters volunteered their services to nurse the sick and wounded soldiers, hundreds of whom, moved to sentiments of purest piety by the words and example of their angel nurses, begged to be baptized in *articulo mortis*—at the point of death. The labors and self-sacrifices of the Sisters during the war need no praise here. Their praise is on the lips of every surviving soldier who experienced their kind and careful ministration. Many a soldier now looks down from on high with complacency on the worthy Sisters who were instrumental in saving the soul when life could not be saved. Nor was it alone from the Order of the Sisters of the Holy Cross that Sister-nurses engaged in the care of the sick and wounded soldiers. Many other orders made costly sacrifices to save life and to save souls, notably the noble Order of the Sisters of Charity. To members of this order I am personally indebted. When prostrate with camp-fever, insensible for nearly three days, my life was intrusted to their care. Like guardian angels these daughters of St. Vincent watched every symptom of the fever; and by their skill and care I was soon able to return to my post of duty. I subjoin an enthusiastic eulogy pronounced by a non-Catholic officer whose enthusiasm on this subject is shared by all who came under the care of these daughters of Christ:

"SISTERS IN THE ARMY."

[From a speech made by Capt. Crawford, the "Poet Scout."]

"On all of God's green and beautiful earth there are no purer, no nobler, no more kind-hearted and self-sacrificing women than those who wear the sombre garb of Catholic Sisters. During the war I had many opportunities for observing their noble and heroic work, not only in the camp and the hospital, but in the death-swept field of battle. Right in the fiery front of dreadful war, where bullets hissed in maddening glee, and shot and shell flew wildly by with demoniac shrieks, where dead and mangled forms lay with pale, blood-flecked faces, yet wearing the scowl of battle, I have seen the black-robed Sisters moving over the field, their solicitous faces wet with the tears of sympathy, administering to the wants of the wounded, and whispering words of comfort into the ears soon to be deafened by the cold, implacable hand of death. Now kneeling on the blood-bespattered sod to moisten with water the bloodless lips on which the icy kiss of the death angel had left its pale imprint; now breathing words of hope of an immortality beyond the grave into the ear of some mangled hero, whose last shots in our glorious cause had been fired but a moment before; now holding the crucifix to receive the last kiss from somebody's darling boy from whose breast the life-blood was splashing, and who had offered his life as a willing sacrifice on the altar of his

country; now with tender touch and tear-dimmed
eyes binding gaping wounds from which most women
would have shrunk in horror; now scraping together
a pillow of forest leaves upon which some pain-racked
head might rest until the spirit took its flight to
other realms—brave, fearless of danger, trusting
implicitly in the Master whose overshadowing eye was
noting their every movement; standing as shielding,
prayerful angels between the dying soldier and the
horrors of death.   Their only recompense, the sweet,
soul-soothing consciousness that they were doing
their duty; their only hope of reward, that peace and
eternal happiness which awaited them beyond the
star-emblazoned battlements above.   Ah! my friends,
it was noble work.

"How many a veteran of the war, who wore the
blue or gray, can yet recall the soothing touch of a
Sister's hand, as he lay upon the pain-tossed couch
of a hospital!   Can we ever forget their sympathetic eyes, their low, soft-spoken words of encouragement and cheer when the result of the struggle
between life and death yet hung in the balance?
Oh! how often have I followed the form of that good
Sister Valencia with my sunken eyes as she moved
away from my cot to the cot of another sufferer, and
have breathed from the most sacred depths of my
faintly-beating heart the fervent prayer, 'God bless
her! God bless her!'

"My friends, I am not a Catholic, but I stand
ready at any and all times to defend those noble

women, even with my life, for I owe that life to
them."

The following tribute also, taken from the *Philadelphia Sunday Times*, I feel impelled to quote:

"WHAT THEY DO WITH THEIR BEGGINGS."

"During the late war, and while Gen. S. was in
command of the department at New Orleans, the
Sisters of Charity made frequent applications to him
for assistance. Especially were they desirous to
obtain supplies at what was termed 'commissary
prices' — that is, at a reduction or commutation of
one-third the amount which the same provisions
would cost at market rates. The principal demand
was for ice, flour, beef, and coffee, but mainly ice, a
luxury which only the Union forces could enjoy at
anything like a reasonable price. The hospitals were
full of the sick and wounded, of both the Federal
and Confederate armies, and the benevolent institutions of the city were taxed to the utmost in their
endeavors to aid the poor and the suffering, for
those were trying times, and war has many victims.
Foremost among these Christian workers stood the
various Christian sisterhoods. These noble women
were busy day and night, never seeming to know
fatigue, and overcoming every obstacle, that, in so
many discouraging forms, obstructed the way of doing
good—obstacles which would have completely dis-
heartened less resolute women, or those not trained
in the school of patience, faith, hope, and charity,

and where the first grand lesson learned is self-denial. Of money there was little; and food, fuel, and medicine were scarce and dear; yet they never faltered, going on in the face of all difficulties, through poverty, war, and unfriendly aspersions, never turning aside, never complaining, never despairing. No one will ever know the sublime courage of these lowly Sisters during the dark days of the Rebellion. Only in that hour when the Judge of all mankind shall summon before Him the living and the dead will they receive their true reward, the crown everlasting, and the benediction: 'Well done, good and faithful servant.'

"It was just a week previous to the Red River campaign, when all was hurry and activity throughout the Department of the Gulf, that Gen. S., a stern, irascible old officer of the regular army, sat at his desk in his office on Julia Street, curtly giving orders to subordinates, dispatching messengers hither and thither to every part of the city where troops were stationed, and stiffly receiving such of his command as had important business to transact.

"In the midst of this unusual hurry and preparation, the door noiselessly opened, and a humble Sister of Charity entered the room. A handsome young lieutenant of the staff instantly arose, and deferentially handed her a chair, for those sombre gray garments were respected, if not understood, even though he had no reverence for the religious faith which they represented.

"Gen. S. looked up from his writing, angered by the intrusion of one whose 'fanaticism' he despised, and a frown of annoyance and displeasure gathered darkly on his brow.

"'Orderly!'

"The soldier on duty without the door, who had admitted the Sister, faced about, saluted, and stood mute, awaiting the further command of his chief.

"'Did I not give orders that no one was to be admitted?'

"'Yes, sir; but—'

"'When I *say* no one, I *mean* no one,' thundered the general.

"The orderly bowed and returned to his post. He was too wise a soldier to enter into explanations with so irritable a superior. All this time the patient Sister sat calm and still, biding the moment when she might speak and meekly state the object of her mission. The general gave her the opportunity in the briefest manner possible, and sharply enough, too, in all conscience.

"'Well, madam?'

"She raised a pair of sad, dark eyes to his face, and the gaze was so pure, so saintly, so full of silent pleading, that the rough old soldier was touched in spite of himself. Around her fell the heavy muffling dress of her order, which, however coarse and ungraceful, had something strangely solemn and mournful about it. Her hands, small and fair, were clasped almost suppliantly, and half hidden in the

loose sleeves, as if afraid of their own trembling
beauty; hands that had touched tenderly, lovingly, so
many death-damp foreheads, that had soothed so
much pain; eyes that had met prayerfully so many
dying glances; lips that had cheered to the mysterious land so many parting souls, and she was only a
Sister of Charity—only one of that innumerable
band whose good deeds shall live after them.

"'We have a household of sick and wounded whom
we must care for in some way, and I came to ask of
you the privilege, which I humbly beseech you will
not deny us, of obtaining ice and beef at commissary
prices.'

"The gentle, earnest pleading fell on deaf ears.

"'Always something,' snarled the general. 'Last
week it was flour and ice; to-day it is ice and beef;
to-morrow it will be coffee and ice, I suppose, and all
for a lot of rascally rebels, who ought to be shot,
instead of being nursed back to life and treason.'

"'General!'—the Sister was majestic now—'Rebel
or Federal, I do not know; Protestant or Catholic, I
do not ask. They are not soldiers when they come
to us—they are simply suffering fellow-creatures.
Rich or poor, of gentle or lowly blood, it is not our
province to inquire. Ununiformed, unarmed, sick, and
helpless, we ask not on which side they fought. Our
work begins after yours is done. Yours the carnage,
ours the binding up of wounds. Yours the battle,
ours the duty of caring for the mangled left behind
on the field. Ice I want for the sick, the wounded,

the dying. I plead for all, I beg for all, I pray for all God's poor suffering creatures, wherever I may find them.'

" 'Yes, you can beg, I'll admit. What do you do with all your beggings? It is always more, more! never enough!'

" With this, the general resumed his writing, thereby giving the Sister to understand that she was dismissed. For a moment her eyes fell, her lips trembled—it was a cruel taunt. Then the tremulous hands slowly lifted and folded tightly across her breast, as if to still some sudden heartache the unkind words called up. Very low, and sweet, and earnest was her reply.

" 'What do we do with our beggings? Ah! that is a hard question to ask of one whose way of life leads ever among the poor, the sorrowing, the unfortunate, the most wretched of mankind. Not on me is it wasted. I stand here in my earthly all. What do we do with it? Ah! some day you may know.'

"She turned away and left him, sad of face, heavy of heart, and her dark eyes misty with unshed tears.

" 'Stay!'

"The general's request was like a command. He could be stern, nay, almost rude, but he knew truth and worth when he saw it, and could be just. The Sister paused on the threshold, and for a minute nothing was heard but the rapid scratching of the general's pen.

" 'There, madam, is your order on the Commissary for ice and beef at army terms, good for three months. I do it for the sake of the Union soldiers who are, or may be, in your care. Don't come bothering me again. Good-morning!'

"In less than three weeks from that day the slaughter of the Red River campaign had been perfected, and there neared the city of New Orleans a steamer flying the ominous yellow flag, which even the rebel sharp-shooters respected and allowed to pass down the river unmolested. Another and still another followed closely in her wake, and all the decks were covered with the wounded and dying, whose bloody bandages and, in many instances, undressed wounds gave woeful evidence of the lack of surgeons, as well as the completeness of the rout. Among the desperately wounded was Gen. S. He was borne from the steamer to the waiting ambulance, writhing in anguish from the pain of his bleeding and shell-torn limb, and when they asked where he wished to be taken, he feebly moaned:

" 'Anywhere, it matters not. Where I can die in peace.'

"So they took him to the Hotel Dieu, a noble and beautiful institution in charge of the Sisters of Charity. The limb was amputated, and there he was nursed for weeks through the agony of the surgical operation, the fever, the wild delirium, and for many weary days no one could tell whether life or death would be the victor. But who was the

quiet, faithful nurse, ever at his bedside, ever ministering to his wants, ever watchful of his smallest
needs? Why, only 'one of the Sisters.'

"At last life triumphed, reason returned, and with
it much of the old, abrupt manner. The general
awoke to consciousness to see a face not altogether
unknown bending over him, and to feel a pair of
small, deft hands skilfully arranging a bandage, wet
in ice-cold water, around his throbbing temples,
where the mad pain and aching had for so long a
time held sway. He was better now, though still
very weak; but his mind was clear, and he could
think calmly and connectedly of all that had taken
place since the fatal battle—a battle which had so
nearly cost him his life, and left him at best but a
maimed and mutilated remnant of his former self.

"Yet he was thankful it was no worse—that he had
not been killed outright. In like degree he was
grateful to those who nursed him so tenderly and
tirelessly, especially the gray-robed woman, who had
become almost angelic in his eyes, and it was like
him to express his gratitude in his own peculiar way,
without preface or circumlocution. Looking intently
at the Sister, as if to get her features well fixed in
his memory, he said:

" 'Did you get the ice and beef?'

"The Sister started. The question was so direct and
unexpected. Surely her patient must be getting
—really himself!

" 'Yes,' she replied, simply, but with a kind glance

of the soft, sad eyes, that spoke eloquently her thanks.

"'And your name is—'

"'Sister Francis.'

"'Well, then, Sister Francis, I am glad you got the things—glad I gave you the order. I think I know now what you do with your beggings—I comprehend something of your work, your charity, your religion, and I hope to be the better for the knowledge. I owe you a debt I can never repay, but you will endeavor to believe that I am deeply grateful for all your great goodness and ceaseless care.'

"'Nay, you owe me nothing; but to Him, whose cross I bear, and in whose lowly footsteps I try to follow, you owe a debt of gratitude unbounded. To His infinite mercy I commend you. It matters not for the body; it is that divine mystery, the soul, I would save. My work here is done. I leave you to the care of others. Adieu.'

"The door softly opened and closed, and he saw Sister Francis no more.

"Two months afterward she received a letter sent to the care of the Mother Superior, inclosing a check for a thousand dollars. At the same time the general took occasion to remark that he wished he were able to make it twice the amount, since he knew by experience, 'what they did with their beggings.'"

CHAPTER XLIII.

IN the summer of 1861, the Rev. Father Dillon was in New York, on business for Notre Dame. While there, he became acquainted with several of the officers who were then organizing the Sixty-third Regiment of the Irish Brigade, and took a deep interest in the officers and men, who were almost exclusively Catholics, and were offering their lives for the safety of the nation. At the urgent request of these officers, he volunteered to go as chaplain, provided I would go with him. He wrote to me requesting my consent, and, by return mail, I sent an affirmative answer. Father Dillon was young, but of mature mind, and quite eloquent. He was impulsive and ardent, and threw his whole soul into any good work he undertook. He helped to organize the command, and spared no labor to form his men in virtuous habits from the very start. The following facts, concerning Father Dillon's first official acts in the regiment, have been kindly furnished me by Maj. John Dwyer, an officer of the Sixty-third, Irish

REV. JAMES DILLON, C. S. C.,
Chaplain 63d N. Y. Vol.

Brigade, during the war, now editor and proprietor of the Sandy Hill *Herald*, New York. These facts show the zealous and active part taken by Father Dillon. Whatever concerned the welfare of his men he was foremost in promoting, and this disposition he retained during the time he was able to stay in the service.

THE CHAPLAIN IN COMMAND BRINGS ORDER OUT OF CONFUSION.

While the Irish Brigade was entering the bloody battle at Malvern Hill, July 1, 1862, the regiment being advanced in line, a general (who proved to be Fitz John Porter) came dashing from the front, accompanied with a numerous staff.

"What regiment is this?" was his inquiry.

"This is the Sixty-third, of Gen. Meagher's brigade," was the response of Lieut.-Col. Fowler.

"I am Gen. Porter, in command of this part of the field. I order you to remain here until a field battery comes up, which I have sent for. Support the battery until ordered to the contrary."

Col. Fowler saluted, and said he would see that the order was obeyed.

Porter and his staff then disappeared in the darkness toward the front. Col. Fowler gave the order:

"Battalion! order arms! In place rest!"

Gen. Meagher and his staff at this time came hastily from the front.

"Who is in command here? What regiment is it?" he asked.

Lieut.-Col. Fowler rode up and said he was in command, and that it was the Sixty-third.

"What are you doing here, while your comrades are being slaughtered? Follow me!"

Fowler said that Gen. Porter had directed that the regiment remain here until a battery came up, which he must support.

"Do you refuse, sir, to obey the orders of your general?" was Meagher's question.

"I do not refuse, general, but I must obey the prior orders of Gen. Porter, who is in command here," was the answer.

The fiery Meagher was wild with rage, while he dashed down the front of the regiment and back again to the right where Fowler stood.

"Give me your sword, sir! You are a disgrace to the Irish Brigade. I place you under arrest, sir!"

Then turning to an officer, one of his own staff, who was near:

"Capt. Gosson, take that man's sword!" which was done.

Capt. Joseph O'Neil, the senior officer present, then took command. Meagher called on the men to follow him. Some were for doing so, and the two right companies, (A) First Lieut. Joseph McDonough, and (G) Capt. P. J. Condon, gave orders to their men, and the two companies followed their general to the front. Having reached the top of the hill, the companies were halted, when it was decided to return to the regiment, that all might act together.

Having taken their place in the ranks again, the command was found to be somewhat demoralized in consequence of the loss of Col. Burke and the retirement of Lieut.-Col. Fowler. (Maj. R. C. Bentley was absent.) Add to this the exposed condition of the men, who were being constantly hit by fragments of shell, round shot, and musketry fire. In the confusion O'Neil's voice could not be heard, and only a limited number of the companies on the right knew that he was in command. At this juncture some one shouted:

"Who is commanding officer, anyhow?"

"Col. Burke!" some one responded.

"No, Col. Fowler is!" shouted a soldier from the left.

"Men, neither is!" said an officer in Company D. "Capt. O'Neil will lead this regiment to-night."

"This is Father Dillon's regiment!" a rough voice from the center called out.

"Yes, yes! We want Father Dillon! Give us Father Dillon!"

The chaplain was a few paces to the rear, giving the consolation of his holy office to a badly wounded soldier, who was stricken down a few moments previous.

This good man promptly responded. He passed down the ranks, and told the men he was with them, and would remain here.

"I will take command, if no one else does so. Lie down, boys, and wait for orders!"

19

The order was promptly obeyed. While they were lying down, he went from right to left and informed the men that Capt. O'Neil was now in command, being the senior officer on the field.

The battery had by this time put in an appearance, coming like a whirlwind from the right, regardless of the dead and wounded lying thick on the ground. "Attention, battalion!" rang out from O'Neil. "Forward! By the right flank! Double quick! March!"

And the Sixty-third hung on to the rear of the flying battery, taking position in front of the guns. Every man lay flat on the ground. The cannon continued to fire for an hour at least, their aim directed by the flash of the enemy's guns. Two attempts were made to capture the battery, but their well-directed fire sent the desperate Confederates back in confusion, aided by a volley from the rifles of the Sixty-third.

This ended the battle of Malvern Hill, and the last of the famous "Seven Days." Before daylight, nothing remained on the field held by the Union hosts but the dead and badly wounded, and the wreck and ruin caused by the struggle of 200,000 men.

The next day saw the Army of the Potomac resting at Harrison Landing, on the banks of the James, where it recruited previous to its retirement from the Peninsula, to enter on the second Bull Run campaign.

TEMPERANCE SOCIETY.

To prepare for the realities of war, the Sixty-third, N. Y. V., was encamped on David's Island, in the East River, Long Island Sound, in November, 1861. R. C. Enright was colonel of the regiment, and the Rev. James M. Dillon, C. S. C., was the chaplain. Camps of Union troops were abundant in the neighborhood of New York, filling up companies and regiments for the inevitable struggle soon to come with the rebellious Southern States. Seeing the result of camp life on the young men composing these skeleton commands, the good chaplain of the Sixty-third was determined to guard his boys against the prevailing vices, especially that of drunkenness, which was the predominant failing, and always characteristic of camp life.

A talk of organizing a Temperance Society in the regiment was rife for several days, and assumed formal shape on Sunday, November 17. The Holy Sacrifice was offered, as usual, that morning in the dining hall, where probably 700 officers and men were present. (The regiment was composed almost entirely of Roman Catholics.)

Chaplain Dillon, at the close of the service, took as his text the subject of "Temperance." He went on, in his usual eloquent style, depicting the evils of intemperance. He said it was the father of all crimes, especially among those with Irish blood in their veins. "Show me," he said, "an Irish Catholic who is not addicted to the vice of drunkenness, and I will find a good citizen of the Republic. Give me an abstainer from the cup that inebriates, and I will show you an obedient, brave soldier willing to die for the flag. History is full of incidents where ignominious defeat has followed dearly-bought victory, owing to the indulgence in strong drink. I have in my mind," he went on to say, "one conspicuous example in the hopeless struggle of Ireland, in '98, where the insurgents met disaster after routing the enemy, because they gave way to festivity when they should have taken advantage of their dearly-bought success.

"You are going to the war, my comrades. Many of you will find a grave in the sunny South. I can not say how many, but the number will be large, as it will not be a holiday excursion. The South has a population of five millions, and vast wealth. So has the North. Believe me, the longest purse will carry the day. It is my honest opinion that the Irish Brigade, to which you will be attached, under the leadership of the chivalrous Thomas Francis Meagher, will be always in the van, in the post of danger, the post of honor. It has been ever thus. It is a tribute to your Irish valor, and you should be proud of it.

"Go, then, to the front as temperate men. If you do, you will be equal to all emergencies. I will give you an opportunity to be temperate soldiers, for I propose this very day—now and here—to organize a temperance society *for the war.*

"How many will join it? Let every officer and man present do so, and God will bless you!"

All who would not fall in under the temperance banner he requested to fall back.   Not one did so.

The enthusiastic priest said much more, being visibly affected, as were his hearers.   There was a rush for the front, and the aid of several secretaries was required to take the names.   Father Dillon was surprised at the success of his efforts, and when all the names had been taken, he recited, slowly, and in a distinct voice, the words of the pledge, which all were requested to repeat after him.   They did so, and the voices of those 700 stalwart men sounded like surf on the beach, only a few rods distant.

The speaker announced that in a few days they would elect their officers and get in working order for the temperance campaign.

Accordingly, on the following Thursday, November 21 (a feast of the Blessed Virgin), after Mass, the chaplain spoke again on the subject of "Temperance," after which the following officers were elected for the society: President, the Rev. J. M. Dillon; Vice-President, Dr. Michael G. Gilligan; Recording Secretary and Treasurer, Lieut. Patrick Gormerly; Corresponding Secretary, Capt. Michael O'Sullivan.

The effects of the "Temperance Society" were soon apparent in the regiment.   Daily and Sunday attendance at Mass was sensibly augmented, and there was a decided diminution in camp carousals. So elated was Father Dillon that he decided to have a medal struck to commemorate the event.   A design was prepared and placed in the hands of an engraver in New York City, and several hundred were cast. They had an appropriate inscription on each side, and in size resembled a silver dollar. Even at this day, thirty years after the incident above alluded to, "Father Dillon's Temperance Medals" are frequently met with in the hands of the remnant of the Sixty-third or their descendants.

It is not to be supposed that all who "took the pledge" on that Sunday morning in November, 1861, kept it inviolate, but it is equally certain that many did. This incident will illustrate:

McClellan's grand army of over 100,000 fighting men invested the Confederate capital the summer succeeding (June, 1862). The Irish Brigade was among them, including the "Temperance Regiment." The camps were right in the swamps of the dreaded Chickahominy, a disease-breading and poisonous spot. The water was so execrable that commissary whiskey was dealt out daily to officers and men, at the expense of the government. Even then malaria, dysentery, fever and ague, and kindred troubles were fearfully prevalent.

The men who wore the temperance medals received their rations with the rest, but they absolutely refused to touch the stuff. The writer remembers distinctly (he was a "Medal Man") what a scramble there was daily for his whiskey ration. And the same was true of others. On one occasion Sergt. Quinn, a six-footer, thought he had a prior claim to Sergt. Dwyer's ration. Private Rutledge—short but gritty

TEMPERANCE MEDAL.

—of Co. K, Albany company, differed from his big comrade. It was decided, as the only way to solve the problem, that they fight for it. A ring was formed of too-willing soldiers, both contestants stripping to the waist. In about three minutes, the little Albany soldier laid out the big fellow, who went sprawling his full length on the grass.

Private Rutledge then received his whisky ration, having won it in a fair encounter. From that day forth, until the army left the sluggish Chickahominy far behind, and the whisky rations were stopped, Private Rutledge had a mortgage on Sergt. Dwyer's "commissary."

The Sixty-third regiment was on David's Island, and on the 6th of November, 1861, a delegation of Irish-Americans, ladies and gentlemen, came to the Island, headed by Gen. Thomas Francis Meagher. All were residents of the metropolis. They came in a chartered steamer, accompanied by Dodsworth's famous band. They had with them two beautiful silk flags: one the national colors, the other Erin's immortal green—the "Sunburst." The ten companies of the regiment were drawn up on the parade ground, when Gen. Meagher, in behalf of the donors, presented the flags in a patriotic speech that called forth repeated cheers from the soldiers. Col. Enright of the Sixty-third responded briefly.

The chaplain, the Rev. James M. Dillon, being called upon, addressed the command. He reminded the officers and men of the great compliment paid the

regiment by their New York friends, who, instead of
waiting for the United States Government to do it,
generously contributed the beautiful standards, which
were to be borne in the forefront of battle. To
defend these flags was their duty—even at the sacrifice of their lives. "They are fit companions in
freedom's battle." Then he asked, in stentorian
tones:

"Officers and men: Are you willing and ready to
defend these emblems of freedom with your lives?"

The response came from a thousand throats:

"We are! We are!"

"Then go forth to battle, my friends and comrades,
and never let it be said that the Sixty-third regiment
—which is to hold the second place of honor in the
Irish Brigade—permitted their flag to fall into the
hands of the enemies of the Union and liberty.

"Let me impress on you the fact that to be faithful,
brave soldiers, you must be practical Christians.
There is no braver soldier in this world, in any
country, under any form of government, than a
consistent Catholic. The fathers of most of you have
fought on every battlefield, from Fontenoy to Cha-
pultepec, and their bayonets were ever in the van.
Let it be said of you, ere this causeless rebellion is
suppressed, that the soldiers of the Irish Brigade
have emulated the heroism of their forefathers.

"Ours is a country and cause worth fighting for
—dying for!"

The glowing words of the chaplain were vociferously

cheered, again and again, and when he concluded, the ceremonies were brought to a close.

Father Dillon was a young man in the prime of manhood at the time—about twenty-eight years old. He was mustered into the service October 30, 1861, and was discharged for disability (sickness), October 18, 1862.

I give the following account of a presentation to my dear friend and companion, Father Dillon, with the foregoing, as a kind memento of him. Moreover, this account will help to show how popular he was, and how enthusiastic in everything that pertained to his men and the organization to which he belonged:

PRESENTATION TO THE REV. J. M. DILLON, CHAP-
LAIN OF CORCORAN'S IRISH LEGION.

On Monday, February 9, 1863, the Rev. Father Dillon, chaplain of Corcoran's Irish Legion, was presented with a splendid set of horse equipments, consisting of bridle, saddle, spurs, and gauntlets. The spurs are of a very superior style and worth. The presentation took place in the Clerk's Office in the City Hall, Alderman Wm. Walsh making the presentation speech in the presence of the Aldermen and Councilmen and a few select friends. Alderman Walsh's address was brief, and in substance this: That these offerings were testimonials of their late visit to Suffolk, where they spent such a pleasant time, and a mark of their esteem for the Reverend Father who so creditably filled the position to which he was assigned, and he hoped whenever the Father used these gifts he would be pleased to remember the donors.

In reply Father Dillon said:

" MR. PRESIDENT AND GENTLEMEN:—You will believe me when I tell you I that can not find words to express my

feelings to you on this occasion, for they are feelings of the
heart, and to these no human language can give utterance.
'The language of the heart,' it is said, and truly, ' is silence.'
But this I will say, that when you came to Suffolk to pay
honor to our Irish nationality in the person of our great
and worthy Irish chieftain, Gen. Corcoran [applause], it
became a matter of duty to me to do all I could to honor
you, the representatives of the great city of New York, and for
the doing of which I deserve no credit. You, though, have been
pleased to think otherwise; and I, gentlemen, am glad of it, not,
indeed, because of the value of these gifts, valuable as they
may be and are, but because of the feeling that prompted the
offering. But this presentation is not only a subject of pleasure
to me, it is one also of honest pride. For, gentlemen, you do
not know how proud I am to hear my name mentioned in connection with a man and an organization so eminently calculated
in the future as in the past to do good service in the great
struggle in which we are now engaged and to reflect undying
credit on our nationality. [Applause] Then, gentlemen, I accept
these gifts, and I thank you; and whenever I use them, whether
on the tented field, or on the broad prairies of my Western
home, my only regret will be that I will not have the pleasure
of the company of the munificent donors."

The Joint Committee of the Common Council also gave, on
the evening of February 7, a dinner at the "Maison Dorée" to
the Rev. James M. Dillon, chaplain of Corcoran's Legion, who
was assiduous in his attentions to the comfort of the committee
while they were at Suffolk, and who is now in the city on a
brief business visit connected with the Irish Legion. The
dinner was of the most elegant description. In addition to the
Rev. Mr. Dillon and Alderman Walsh—the latter occupying the
head of the table—there were present several other aldermen
and other prominent gentlemen. The entertainment passed off
very agreeably. Addresses were made by several of the gentlemen present, the Rev. Mr. Dillon responding for the "Irish
Legion," Alderman Mitchell for " Gen. Corcoran," Mr. Walsh
for "The Board of Aldermen," Mr. Healy for " The Board of
Councilmen," Mr. Manning for " The Press," and Mr. Hardy,
in a very handsome manner, for "The Ladies."

REV. THOS. OUELLET, S. J.,
Ex-Chaplain 69th N. Y. S. V.

CHAPTER XLIV.

ROMAN CATHOLIC CHAPLAINS IN THE WAR—THE REV.
THOMAS OUELLET, S. J., IRISH BRIGADE.*

THE Rev. Thomas Ouellet, S. J., though not of
our race, having been born in Lower Canada,
of French parents, was one of the most zealous
priests in the army. When the war commenced,
Father Ouellet was attached to St. John's College,
at Fordham, and, hearing that a Catholic regiment
required a chaplain, offered his services to Archbishop Hughes, the Nestor of the Catholic Church of
America, who assigned Father Ouellet to the Irish
Brigade.

Father Ouellet was the direct antithesis of Father
Corby in manner, and in dealing with the men
intrusted to his spiritual charge. Father Corby was
gentle and conciliating, while the subject of this
sketch was a perfect martinet in everything that

---

* Written for the New York *Tablet* by GENERAL DENNIS
BURK, I. B.

pertained to his sacred duties; full of energy, and possessing, in a high degree, the positiveness of his race. We remember forming our first opinion of this clergyman at Camp California, Va., in the winter of 1862. The brigade was assigned to the division commanded by that brave and accomplished old soldier, Gen. E, V Sumner, then lying near Alexandria, Va. The brigade consisted at this time of the Sixty-ninth, Sixty-third, and Eighty-eighth, New York Volunteers.

The Sixty-ninth was commanded by Col. Nugent; Sixty-third by Col. Burke, and the Eighty-eighth by Col. Baker. It was customary on every Sunday to hold a joint assemblage of the entire command at the celebration of the Holy Sacrifice of the Mass. One Sunday morning, on our way to Mass, we heard an altercation between Father Ouellet and a captain of the Sixty-ninth. The captain had been using language toward some members of his company that offended the sensibilities of the good priest's ear, and he was reproving the captain for his words. The captain had a very exalted opinion of himself and the position he occupied in the army. When reproved by the good Father, he said: "Do you know, sir, I am a captain of this regiment, and you are only a captain of cavalry on detached service?" (A chaplain of the army receives the same pay and allowances, as a captain of mounted troops.) Father Ouellet, seeing the consequential gentleman he had to deal with, ceased his argument with him, and went to the church to perform his sacred duties. When the time for exhortation came Father Ouellet paid his respects to the captain in a form that ever afterward made him dreaded by the backsliders of our organization. He said, in his peculiar French accent: "I have been told to-day, by an officer of my regiment, when reproving him for profanity in the presence of his men, who are to share with him on the battlefield the dangers of a soldier's life, that I was only a captain of cavalry, and had no business to interfere in the discharge of his duties. I never intended to interfere in the discipline of the regiment, but I want to tell that captain, as well as all here assembled to worship God, that I did not enter the army as a captain of cavalry, but as a soldier of the Saviour to preach the doctrine of our holy Church, and I shall, on all occasions, as one of the spiritual directors of this command, reprove vice, and preach to you, undefiled, the religion of your fathers."

From that occasion to the end, Father Ouellet enjoyed the esteem and confidence of the entire body of men composing the organization of which he was in part the spiritual guide. No matter at what time, or how much it would inconvenience him, he was always ready for duty. On the march, in bivouac, or in battle, Father Ouellet was distinguished for zeal, and indefatigable in the performance of his sacred mission. He was an intense lover of the Union and

believed in the war for the suppression of the rebellion. He hated cant and duplicity. Honesty of purpose, combined with a high belief in true Christian
character, always guided this remarkable man.

Father Ouellet was in build small of stature and
lithe of frame, but immense in energy. He loved his
sacred calling, and never neglected its important
duties. During Gen. McClellan's famous seven days'
retreat before Richmond, he was always to the front
on every occasion ministering to the wounded, and
always predicting, to those who happened to be faint-
hearted, the certainty of final success. It was after
this terrible trial of the Army of the Potomac that
Father Ouellet made use of two expressions that are
to-day in the mouth of every soldier who served in
that army; and we doubt if one out of a hundred
knows the author. On the first Sunday after the
retreat to Harrison's Landing, after the permanent
establishment of the camp, the good priest, in his usual
energetic manner, had a chapel erected and summoned the brigade to attend Mass. Father Corby was
the celebrant, and Father Ouellet was to preach the
sermon of the day. The men were tired, and, as it
was about breakfast time, some of them sat down in
their shelter tents, placing their repast outside, as
there was but little room inside the modern army tent
for any purpose but to lie down. The energetic
priest noticed the action of the backsliders, and,
suddenly descending from the hill where the church
was situated, walked along the company streets and

kicked the vessels containing the coffee over, spilling their contents, amid the general howls of the hungry soldiers. He then ascended the altar and addressed the assembled veterans as follows: "I know all who are regardless of your regimental designation. I can tell the good and bad of you. The good came here this morning to thank God for their deliverance from death, and the rest who remained to satisfy their appetites were fellows that were *coffee-coolers* and *skedaddlers* during our retreat." Ever afterward, there was little necessity for the chaplain to call the attention of the men when circumstances permitted the celebration of the Mass. They all attended, particularly if Father Ouellet was in camp.

Father Ouellet was loved by all that remained of the Irish Brigade, and respected by every member of the Second Army Corps, from the gallant commander, W. S. Hancock, to the humblest private in the ranks.

FATHER OUELLET TRIES HIS HAND AT HOUSE BUILDING.

[From Notes by St. John Dwyer, Sixty-third New York.]

In December, 1862, Burnside stormed the heights of Fredericksburg with 50,000 men — the Right Grand Division of the Army of the Potomac. The attack was a total failure, as was the attempt of Franklin's Left Grand Division, below the city proper, to turn the Confederates' right flank. On the night of the 15th, the ill-fated but gallant army recrossed the Rappahannock, on the ponton-bridges, leaving the city filled with the Union wounded, and the slopes of Mary's Heights littered with the heroic dead.

The morning of December 16 found the troops occupying their old camps again, minus 12,353 men than when they were there less than one week previous. (Union loss: Killed, 1,180; wounded, 9,028; missing, 2,145—12,353. Confederate loss: Killed, 579; wounded, 3,870; missing, 127—4,576.) It was discouraging to the men; and, besides, they were compelled to rebuild their huts in many instances, having destroyed them when leaving. Not an officer or man in the army believed for a moment that we should be under the necessity of re-occupying our temporary homes.

Passing an abandoned winter hut on the morning of the 16th, the attention of the writer was attracted to the efforts of an individual to put his house in order once more. The sides were there, but the canvas roof was missing, as were its frail rafters. It proved to be Father Thomas Ouellet, chaplain of the Sixty-ninth New York, of the Irish Brigade. The writer reined up a moment to witness the novel sight —a priest rebuilding his "homestead" unaided! He made sorry work of it, but appeared to be in no way disconcerted. Addressing him, the writer said:

"Good-morning, Father Ouellet."

"Oh, good-morning, Lieutenant."

"I fear, Chaplain, you are but an indifferent carpenter. The Sixty-ninth men would be only too glad to do that work for you. Why don't you ask Adjutant Smith for a detail?"

"Indeed, he furnished me with a detail, but the poor fellows are so used up with our experience at the Heights, there are hardly enough of them left to put up their own huts, and furnish men for guards and picket. They would willingly help me, but I sent them away."

"Then let me send you a dozen men of the Sixty-third. Several of them are carpenters."

"Thank you very much, Lieutenant. But, I am sorry to say, you are no better off than the Sixty-ninth boys. You have not 100 men left in your whole regiment. You passed me Wednesday on the dock over in Fredericksburg, as you came out of the fight."

The good man was correct. The Sixty-third did not muster fifty muskets after the assault.

As I turned to leave, seeing that he would not accept the proffered aid, he remarked:

"I will get along slowly; all I want is a roof to keep out the cold and rain."

He did "get along" in some way, as toward evening the tent roof was in place, his sheet-iron stove going, and he was apparently as happy as though he were in a cozy rectory in a northern city.

I put my head in at the door and remarked:

"I see you are all right again, Father. 'Where there's a will there's a way!'"

20

He laughed and invited me in to enjoy the warmth of his "home," which could not compare with that of the humblest private.

Father Ouellet was in the terrible carnage of the Seven Days on the Peninsula. Soldiers who witnessed the scene tell that when bullets came thick and fast he was there, and paid no attention to the danger, announcing that he was not only a soldier of McClellan's army, but that he was also a soldier of Christ. An incident which occurred at the battle of Malvern Hill is related by Major Haverty. The soldiers were in a fierce conflict and were fighting and firing by the light of Confederate guns and bursting shells. Father Ouellet, with his stole on and a lantern in his hand, was out at the very front of the line of battle. To the wounded he would say: "Are you a Catholic? and do you wish absolution?"

One man, whom he asked, was badly wounded, but replied: "No, but I would like to die in the faith of any man who has the courage to come and see me in such a place as this."

Father Ouellet gave the poor. man conditional baptism, and then went on in his work of mercy, giving the wounded absolution, and exhorting them to have courage and to put their trust in Christ, who, for love of them, was wounded so "there was not a sound spot in Him." The love which the "boys" had for Father Ouellet could be equalled only by his zeal for their salvation. Father Ouellet resigned in 1862, and re-enlisted in 1864, as has been stated in a previous chapter.

REV. PAUL E. GILLEN, C. S. C.

CHAPTER XLV.

THE REV. PAUL E. GILLEN, C. S. C., AS CHAPLAIN.

THE Reverend Paul E. Gillen, one of the Fathers of Holy Cross, left Notre Dame in the early part of the war of '61-5 to accomplish what good he could among the soldiers in the Army of the Potomac. In the beginning he accepted no commission and wanted none. A commission, in his opinion, would be an impediment rather than a help to his work, wishing to be free to pass from one portion of the army to another. He had a singular faculty for finding the Catholic soldiers, and among them he did a remarkable amount of good. His way of going through the army was thoroughly practical, and by his own ingenious plans he had a very successful time of it until Gen. Grant spoiled his fun. The mode of travel adopted by him was this. Having secured a strong horse he purchased also an old-fashioned, flat-bottomed rockaway in Washington, D. C. From this vehicle he had the front seat removed and from the back seat he drove his faithful horse whom he called "Sarsfield." In this rockaway were transported a few army blankets for sleeping purposes, a small amount of provisions, a chapel tent — constructed according to his own architectural plan—and a folding altar. In this conveyance he lived. He travelled in it by day and slept in it at night. By turning the "north-end," as he called it, to the storm, after the fashion of the buffalo in the West, he could stand against the chilling winds with great security.

Father Paul Gillen, before his ordination and before the war, was well known in Virginia for his piety and general zeal. Being a man "in whom there was no guile," he seemed to have the freedom of the State, war or no war. Once, during the war, he fell into the hands of the notorious Mosby men; but when they learned who he was they let him go, taking nothing from him, but sent him on his way rejoicing. In 1862, after his chapel tent was finished in Philadelphia, he went to get it and take it with him to the front. He tied it to the center of a long "tent pole," and, moreover, had some clothing, a small demijohn of Mass wine, and a quantity of prayer-books and other articles, suspended also from the pole. All this was quite bulky and pretty heavy. He induced a friend (B. E.) to help him carry it to the railroad depot. Placing one end of the pole on his friend's shoulder and the other on his own, they started through Philadelphia at half-past eleven o'clock, p.m. All this was done so as not to keep a poor expressman out late at night, but principally to save expenses. Our good men got on well enough

until they reached a business street, where some police-
men, not asleep, regarded the proceeding with suspi-
cion. "How is it that these men are carrying so much
plunder at midnight?" they asked. Our travelers
were arrested and taken to the lock-up. I must say
when the police heard the simple story, examined the
goods in question, and learned the use to which they
were to be put, they were much ashamed of the
arrest; still they felt that they had only done their
duty. Of course Father Gillen was not only released,
but helped and directed on the balance of his journey
to the depot.

His work in the army consisted in going from
regiment to regiment, and wherever he found a
few dozen Catholics, there he "pitched his tent,"
staid a day or two, heard all their confessions, celebrated holy Mass, and communicated those ready to
receive. Then "striking his tent" he pushed on to
another regiment. After a time he acquired a perfect
knowledge of the various organizations which had no
Catholic chaplain, and he made compacts to attend
them periodically, as far as practicable. Maj.-Gen.
Hancock often met good Father Gillen on the march,
and, although he perhaps never spoke to him, he still
conceived a great admiration for the venerable priest
who showed such zeal and earnest unselfishness
in his labor of love. Frequently I had occasion to
see Gen. Hancock on business, as he was my corps
commander, and he invariably inquired after the
health and welfare of Father Gillen. But after a

time, a general order was issued, forbidding any
"citizen" to come and remain within army limits,
and, as he was not commissioned, he came under this
order. Moreover, the same order excluded all vehicles
which were not provided for by the army regulations
—under this came Father Gillen's rockaway. One
day, at a distance, Grant saw the strange-looking
land-boat in which Father Gillen was making his
way, and ordered him arrested and sent out, rockaway
and all. After this, Father Gillen went to the Corcoran Legion, then at Norfolk, Va., and accepted a
commission of one of the regiments of that organization. They were only too glad to receive the experienced war chaplain. In this command he labored
with marked success, and gave general satisfaction
until the end of the war. He was beloved and
respected by Catholics and non-Catholics. He could
do double the work, and endured twice as much
hardship as ourselves—much younger men and much
more pretentious. Father Gillen, C. S. C., lived and
labored many years after the war, and finally died,
at an advanced age, on October 20, 1882. He is
buried within gunshot of where I write these lines,
under the shadow of the cross, his banner in the
army of Jesus Christ, carried fearlessly and zealously
in the desperate struggle against sin and Satan.

I regret I have not material for a longer history of
good Father Gillen's labors. I give only what came
to my personal knowledge; and, as most of the time
we were in very different parts of the army, I did not

learn as much as I could wish. Perhaps, when these lines go out in print, some friendly war companion, who knew him intimately in his army work, may give many more interesting facts concerning him. Besides, I am in hopes that what I write in this modest book will serve to refresh the memories of officers and men, and induce them to give their experiences on many points touched upon, as I am now jotting down simply my own observations and impressions, so indelibly printed on the tablets of my memory that I shall not forget them until I forget my prayers.

CHAPTER XLVI.

THE REV. CONSTANTINE L. EGAN, O. P.

The following facts were furnished by the Rev. Constantine L. Egan, O. P. They are full of interest, and one can not help admiring the noble self-sacrificing spirit with which he fulfilled his arduous duties. He entered the service as a regular chaplain in September, 1863, and would have entered in the early part of the war had he realized the great want in the army of Catholic chaplains.   W. C.

Toward the end of August, 1863, a messenger came to our convent, in Washington City, from the War Department, asking me to call at the department the next morning. I called, as requested, and was informed by Gen. James A. Hardee, then assistant secretary of war, that Gen. Meade had dispatched to the secretary of war to send, if possible, a Catholic priest down to the army, to minister to two of the five soldiers who were to be shot on the Saturday following for the crime of desertion. I told him 1 would willingly comply with the request, so he gave me a pass, and the next day I started, taking the train at Alexandria, Va.

Having arrived at Bealton Station, a few miles north of the Rappahannock River, I was met by a

REV. C. L. EGAN, O. P.,
Ex-Chaplain 9th Massachusetts Vol.

chaplain of the One Hundred and Eighteenth Pennsylvania Volunteers, and escorted to the headquarters of his regiment. He introduced me to Col. Herring, commander of said regiment, who received me very kindly, and gave orders to the guards to let me have free access to the prisoners. I went to the tent where the prisoners were confined, heard their confessions that evening, and came back to the colonel's tent. He kindly tendered me his hospitality; told me I was to sleep in his tent that night, and while I remained with his regiment in the performance of the sad mission for which I had been called. Thanking him, I accepted his hospitality.

Next morning a tent was erected, where I said Mass for the condemned men, and administered to them Holy Communion, I spending the greater part of that day with them in their tent. Next morning I celebrated Mass for them, and both men received Holy Communion. During the forenoon, preparations were going on for their execution. About one o'clock, the Fifth Corps, to which the prisoners belonged, were drawn up on a slope of a hill, from which all could witness the execution. Then a death procession, composed of the culprits, a Jewish rabbi, Chaplain O'Neil, a Methodist preacher, myself, the guard, the shooting party, and the band, playing a solemn dirge, passed down the line, and halted in front of the graves.

The religious belief of the prisoners varied; one was a Jew, two were Methodists, and two were

Italian Catholics. We were allowed fifteen minutes to pray, and the poor doomed men made good use of the short time they had to live in the fervency of their prayers to Almighty God. The time having expired, the officer in charge of the soldiers detailed for the shooting placed a white bandage over the eyes of each prisoner, read the death-warrant, and gave the order to his company: "Make ready! Aim! Fire!" Down fell the five men on their coffins, on which they sat, and in less than three minutes they were pronounced dead by the surgeon of the regiment. Their lifeless bodies were placed in coffins and lowered to their graves; then the troops marched back to their camps, with the bands playing merry tunes.

After performing the funeral service over the graves of the two men, Col. Patrick Guiney, of the Ninth Massachusetts Volunteers, invited me to his regiment. The Ninth Massachusetts enlisted at the commencement of the Rebellion, with Father Scully as their chaplain; but he, on account of bad health, had been compelled to resign. This regiment was composed entirely of Irishmen. After Father Scully left them, they had no priest; nor, in fact, was there any priest in the Fifth Army Corps, nor in any of the whole Army of the Potomac, except Father William Corby, C. S. C., who was chaplain in Meagher's brigade, in the Second Army Corps. Father Corby joined the army after the breaking out of the war, and remained as chaplain of the Eighty-eighth New York, Irish Brigade, until the war terminated.

Next day being Sunday, I said Mass for the Ninth regiment, and announced, after Mass, that I would remain with them during the week, thus giving them an opportunity to approach the Holy Sacraments; during each day of the week I would hear confessions in the tent chapel erected for me, and on each morning, at seven o'clock, would say Mass. That evening Col. Guiney and myself rode to the headquarters of Gen. Griffin, commander of the First Division of the Fifth Army Corps. The general received us very cordially. I said to him that I would remain eight or ten days in the army in order to give the Catholic soldiers of his division an opportunity of attending their religious duties. He said he was glad I could do so, adding that it seemed to him very strange that his division was left without a Catholic priest, so many of the soldiers in his command being Catholics. He then issued an order suspending the drill during the week, in order, as he said, "to let the Catholic soldiers in his division attend their religious duties." I thus spent ten days on this mission, hearing soldiers' confessions each day, celebrating Mass each morning, and administering Communion to all who were at confession the previous day, thus giving to all an opportunity of approaching the Holy Sacraments, of which opportunity not only the soldiers of the Ninth regiment availed themselves, but numbers of the three divisions of the Fifth Corps. My mission then being finished, I prepared to leave for Washington.

Previous to my departure, Col. Patrick Guiney

and the officers and soldiers of his regiment, and many others from the Fifth Corps, came to me, and entreated me to remain in the army, saying: "It is not just or religious to have so many Catholic soldiers, subject as they are every day to the danger of death, without the services of a priest;" that they were fighting in a just cause, to preserve the integrity of the United States Government they loved so well, which gave them a friendly welcome and a home when driven from their own native land by the tyranny of a cruel and oppressive government, such as England had always been to them. Seeing, therefore, the need of my services in the army — the good I could do for such brave men — and being myself patriotic in the cause — sharing the feelings and sentiments of my own countrymen — I told Col. Guiney I would become their chaplain; but it was necessary for me, first of all, to get permission from the Provincial of my Order. On my return to Washington, I met our Provincial, and earnestly entreated him to give me permission to accept a chaplaincy in the army, pointing out to him the great need of a priest's services. He willingly granted me this permission, giving me a letter to that effect, of which the following is a copy:

"St. Dominic's Church, Washington, D. C.,
"September 13, 1863.

"From motives of Christian charity to the soldiers of the Army of the Potomac, I freely grant permission to the Rev. Constantine L. Egan of our Order to accept the chaplaincy of the Ninth Massachusetts Regiment.   M. A. O'Brien,
"Vice Provincial of the Province of St Joseph's. "

I wrote immediately to Col. Guiney to procure my commission as chaplain of his regiment. Some time after, I was asked by the Secretary of War to go to Gen. Newton's corps, which was camped near Culpepper Court House, Va., to minister to another deserter sentenced by court-martial to be shot. I started the next morning, and reached Gen. Newton's headquarters about ten o'clock that night. The general told me I had better see the prisoner soon, as he would certainly be shot the next morning. I started at once to where the prisoner was confined, heard his confession, and staid the remainder of that night at Gen. Robinson's headquarters. Next morning I said Mass for the prisoner in the provost-marshal's tent, administering to the poor condemned man Holy Communion. Afterward, I was invited by the provost-marshal to partake of a cup of coffee and some hard-tack—such as he had for breakfast himself. After breakfast, the provost-marshal commenced loading the twelve rifles for the shooting party, one of the rifles being loaded with a blank cartridge only—the other eleven were loaded with bullets. After a while, an ambulance was in readiness, accompanied by a squad of soldiers to guard the prisoner to the place of execution. The prisoner was placed in the ambulance, and I took my place by his side. During the sad journey, of about two miles, we were occupied saying the rosary and litanies, the poor prisoner praying with much fervor during the short time he had to live.

Arriving at the place of execution, we saw a coffin ready and a grave prepared for the reception of the poor soldier's remains, and the whole of the First Army Corps drawn up in a position to witness the prisoner's death. We got a few minutes to pray, and before the white bandage was placed over his eyes, the prisoner stood up, and in a steady voice said: "I ask pardon of all whom I have offended; I forgive every one who has offended or injured me; boys, pray for me."

The officer then read the death-warrant, and placing the white bandage over the prisoner's eyes, gave the order to the firing party: "Make ready! Aim! Fire!" The poor soldier fell on his coffin, and death was almost instantaneous. After the burial service was performed, I went to the corps' headquarters, where I got dinner, and after that was escorted in an ambulance to the railroad, and returned some time at night to Washington.

A few days after this, I received a letter from Col. Guiney, with my commission as chaplain from Gov. Andrews, of Massachusetts. I then made preparations to join my regiment, procuring a light set of vestments and things necessary for divine service, and started as soon as I could, joining my regiment in the vicinity of Warrenton, Va. During the month of October our corps had considerable marching from one point to another, and on the 14th we had a sharp battle at Bristow Station, repulsing the enemy, who left their dead and wounded on the field. We captured several hundred prisoners and seven guns — two of which the Confederates subsequently recovered. During the remainder of October not much fighting was done, but on November 7 a battle was fought at Rappahannock Station and Kelly's Ford, in which our troops were victorious, capturing four guns and 2,000 stands of arms, and about one thousand six hundred officers and men were taken prisoners. We remained here in camp until November 24. On this morning we broke camp, and marched in the direction of the Rapidan River, but, on account of the violence of a rainstorm that set in, we countermarched and returned to our old quarters, where we remained until the 26th.

When we again marched from our headquarters toward the Rapidan, we crossed at Culpepper Ford, moving on the Culpepper plank-road. On the evening of this day, Greg's cavalry, in our advance, had a sharp fight, in which many of the troopers fell. The wounded were gathered into Newhope church, where I spent a good part of the night ministering to the wounded and dying. I recollect a kind-hearted surgeon, belonging to the cavalry, who held a lighted candle for me as I was reading the prayers of the ritual in administering extreme unction to the dying men. On the 29th, we advanced to Mine Run and formed a line of battle, and bivouacked for the night. The enemy were posted on the east side, about one mile from the stream called Mine Run, on a center ridge nearly one hundred feet above the surface of the stream. Their works could easily be seen by us posted on the west ridge of the run. They were strongly fortified, their works bristling with abatis, infantry parapets, and epaulements for batteries. About three o'clock on the evening of the 30th, the order was given to charge the enemy's line. At four o'clock the soldiers stacked their knapsacks, so that the field resembled a meadow covered with stacks in the shape of soldiers' knapsacks, overcoats, etc., piled in large heaps.

Seeing the danger of death before us, I asked the colonel to form his regiment into a solid square so that I could address the men. He did so. I then spoke to them of their danger, and entreated them to prepare for it by going on their knees and making a sincere Act of Contrition for their sins, with the intention of going to confession if their lives were spared. As the regiment fell on their knees, other Catholic soldiers broke from their ranks and joined us, so that in less than two minutes I had the largest congregation I ever witnessed before, or even since. Having pronounced the words of General Absolution to be given in such emergencies and danger, I spoke a few words of encouragement to them, exhorting them to remember that they were fighting in a just cause to preserve the integrity of the United States Government, which had never committed an act of tyranny toward any of its citizens; that they were fighting the battle of liberty, justice, and even for the rights of humanity itself, not only for those under our own government but for the poor oppressed of all nations; that the tyrannical and oppressive governments of Europe were aiding and abetting in every way possible the misguided people of the South in their revolt against the best of governments; that England, who largely fomented the Rebellion by her emissaries in this country, hypocritically crying out against the barbarity of slavery, was now aiding, by her cursed, ill-gotten gold, the Southern people to maintain in perpetual slavery 4,000,000 human beings. All this in order to divide us and break up our glorious principle of self-government, wrested from her tyrannical hand by the brave heroes of the Revolution, who won for us our inheritance of liberty.

After talking to the soldiers and finishing my remarks, they arose from their knees, grasping their muskets with a firm clinch, and went back to their respective commands, awaiting the hour to expire to make the assault. In the meantime, Maj.-Gen. Warren, who made a closer reconnoissance of the enemy's works than he had made the day before, when he urged Gen. Meade to make a general assault on the enemy's works, now reported that their works were so strong they could not be taken. Accordingly, Gen. Meade, being a prudent, humane, and cautious man, rescinded the order, which saved his army; for if the attack had been made, our army would have been slaughtered worse than it had been the year before at Fredericksburg. A retrograde movement was decided upon, however, and the next

21

evening at nightfall we retreated, the Fifth Corps in the advance, and crossed the Rapidan. In the morning, about two hours before daylight, we bivouacked on the north bank of the Rapidan, and, after resting a few hours, resumed our march, crossing the Rappahannock on December 3, and camped along the Orange & Alexandria railroad for its protection, where we remained until the month of March following.

Previous to our march to Mine Run, I received a petition from the Fourteenth regulars to visit their brigade and minister to their spiritual wants; but on account of the movements of the army and camp rumors that were rife of an immediate move of the whole army toward Richmond, I could not comply with their request. The following is a copy of the petition I received:

"CAMP NEAR BEALTON, VA., Nov. 14, 1863.

"REVEREND AND DEAR SIR:—At the request of several Catholic soldiers, with my brother officers, who are Catholics, I have ventured to urge your paying the regiment, the Fourteenth U. S. Infantry, with which I am connected, a visit. You, no doubt, are aware that a majority of the enlisted men composing the troops of the regular army are of our, the Catholic, faith, and that there is a respectable number of officers included in its membership. We are without a chaplain, and have had no visitation from one since Father Tissot, S. J., left the field— nearly nine months ago. This gentleman, at that time chaplain of the Thirty-seventh N. Y. Volunteers, visited our regiment and brigade at such hours as he had convenient opportunity, and was always welcomed and appreciated with the same apparent warmth by the dissenters as by the sons of the Church. His missions were undoubtedly productive of good, and I shall be exceedingly glad if you can, like him, visit us, even if you can not devote as much time as he did. A soldier of the company I command, was yesterday, I fear, fatally wounded by accident. He has begged pitifully for a priest, and we know of no other one than yourself in our corps to ask to come and see him. Will you come ? I am with respect,

"Yours sincerely,

"REV. C. L. EGAN,   I. F. MILLER,
"Ninth Mass. Vols.   Capt Fourteenth U. S. Infantry."

After settling down in winter-quarters, I decided to visit the brigade of regulars, who were mostly Catholics, and also other brigades of the Fifth Army Corps. A corps is divided into three divisions, each division into three brigades, and each brigade into five regiments. During the winter I gave missions through the whole corps, pitching my little chapel tent in each brigade, having a soldier with me from my own regiment to take care of my horse, cook our rations, and, of course, do our washing in as good style as a big, rough Irish soldier could perform an art to which he was unaccustomed.

Finishing my visits and missionary duties in this corps, I moved on in the month of February, 1864, to Culpepper, where the First Army Corps, commanded by Maj.-Gen. John Newton, was camped. Also in that vicinity were several brigades of cavalry under the command of Gens. Custer, Merritt, and McKenzie. Calling on Gen. Newton, I told him I came from my own regiment to perform missionary duties for the Catholic soldiers in his command, knowing there was no Catholic priest in his corps.

He said he was very glad, and thanked me for doing so, at the same time remarking, that he was very much chagrined and displeased with the Catholic bishops for their gross neglect of the Catholic soldiers, whom they left, subject as they were every day to death, without the service of a priest to administer to them in their dying moments the Last Sacraments. The general ordered for me a tent and a requisition from the quartermaster for forage for my horse, telling me if I needed anything he would most willingly have my wants supplied, in order to help on the good work in which I was engaged.

My tent was pitched where the greater number of the troops were camped, each day hearing confessions, celebrating Mass the following morning, and administering Communion to those at Confession the day previous. Having finished my mission in the First Army Corps, and also in the cavalry brigades, where I met a large number of Catholics, especially among the New York regiments, I returned in the month of March to my regiment, thereby giving them an opportunity to prepare and put their souls in order for the danger to be met during the summer campaign. Gen. Grant, and Sheridan, his chief lieutenant, were now destined to take command of the Army of the Potomac. According to camp talk, there would soon be hard fighting under these generals; no more retreating and falling back as there had been during the previous year. Gen. Lee would not be permitted to follow his old tactics of whipping and driving us back, and then sending the prime of his army to reinforce other points of the Confederate army as he did at Chicamauga, when, driving Meade's army to Centerville, Va., in the month of September, he sent Longstreet's heavy corps of veterans to aid Bragg against Rosecrans at Chicamauga.

On April 28, 1864, we broke camp, marched to the Rappahannock, and bivouacked for the night; next morning, crossing the river, we marched to Brandy Station and camped there for about four days. The Sixth Army Corps were all camped in that vicinity. I erected my chapel tent in order to give the Catholics of the Sixth Corps, who had no priest, an opportunity of approaching the holy sacraments, hearing confessions each day and a good part of the night, and giving them Communion each morning at Mass. On May 3, in the afternoon, we received orders to march, the army moving in the direction of Culpepper. About sundown our corps halted, lighted our camp-fires, cooked our supper, got our little dog tents, as they were called, in readiness, and went to sleep. About midnight we were aroused from our slumbers and told to move quickly. In about fifteen minutes we were in motion, moving to the left in the direction of the Rapidan river. At daybreak we reached the river, crossing at Germania Ford and advancing about five miles, where our column halted on the Lacy farm, and bivouacked near the Lacy House the remainder of that day and night.

On the next morning, May 5, our corps was ordered to move to Parker's store, five miles distant southwest of our camping ground. We had advanced about one mile when we were attacked by an unlooked-for advance of Confederate infantry under Gen. Hill. Getting into position as best we could, the battle commenced, striking heavily against Gen. Griffin's division, in which division was my regiment. In about ten minutes my regiment lost, in killed and wounded, 150 officers and men, among whom were Col. Guiney, who received a bullet in the right eye, and Capts. Phelan and McNamara, who, in advance of their companies, were urging their men to retake the guns which the rebels had captured from one of our batteries. Capt. Phelan was killed instantly; Capt. McNamara was brought off the field alive, but died that night. In the rear, a corps field hospital was established in an old deserted farm-house. Here the wounded were gathered. I got as many of the wounded officers and men of my regiment into the old house as could find room, and the rest were put under cover of the tents. After attending to their spiritual wants and alleviating their bodily suffering as much as I could, my services were needed by other Catholics belonging to our corps. The ambulances came in droves bringing in the wounded all day and far into the night. Surgeons were busy at work amputating broken limbs; men were employed digging long trenches where we

buried our dead. All this was fearful to see, and
it was awful to hear the groans and screams of our
wounded men, wrestling all night in their agony.
At daylight next morning, May 6, the shrill rattle
of musketry was heard in our front and soon extended
along the line. This was to be the great day of
test between the two armies, for both had resolved
to take the offensive.

It might be called almost a hand-to-hand fight
the day through, between the two conflicting lines
of men, who were irregularly formed among the
dense thickets, and swayed back and forth during the whole day, first at one point and then at
another. But the most desperate effort of the enemy
was made just at night-fall, the rebels making a
furious dash on our extreme right, and driving
before them two entire brigades. The rebels were
soon checked and compelled to fall back, but succeeded in taking with them about four thousand
prisoners. If they had succeeded in turning our
right wing, which was their object, our whole army
would have been severed from its supplies across the
Rapidan, and our defeat would have been almost
inevitable. Thus ended the battle of the Wilderness,
which was indecisive.

Both armies rested upon their arms in their
respective positions on the field. During this day
our field hospital of the Fifth Army Corps was greatly
crowded by the numbers of wounded men who were
brought off the field. I suppose we must have had

in the neighborhood of at least four thousand men. Early next morning some guns opened fire on the right of our line, but there was no reply. As Gen. Lee had intrenched his whole front and was unwilling to fight except behind his breastworks, Grant resumed his march to Spottsylvania Court House. And our corps started, preceded by cavalry. During the day we were confronted by Longstreet's Corps where we lost heavily, in all about fifteen hundred officers and men. The loss in my own regiment in this fight, in killed and wounded, was also very great.

Next day, May 8, commenced the battle of Spottsylvania, which lasted from the 8th until the 19th of May. Our corps field hospital was established in the rear, about the center of our whole army line of battle, with Hancock on the right, Sedgwick on the left, and Warren commanding our corps in the center. In the afternoon the battle became furious, ambulances bringing in the wounded until a late hour that night. The next day, the 9th, opened comparatively quiet; but in the afternoon there was sharp skirmishing at various points of the line. On this evening Gen. Sedgwick was killed—a great loss to his corps, and severely felt by the army. The morning of the 10th, a sharp cannonade commenced, preparatory for a general attack to be made along the entire line. The battle during the whole day was furious, yet indecisive in its results.

On the 11th, it rained very heavily during the day, and all remained quiet until the afternoon, when some slight skirmishing took place. On May 12, it was fearful; the rain falling heavily, the dark clouds lighted now and then by flashes of lightning, and the loud peals of thunder were hardly to be distinguished from the roaring of the cannons. Ambulances came from every direction, plowing their way as best they could through the undergrowth and brush. Surgeons had their long tables, practising their art in sawing off the broken limbs of our brave soldiers. The fighting on this day was of the most obstinate nature until after dark; was renewed again about nine o'clock, and continued off and on, with more or less vigor, all night.

On the 14th, 15th, 16th, and 17th, there was considerable marching and counter-marching in quest of a weak point on the enemy's defenses. On the 18th, there was heavy fighting, but after that the army moved to the left and resumed next night its march to Richmond. On the 23d, Griffin's division of the Fifth Corps crossed the North Anna River at Jerico Ford and entrenched on the bank of the river in a kind of works hardly breast high, when we were soon attacked by a strong force of infantry, who were repulsed. We remained there that night until the Second Corps could cross at the Chesterfield Bridge; but Hancock was confronted by a division of Longstreet's Corps on the south bank of the river. A vigorous attack was made by Egan and

Pierce's brigades of Birney's division, who swept over the plain on the double-quick and swarmed over the parapets, driving out the garrison. The passage across the river was then quietly made by Hancock's Corps, on the south side of the river.

Lee had chosen a strong position, having the inside track in the march, and crossing the North Anna before us. Grant, seeing that Lee's position was absolutely invulnerable, withdrew from the enemy's front and recrossed the river, taking our line of march on the road to Richmond. After about two days we reached the Pamunkey without loss, and crossed the river to Cold Harbor. But Gen. Lee, as usual, had a much shorter road and was already in a strong position in our front. Notwithstanding his strong position, our generals unwisely determined to assault his lines on June 3, an attack being ordered along the whole line, and in less than an hour 10,000 of our brave fellows were either killed or wounded — more in proportion even among the killed than we had in any of our previous battles.

Some hours after, Meade gave orders to the different corps commanders to renew the assault, but the men unanimously refused to obey his orders — knowing it was murder to themselves to attempt it. A few days after, the time of my regiment's three years' service expired, so they were relieved from duty, and made preparations to return home to Boston. The day before we left, Gen. Griffin sent for me. When I reported to him he said: "You ought not

to leave the Catholics in my division without the
services of a priest." I told him I would like to
remain, but it would be difficult for me to stay in
the army without being connected with it officially.
He told me to write out an application to the President for a commission and that he would endorse it,
and also get the commander of the Army of the
Potomac to endorse the application. So I immediately wrote out an application, which was sent to
Washington for action.

CHAPTER XLVII.

CONTINUATION OF FATHER EGAN'S NARRATIVE.

IN the meantime I returned to Boston with my regiment; but on account of some delay in the mustering out of the regiment, I went home to Washington before the formalities were gone through with, to make sure accompanying the army again, where I knew my services were so much needed by the Catholic soldiers. At Washington I met the Rev. James Dillon, C. S. C., on his way to City Point, Va., to join his regiment in the Second Corps. He had accompanied me to the army, but went home some time previous to this meeting to Notre Dame University, in a bad state of health; being, in fact, far gone in consumption; but his great zeal for the soldiers of his regiment, who needed his services, caused him to return to them again.

He joined his regiment at their camp, before Petersburg, but could not remain; and, returning to Notre Dame, he died a short time afterward from the dire disease contracted in the army during the first two years of the war. He was truly a noble, self-sacrificing priest.

A general field hospital now being established at City Point, where all the wounded soldiers of our army before Petersburg were being taken care of, I remained for some weeks attending to the spiritual wants of our Catholic soldiers until I received my commission from the war department. I then left the hospital and reported to Gen. Griffin, whose headquarters was about twenty miles distant, near the Weldon railroad. From this time to the termination of the Rebellion, I remained attached to Gen. Griffin's staff, having full freedom to attend not only the Catholics of the Fifth Army Corps, but also those of the Ninth Army Corps, who had no Catholic chaplain among them from City Point. During the months of July and August, a railroad was built in the rear of our line up to the Weldon railroad, a distance of about twenty-three miles. This transit gave me free access to the general field hospital at City Point, and to the troops along the line, in breastworks and in forts, about one mile distant from each other.

On the 30th of July heavy cannonading was heard in the evening all along our line. It was occasioned by the explosion of the mine before Petersburg, where a breach was made in the rebel lines, dashing into the air and killing several hundred poor human beings, leaving a great hollow or crater of loose earth 150 feet long by 60 feet wide and 25 deep. The only thing effected by this was a death-trap for our own brave men, who were massed into the gap of the crater and slaughtered or made prisoners of by the rebels. Our loss, in killed and wounded, in this affair was 4,400; while that of the enemy, including 300 blown up in the fort, was barely one thousand.

On the 18th of August our corps moved on to take the Weldon railroad, only about three miles distant. Advancing about a mile, the enemy was met and attacked; and, after a spirited fight on both sides, our men planted their colors on the railroad and held it, which was a great loss to the enemy. Our loss in this engagement was about one thousand, including 200 prisoners, captured in the commencement of the fight. Everything remained quiet along the line until the 29th of September, when a movement was made to our left. Warren moved with two divisions of his corps, and two on the Ninth, under Gen. Park, with Greg's cavalry in advance, reaching the Squirrel Level road, and carrying two or three small works at different points. There was sharp fighting throughout this and the following day, we holding the newly gained ground and intrenching on it. Breastworks were immediately made to connect with our former position across the Weldon railroad.

On the 27th of October another advance was made toward Hatchers' Run, but it failed in effecting its object, and ended with our whole army falling back to our old intrenchments before Petersburg, and thence to Warren's works, covering the Weldon railroad and the Vaughn and Squirrel Level highways. During the months of January, February, and March

there were few movements of the army, which gave
me an opportunity of giving missions through the
Fifth and Ninth Corps, holding our lines from near
Hatchers' Run down to Fort Steadman on the way
to City Point.

On March 25, 1865, my missions ended at Fort
Haskel. On the 24th I heard confessions for
about four hours in the fort, and early next morning a place was erected for me in which to celebrate
Mass. I began to say Mass before daylight on the
25th, and, before finishing Mass, I heard some sharp
rattling of musketry, followed by loud cannonading.
I hurried through Mass and the administering of
Communion to about sixty soldiers, then, getting my
vestments together and placing them in my saddle
bags, mounted my horse and rode out of the fort,
just as the gunners were ordered to mount the parapets. Fort Steadman, the next fort on the right, was
attacked and taken by assault, the Confederates surprising the Fourteenth New York Artillery, who were
in Fort Steadman, in front of which the Ninth Corps
were camped. The fort was taken and carried at a
single bound, and its guns turned on our troops.
Three mortar batteries adjoining it were also taken;
however, the rebel victory was of short duration, for
our surrounding artillery, supported by the Ninth
Corps, were brought to bear upon Fort Steadman, the
fire of which became so hot that the victors had to
abandon the fort, and many of them, afraid to recross
the intervening space to their own lines, surrendered.

When I returned to camp, meeting Gen. Griffin and staff in advance of the division, moving out after breaking camp, I fell in with the staff. Advancing about seven miles on the left towards Hatchers' Run, we were met by Gen. Meade and staff. Making short halt, Gen. Meade gave a verbal order, saying: "Griffin, you advance with your command and attack the enemy where you meet him. If you drive him do not go beyond the Boyton plank-road until you connect with the Second Corps."

Immediately our line of battle was formed, with a skirmish line in our front, Bartlett's brigade on our right, Pearson's on the left, and Chamberlain's brigade in the center. Advancing about a mile through open fields, our skirmishers were met by the enemy, and, with sharp firing on both sides, our skirmishers were driven back to the line of battle. The rebel infantry, advancing out of the woods with their accustomed rebel yell, came nearer to our line, and so impetuous were they, that one man would crowd before another, not keeping steady or closed ranks in their line of battle. On the other hand, our troops advancing slowly, and in a steady, closed line, took deliberate aim, our officers shouting to their men: "Steady, close up, aim low." Griffin ordered our right and left wing to advance, as the rebels approached, seemingly determined to break through our center. Gen. Chamberlain, who held the center, advanced before the troops, waving his sword and shouting in a shrill voice: "Forward, boys, forward." His horse was riddled with bullets and fell under him, he receiving four wounds. Still he advanced before his command, bleeding profusely from his wounds, but crying out and waving his sword to the soldiers with the command "Forward!" After a few volleys of steady firing from our line, the rebels recoiled and broke, falling back and running, with our men in pursuit of them.

Surgeon De Witt, surgeon chief of our division, and myself viewed the battle as it was progressing, from a little elevated ground, where Gen. Griffin stood directing the fight. As soon as the battle was over, Surgeon De Witt ordered me to go back to the rear and give his commands to the division surgeons to hurry up and attend the wounded. Riding back about a mile I met the doctors and returned with them. After attending to the Catholics who were in danger of death, I helped the wounded into ambulances, which carried them back to the field hospital. It rained very heavily during the evening, but we succeeded in burying the dead, both our own and the Confederate.

Returning from the field wet and weary, just at dark, seeking some place of shelter to bivouac for the night, the sentiments expressed by my countryman, the Irish poet, Col. O'Hara, under similar circumstances, came to mind:

22

" The muffled drum's sad roll has beat
The soldier's last tattoo!
No more on life's parade shall meet
That brave and fallen few.
On fame's eternal camping-ground
Their silent tents are spread,
And glory guards with solemn round
The bivouac of the dead! "

We halted for the night in the old Lewis farm-house, deserted by its inhabitants the day before, our corps resting in front of the rebel intrenchments and covering the White Oak road.   The Fifth Corps was placed by Gen. Grant under Gen. Sheridan's command, and moved in the direction of Five Forks, where Sheridan was and had been fighting, endeavoring to turn the right wing of Lee's army

About three o'clock in the afternoon of April 1, Sheridan and staff rode over to where Griffin's division was resting a few minutes.   After the day's march, Sheridan, alighting from his horse, drew out his plan of attack, tracing the lines on the dust of the road with the point of his sword, also showing Griffin the rebel position.   The plan of battle was to attack the enemy's whole front, Merritt's two divisions to make a feint of turning the right flank of the enemy, while the Fifth Corps should vigorously assail his left. Having mounted his horse again, Sheridan remarked before starting: "Griffin, your right flank will be taken care of by McKenzie, who will be pushed over toward the Ford road and Hatchers' Run. We'll have them," he said, as he gave spurs to his horse, "in an hour and a half from this." And sure enough we had, capturing the rebel works and turning their right flank, which caused Lee the next night to leave his whole line of works before Petersburg.

After the battle was over, De Witt, chief surgeon of the division, told me to take care of the wounded and to gather them over to a farm-house on the battle-field, and he would go after the doctors and bring them up as soon as he could. I rode along, collecting all the straggling soldiers who were on the field, and ordering them to take the wounded over to that house near by. The inhabitants had already left the house, locking the door. Breaking open the door, we got all the beds that we could find down on the first floor, and placed our dying soldiers on them and outside on the porch. The other wounded men were placed in rows on the ground inside the picket fence, inclosing an area of about half an acre or more around the house.

All the linens and calicoes that could be found about the place were torn up in strips to bind the wounded limbs of our men and to keep them from bleeding to death until the surgeons could give them proper treatment. About twelve o'clock at night the surgeons and our ambulances arrived. I told my orderly to get our horses ready, for we should be obliged to go down to headquarters in order to be up with our command, as soon as they moved; for I knew that Sheridan would have us on the go before daylight. Seeing him on the evening of the battle riding from one division commander to another, as he was directing the whole movement along the line, it gave me an impression of his ceaseless activity of body, with his mind intently fixed on the business he had to do, and his indomitable will pledged to execute it. I, therefore, concluded there was very little rest for us until Sheridan had accomplished his work of capturing Lee's army, and so it happened. The advance was sounded next morning before daylight, Sheridan ordering our corps to connect with the army in the neighborhood of Sutherland Station.

The next day we had a fatiguing march to Petersburg, south of the Amelia Court House, where we arrived at sundown and spent the night until about eleven o'clock throwing up intrenchments across the Burksville road. Meade's whole army joined us toward evening on the 5th. Gen. Lee's army, leaving the Amelia Court House, moved that night around on our left, striking out for Farmville, in order to recross the Appomattox and, if possible, escape his pursuers. He crossed the Appomattox on bridges at Farmville, marching all night, and leaving us well in the rear. But Sheridan, with his usual swiftness, headed him off and detained him by harassing his front, at one time capturing nearly the whole of Ewell's corps—Ewell himself and six other generals being among the prisoners, of whom 6,000 fell into the hands of Sheridan's troopers.

On the morning of April 8, our Corps, the Fifth,

Gen. Griffin commanding, and Gen. Ord commanding the Twenty-fifth Corps, with one division of the Twenty-fourth, made a forced march all day and night until about four o'clock in the morning, when we connected with Sheridan's cavalry, who were right in front of Lee's whole army across the railroad, holding three train-loads of provisions — captured that night by Sheridan's cavalry — on their way to Lee's army. We bivouacked on the road and rested for about two hours, when the bugle sounded the advance at dawn of day.

A line of battle was immediately formed, Gen. Ord on the left, and Gen. Griffin's corps on the right. The line of troops advanced to where Sheridan's troopers were engaged with Lee's advance, endeavoring to cut their way through Sheridan's cavalry. As soon as our heavy lines of infantry came supporting Sheridan's cavalry, his troopers moved to the right and left flanks of the infantry line. The advancing rebel line of soldiers, seeing the heavy force of infantry before them, fell back gradually, while our troops steadily advanced after them.

As I was riding behind the line, I noticed a wounded rebel soldier stretched on the ground. I alighted from my horse and went over to him to aid him spiritually if he wished, and if not, at least to render him all the temporal aid I could in consequence of his great suffering. He was in terrible pain, having been shot in the abdomen by his own officer. He told me that when the cavalry moved from their front, and a heavy line of infantry came before them, seeing that it was useless to contend further, he fell back. His officer at once ordered him to "About face"; and, refusing to do so, the officer drew his revolver and shot him, leaving him there on the enemy's field.

Examining his wound, I found it was fatal, and from his agony and suffering I concluded that the poor fellow had not long to live; I told him so and entreated him now to fight the last battle for Heaven. I asked him if he had ever been baptized, he replied in the negative. I told him that baptism was necessary in order to go to heaven, and he seemed willing to be baptized after the instructions I gave him. Then, laying hold of a canteen of water, I baptized him "In the name of the Father, and of the Son, and of the Holy Ghost. Amen."

After receiving baptism he uttered some very fervent ejaculatory prayers, saying: "Oh, my God forever have mercy on me!" The poor fellow was writhing in great pain and agony; I remained with him as long as I could and was sorry to leave him before he had breathed his last. But by this time our troops were out of sight and, not knowing where I should find them, I left the poor, dying soldier and followed up the command. After riding about a mile I overtook the troops and, seeing one of Sheridan's staff officers riding along the line, giving orders to the troops to "Halt!" and "Ground arms!" which

orders were obeyed, I asked an officer what it all
meant. He said that Gen. Gordon had come into
our lines with a flag of truce, asking a little time to
make the surrender.

The troops laid down along the line and rested.
Then they began cooking their rations; that is, any of
them that had rations to cook; for, after making
forced marches since the battle of Five Forks, and
fighting at intervals, their haversacks were light.
About two o'clock it was formally announced to the
troops that Lee's Army of Northern Virginia had
surrendered. Their haversacks were then replenished by the commissary department, and, after
getting a good meal, the soldiers went under their
little dog tents to rest in peace, having no more fear
of being attacked by Lee. The troops remained on
the field that day and night; the next day also was
spent there, many of the Union officers going over
and mingling with the rebels, trading horses, and
the rebel officers coming into our camps, spending
the day, talking over the different battles, our officers treating them to cigars and commissary whisky,
and the best they had themselves. It was interesting to hear the brave combatants discussing matters
in a friendly spirit about in the same manner as
politicians discuss their political issues.

In a few days the bulk of our army moved on
their way to Richmond. The Fifth Army Corps
remained to receive the formal surrender of the
Confederate arms. Maj.-Gen. Bartlett, commanding

the first division of our corps, was ordered to perform the honorable task, which was done a few days after Lee's surrender. The Confederate army moved from their camp in the usual routine of march, major generals and their staff officers at the head of their corps, division generals at the head of their divisions, brigade generals at the head of their commands, and colonels at the head of their regiments.

The Union soldiers formed in line along the side of the road with fixed bayonets, Gen. Bartlett and staff at the end of the line. As each corps came up Gen. Bartlett, in a modest tone of voice, ordered them to "Halt, and about face," "Plant your colors," "Stack arms and equipments." This being done, the rebel veterans mingled with our veterans, who generously shared with them a part of their own rations. It was interesting to see them sitting in squads together, and to hear them talking over their former battles. I overheard a rebel soldier, saying, in a loud, emphatic voice: "It was that Irish devil, Sheridan, that did the work for you fellows. He was the only general you had who struck terror into us; but for him, this war would not be over yet: but now we are glad it is over, for we have had enough of it."

The next day the country about the little village of Appomattox was pretty well cleared, all the rebel veterans returning to their homes as best they could, picking up all the old horses and mules they could find. Our officers and soldiers did not prevent them, knowing that the poor fellows needed them to help

put in a crop, now that it was the spring of the year and such work was in progress.

We remained at Appomattox until about April 18, when all our troops made a very slow march toward Richmond, sometimes staying for several days in camp. Near Farmville, about fifteen miles from Appomattox, we camped a few days. On April 25, the adjutant-general of the division handed me a letter sent to the headquarters, requesting me to go to the Third division. I will transcribe the letter, which fully explains itself:

"HEADQUARTERS, THIRD DIVISION, FIFTH ARMY CORPS,
                                "April 25, 1865.
" FATHER EGAN, Chaplain at Headquarters,
                "First Division, Fifth Army Corps.
    " REVEREND AND DEAR SIR:—We have a prisoner under sentence of death for desertion; the time appointed for his execution is Friday. He desires the attention of a clergyman of your denomination, and I know of no other more acceptable than yourself, nor would I desire any if there were. He wishes much that you would come and see him, if possible, to-morrow. In case you can not come, may I hear from you, that I may look elsewhere? I have the honor to remain,
                "Yours most respectfully,
                    " ALFRED C. ROE,
                        " Chaplain and A. A. D. C."

This letter, on the back of its fly-leaf, had the following indorsement:

" HEADQUARTERS, THIRD DIVISION, FIFTH ARMY CORPS,
                                "April 25, 1865.
            " Respectfully Forwarded.
"Approved.   S. H. CRAWFORD,
            " Brevet Major-General, Commanding."

" HEADQUARTERS, FIFTH ARMY CORPS,
"April 25, 1865.

"Respectfully referred to Brig.-Gen. Chamberlain with the request that he send Father Egan to attend the prisoner, at Third Division Headquarters, now under sentence of death.

" By command of

" BREVET MAJ.-GEN. GRIFFIN.

"F. F. LOCH, Col. Adjt.-Gen."

Next day I rode over to Gen. Crawford's headquarters, about seven miles distant, and reported to the general. He sent an orderly with me to the place where the prisoner was confined, giving orders for me to have free access to the prisoner, and inviting me to return at night to his headquarters, where he would have a tent prepared for me. Having arrived at the guard-house, I introduced myself to the prisoner who was in a very sullen mood; for no person can realize the feelings of a man condemned to die but the poor, condemned man himself. After talking to him for a good while, I told him I would see him next day again; that I would make an effort to have the execution suspended, but advised him, at the same time, to prepare for the worst.

Returning to headquarters I took my supper and went to bed, thinking a good deal, after lying down, as to what plea or what means I should use to get the poor prisoner pardoned. In the morning Gen. Crawford sent for me to have breakfast with him in his tent. During breakfast I commenced my plea for the poor prisoner, adducing arguments well digested and thought over during the night. Finally the general said to me: "I will give you a letter to Gen. Meade, whose headquarters are at Burksville, seventeen miles from here. I will give you my carriage, and order an escort of cavalry to guard you on the way, so that no bush-whackers may molest you."

I thanked him very kindly and said I would act upon his suggestion. After breakfast the carriage was made ready with seventeen troopers, and Gen. Crawford, handing me the letter, we started on our journey. On the way I was thinking and arranging arguments in my mind, and the plea I would make when I should meet the general. After arriving at Gen. Meade's headquarters and asking for the adjutant-general, an orderly went to his quarters, telling him I wanted to see him on important business. The adjutant-general came down to where I was; I told him my business and handed him Gen. Crawford's letter to Gen. Meade; the general, after reading Gen. Crawford's letter, sent an orderly to call me to his quarters.

The general was sitting on a camp-stool in his tent and invited me to sit down on another; I told him my mission of mercy and made as strong pleas and remonstrances as I could, the principal point of my argument representing the prisoner as a reckless half-fool, *non compos mentis*. The general remarked that that fellow was no fool, for he broke away from the guard three times. "Well, general," I said, "do you think that a man of common sense would defy the guards, knowing that loaded muskets were in their hands, that it was their duty to use them in shooting

him, and that if they did not do so, severe punishment
would follow on themselves? "

Before the general had time to make any more
objections I appealed to his humanity, knowing before-
hand his character as a humane and conscientious
man, and followed up my line of argument as I had
previously arranged it in my mind during the journey.
When I finished, the general said: " Well, Father
Egan, I will suspend his execution for to-morrow, but
you will have to get the doctors to substantiate your
claim that the prisoner is *non compos mentis.*" I
thanked the general for his merciful act, and, after a
little more conversation on other subjects, I arose,
bidding him good-bye, he shaking hands with me
in a friendly manner, and went where the cavalrymen
were employed in cooking their dinner and feeding
their horses, telling them the success of my mission,
which pleased them very much, and that we must
start as soon as we could; which we did in a short
time and arrived at Gen. Crawford's headquarters
during the night.

Next morning at dawn of day I went to see the
prisoner, saying to him: "You will not be shot to-day."
"Is dat so, Fader?" he said to me very coolly. After a
little he filled with emotion and began to shed tears,
the poor fellow realizing that his life was spared.
"Vel," he said, " Fader, I tank you so very much;
you have saved mine life. Before you go away I vant
to go to confession, and I vill be a good boy from
dis out." After hearing his confession I bade him
good-bye, shaking hands with him.

I then rode over to headquarters, and after breakfast went to my own command, seven miles distant.
From that day forth the army was on the march to
Richmond, from thence to Washington, and finally
reaching Alexandria, camped in that neighborhood.

Being near my home in Washington, at St. Dominic's Church, South Washington, it was easy to get a
leave of absence to return home until I should be
mustered out of service. On July 15, following, I was
mustered out, receiving an honorable discharge, with
an order for $300 extra, according to a law pre-
viously enacted by Congress, to the effect that all
officers remaining in the army until the war was over
would receive—in addition to their pay—the sum of
$300.

CHAPTER XLVIII.

THE IRISH BRIGADE IN THE WAR FOR THE UNION.

BY MAJ.-GEN. MULHOLLAND.

THE story of the Irish race is the history of a people fearless in danger and peerless in battle. In every age in which they have appeared, in every land where they have fought, under every flag they have defended, they have added to their glory and increased their renown.

"Magnificent Tipperary!" exclaimed Sir Charles Napier when, at Meecanee, after four hours' hard fighting, he saw 800 Irishmen driving before them 20,000 Belooches—the bravest soldiers of India.

"Curse the laws that deprive me of such subjects!" cried George II., when he heard of the whipping that the Irish Brigade, in the service of France, had given his troops at Fontenoy.

"Men," says Washington, "distinguished for their firm adherence to the glorious cause in which we are embarked."

(350)

"I thank the Irish Brigade for their superb conduct in the field," says Gen. McClellan on the Peninsula.

Ah, yes, in every age, in every clime, it has been the same thing. In India, in Africa, in China, and on all the fields of Europe, they have left their footprints and the records of their valor. The shamrock and the fleur-de-lis have blended together on many of the bloodiest and most glorious fields of France. Along the banks of the Guadalquivir the cry of "Fag-a-Bealac!", is echoed even to this day, and Spain still remembers Ireland's sons and Irish intrepidity.

Italy recalls Cremons and the regiments of Dillon and Burke, sweeping before them the Cuirassiers of Prince Eugene. Before their wild hurrah, the strongest defenses of Flanders trembled and fell, and Luxembourg entered Namur when the Irish charged the works. On every field of the old lands, and in every battle in which our own country has taken part, the sons of Erin have been present, gathering fresh laurels and reflecting new lustre on their race.

Light-Horse Harry Lee, writing of the Pennsylvania troops of the Revolution, says: "They were known as the line of Pennsylvania, whereas they should have been called the line of Ireland. Bold and daring, they would always prefer an appeal to the bayonet to a tiresome march. The general (Wayne) and his soldiers were singularly fitted for close and stubborn action. Cornwallis, therefore, did not

miscalculate when he presumed that the presence of
Wayne and his Irishmen would increase the chance
of bringing his antagonist, Lafayette, to action."

Not only Wayne and his brigade were Irish, but
nearly all the general officers of the Revolution from
Pennsylvania were Celts. Gens. William Irvine,
Stephen Moylan, William Butler, Edward Hand,
William Thompson, John Shee, Walter Stewart, and
Washington's surgeon-general, John Cochran, every
one of them hailed from the ever-faithful Isle.

Indeed, we can speak with conscious pride of the
Irish soldier in the United States. Barry, the first
commodore of our infant navy, was Irish. The first
and last commanders of our army, Anthony Wayne
and Philip Sheridan — Sheridan, the beloved of
Grant, "the whirlwind with spurs" (as Hancock
aptly named him)—were of full Irish blood. In
every battle of the Revolution Moylan and his Irish
Dragoons were ever near to Washington. On every
field of those dark hours Irish blood flowed in copi-
ous streams. As it was at the birth of our nation,
so it has continued to our own time.

In the beginning of the struggle of 1861, the first
name that became conspicuous as that of a soldier—
grand, heroic, superbly brave—was Irish Col. Mulli-
gan, the defender of Lexington; and the very last
officer killed in that unhappy war was an Irishman,
noble, gallant, and pure, Gen. Tom. Smythe, of Delaware, who fell near Appomattox but a few hours
before Lee's surrender. On every bloody field of that

awful struggle, the Irish soldier was in the very front.

Who of us does not remember the day after Bull Run, when the whole nation was saddened, depressed, almost terrified, by the appalling disaster that had befallen our cause?

When, at Blenheim, the legions of France went down before the victorious Marlborough, the nation found solace in the splendid valor of Lord Clare and his Irishmen, and rejoiced because of his wresting two standards from the triumphant foe. So, also, after Bull Run, our people could recall with pride the heroism of the Sixty-ninth New York Volunteers, that noble regiment which, after a long day's fight and heavy loss, amid all the confusion of total defeat and ignominious rout, under the command of the brave and modest Corcoran, quietly formed square against cavalry, and with the green flag flying, marched off the field in perfect order. Here, on the first great battlefield of the War of Secession, amid carnage and disaster, the brigade of which I propose to write was born. Around this green flag 5,000 Celtic soldiers afterward gathered, and it is the history of their deeds that I now attempt to tell. The story of their feats of arms would not be, of itself, a true reflex of the Irish Brigade. The Celt prefers to mix a little fun with his fighting, and so I will interlard a few anecdotes of the men in this narrative, and perhaps shall pause to tell of their chivalry.

23

At Fair Oaks the brigade adjourned an improvised horse-race to make a very splendid charge on the Confederate lines, and the hurrahs with which they rushed over the enemy's works were but the continuation of the cheers that had welcomed Major Cavanaugh as he jumped the last hurdle on the winning horse.

"Here's to the Thirty-seventh (Irish) New York, the tirror of the inimy, and the admiration of the faymale sex!" was the toast given by an Irish sergeant at a farewell banquet. Truly, I can recall many touching incidents of knightly courtesy that made the brigade the "admiration of the faymale sex."

In passing over one of the long corduroy bridges that crossed the swamps of the Chickahominy, a company of 100 men met, in the center, two Sisters of Charity. As only two persons could pass on the narrow footway, the ladies were about to turn back; but the commander of the company, saluting, quietly stepped off the roadway into the knee-deep mud and slime, and was promptly followed by everyone of his men, who, silent and respectful, struggled to regain a foothold in the treacherous swamp, while the blushing *religieuses* passed over dry-shod.

Again, I recall a noble soul who fell by my side in the evening, away out by the Stone Wall, at Fredericksburg. He was in the act of firing when a ball went whistling through his lungs. The musket fell from his powerless hands, and while the film of death gathered in his brave eyes, I heard him gently murmur: "Ah! what will become of Mollie and the children now?" With that he passed away. Not a thought of himself, his wound, or his approaching death, only of wife and the little ones. Did ever warrior of old face the grim Reaper more fearlessly?

One dark night, when we were marching away from Falmouth, the brigade was groping along a by-path, the men growling about the roughness of the walking, now and then tripping over a log, and plunging headlong into the darkness. A man remarked to his comrade, who was grumbling and falling more frequently than the others: "Whist, Jimmy, yez'll be on the *main* road in a minute." "Bedad, Barney," replied the unfortunate one, "Oi'll nivir get onto a *mainer* road than this!"

And this brings me back to the *main* subject of this paper. It was the intention of those who organized the Irish Brigade to place Gen. James Shields in command; but the Government designed a larger field of usefulness for that old veteran. Col. Michael Corcoran, who led so well the Sixty-ninth at Bull Run, still languished in a Southern prison, and so it came about that Thomas Francis Meagher assumed command. This son of Waterford had pleaded Ireland's cause with silver tongue when his face was as yet innocent of the beard of manhood; and by reason of his great love of liberty had drawn down upon himself, even at that early age, the very humane sentence: "To be hanged, drawn, quartered, and his remains placed at the disposal of Her Most Gracious Majesty, Victoria R." The last portion of the sentence doubtless saved the boy, for the fresh young queen was sorely puzzled to know what to do with the "hanged, drawn, and quartered" remains, and so escaped the unpleasant duty of handling the mass of blood and bones by transporting the young patriot— all alive—to Van Dieman's land. Had the learned judge but added cremation to the other very dreadful things that he proposed for the youth, Victoria would have been spared the role of undertaker, and the future commander of the Irish Brigade would have gone up in smoke. However, cremation was not thought of forty years ago, and Meagher lived to escape from penal servitude, become an American citizen, and be commissioned a brigadier-general of volunteers. His command at first consisted of the Sixty-third, Sixty-ninth, and Eighty-eighth regiments of New York Volunteers, to which was afterward added the Twenty-eighth and Twenty-ninth regiments of Massachusetts, and the One Hundred and Sixteenth regiment of Pennsylvania Volunteers.

So, on a balmy Indian summer day of 1861, the green flags, with the Harp and Sunburst, and the motto, "No Retreat!" were presented to the three first regiments in the words of John Savage's song of the Sixty-ninth, to

> "Plant that Flag
> On Fort and Crag,
> With the people's voice of thunder..."

And the brigade marched down Broadway through a dense mass of humanity, the bands playing the airs of Ireland; and amid cheers, sobs, prayers, benedictions, and wild enthusiasm, sailed away from the Battery, and was launched on its honorable career.

Many a funny story is told of those early days of the organization before drill and discipline had a chance to make them the perfect soldiers they afterward became. Here is a raw sergeant endeavoring to keep the boys in order with: "I say, kape your heels together, Tim Mullaney, in the rare rank, and don't be a-shtanding wid wan fut in Bull Run and the other in the Sixth ward!" Or another who, on the arrival in Washington, wished the platoon to execute a movement, which he afterward learned was a "Right wheel," gave the model and clear directions: "Now, byes, wid ye're face to the Capitol and ye're backs to the daypo, shwing to the right loike a gate!"

Six months after leaving home, we find the brigade on the Peninsula, thoroughly equipped and ready for the fray. They had passed through the early portion of the campaign, having been present at Yorktown and Williamsburg, and were now breaking the monotony of camp life by a genuine Irish horse-race, with its accompanying side shows.

CHICKAHOMINY STEEPLE-CHASES.

JUDGES:—Gens. Richardson and French.

STEWARDS: — Lieut.-Col. Fowler, Capts. McMahon and Hogan, Dr. Smith, and Lieut. Haverty.

CLERK OF THE COURSE:—Quartermaster O'Sullivan.

FIRST RACE.

A Steeple-Chase.—Open to all horses the property of and ridden by officers of the Irish Brigade. Best of three heats over the course.

Prizes: — A magnificent tiger skin, presented by Gen. Meagher—the spoil of his own gun in South America. Second horse to save his stakes.

Thirteen entries came to the scratch at the judge's stand, and no thirteen jockies so remarkably gotten up or so wonderfully attired had ever appeared on a track. Color was necessary to lend the proper brilliancy to the sport, and every farm-house was ransacked for bits of scarlet, blue, or green. Table-cloths and the bright frocks of the ladies soon became jackets and caps. Window curtains or red blankets were quickly metamorphosed into small-clothes; and stunning indeed was the general effect. Then, after much cheering, laughing, betting, false starts, beautiful jumps, serious tumbles, amusing spills, dislocated shoulders, and all the adjuncts of a well-conducted race, Major Cavanaugh, on Katy Darling, came to the winning post in splendid style, and carried off the tiger skin. Then followed mule races for the drummer boys; foot-ball, sack races, and fun for everybody. But the screaming farce, " The Limerick Boy," which was announced for the after-noon, was indefinitely postponed, for the evening breeze brought from Seven Pines, where Casey's division was suffering sore defeat, the roar of the distant battle. A night march placed the brigade within musket shot of the victorious enemy.

The dawn of June 1 was ushered in by an effort to push our troops still further on and occupy Pamunky & Richmond railroad, but the reinforcements that had come upon the ground during the night had blocked the game. Howard and French went at them before it was well daylight and gave them a taste of what was to follow; and here it was that the former lost his arm under peculiar circumstances. A ball had passed through the fleshy part of it, wounding him quite severely. He refused to leave the field, and while his brother was binding up the limb, he, too, was badly hit. Then a second ball struck the general on the arm, this time smashing the bone to pieces and rendering amputation necessary.

The moment that the Irish Brigade charged at Fair Oaks was one full of anxiety, and extremely critical. The enemy had massed a large force in front of Richardson's division for a final attempt to capture the railroad. Howard and French had given them a check that they had not anticipated, and Meagher was ordered in to give the *coup de grace.* Sumner ordered the brigade forward. Baring his old gray head and choking with emotion, he said to them: " Boys, I stake my position on you. If you run away to-day, I will tear these (pointing to his shoulder straps) off and run with you."

Meagher, knowing that the fight was for possession
of the railroad, thought the best thing possible
was to possess it, and promptly issued orders to that
effect. Nugent quickly advanced under a hot fire,
and deployed his regiment, the Sixty-ninth, right on
the track, planting his colors between the rails.
Capt. McMahon, of Meagher's staff, coolly rode over
the plain which separated the left of the line from
the railroad track, and selected the position for the
Eighty-eighth, where it could take the enemy in
flank. That regiment, under a destructive fire, swept
across the open fields, never firing a shot until the
colors were planted on the railroad track; then, in a
broad sheet of lightening, they threw their fire into
the woods that gave shelter to the Confederates. An
instant, and the reply came quick and sharp. From
out the blackberry bushes and small pines that
tinctured the noble forest came a scorching whirlwind,
tearing, rending, and destroying. The chivalry of
Erin had met the chivalry of the South, and the
exchange of courtesies was earnest and vigorous.
The Harp and Sunburst had come to stay. An Irish
"hurrah," a glorious charge, and the woods were
cleared! Fair Oaks became a victory; and within
half an hour from the moment the Irish Brigade
opened fire, the enemy were everywhere in retreat.

Dr. Ellis says of this battle: "There was the
Irish Brigade in all the glory of a fair, free fight.
Other men go into fights sternly or indifferently, but
the only man who, after all, really loves it, is the green

immortal Irishman. So there the brave lads, with Meagher at their head, laughed, fought, and joked as though it were the finest fun in the world. "

Hoadly says: " Meagher's Brigade, advancing with their well-known war-shout, closed with ferocity on the foe and mowed them down by companies."

Fair Oaks fought and won, McClellan and Sumner joined in showering thanks and congratulations on the command; and that old Spaniard from old Spain, Marshall Prim, visited the camp, his brightened eye showing the soldier's pleasure at the sight of brave men, as he said to them: " Spain has reason to appreciate Irish valor. We have been friends from ancient times, and have fought side by side on many a bloody field."

One of the amusing incidents of the day was the taking prisoner of a big, six-foot Texan, by a very small drummer boy, George Funk, of the Eighty-eighth. The fourteen-year old vagabond, thinking that he could make more noise with a musket than a drum, threw away the latter, and went out skirmishing on his own account. Seeing a "Reb. " blazing away from behind a tree, he waited until he had discharged his piece, then quickly covering him with his musket he commanded him to "ground arms," and marched him into camp. Meeting Gen. Sumner, he called out: "General, I have brought you a present !" It was rather amusing, too, the next day when Gen. Meagher went into the field hospital to console his orderly (who had been shot in both hips), to hear the boy greet him with, "Good morning, general, has Dolly got her oats yet?"—alluding to the General's favorite mare.

During the charge at Fair Oaks, the bayonet and clubbed musket were used quite freely. So ferocious was the hand-to-hand struggle, that some of the pieces were smashed and twisted so they were of no further use. Gen. Sumner was disposed to find fault with the men for having left their guns behind them. Sergeant Granger promptly invited him to walk out to the front and look at the stack of broken muskets. Said he: " Thim rebels wint at our byes wid bowie knives, and the min wint for thim the way they knew best."

GAINES'S MILL.

No battlefield of the war approaches so near our idea of a storm-swept battlefield as that of Gaines's Mill. As the sun went down that hot summer evening, it sank upon a scene of wild grandeur that the tempest and destruction of war alone can present. On the north bank of the Chickahominy, 30,-000 of our men had held in check, for five long hours, the 60,000 Confederates who had been hurled against our lines; but now, when the day drew to a close, the line that they had held so long and well was rent and broken. On our right Sykes was falling back before the divisions of Hill and Ewell.

On our left, Longstreet, led by Hood's Texans, had crushed, and almost annihilated Morell's division. Our cavalry, under Gen. Philip St. George Cook, had made a gallant but hopeless charge, and were falling back, a confused mass of men and horses, breaking through our batteries, and carrying with them to the rear, the gunners and their frantically plunging animals. Our whole force, artillery, cavalry and infantry — defeated, routed, demoralized, and in utter confusion—was hurrying across the plain toward the bridges that spanned the stream. The successful enemy, elated with victory, were pouring out of the dark woods; and with deafening cheers, they swept in long lines over the ground they had won, regardless of the prostrate forms of the dead and wounded, delivering their fire in rapid volleys, and rushing upon our flying men.

As the twilight deepened, the total destruction of the whole force seemed, for a time, almost certain. The enemy, knowing the great advantage they had gained, pressed with still greater energy upon our beaten troops; but at a moment when all seemed lost, a welcome cheer burst upon the ear, at first faint and distant, but soon gathering strength and volume, and then increasing into a roar that deafened the sound of the artillery. Re-enforcements had come, few in number to be sure, but with brave hearts and undiminished courage. It was the brigades of French and Meagher that Sumner had sent to the rescue.

Quickly passing over the bridge and forming line
of battle, Meagher led his brigade to the front. In
order to gain the crest whence our line had been
driven, it was necessary to push their way through the
mass of struggling fugitives; then with wild hurrahs
they closed with the advancing foe, greeting
them with cheers, and showers of leaden hail.
The Confederates, astounded, believing that we
had been heavily re-enforced, paused, halted, and
recoiled, while the Irish Brigade stood, panting and
elated, ready to meet the next onslaught; and as the
darkness crept over the field the men gave one long,
loud cheer to which even the wounded and dying of
the brigade lent their voices, and the battle was over.

That very gallant soldier, the Comte de Paris,
happened to witness this action, and in a letter written to me a few months since, he vividly recalls the
scene:

"VILLA ST. JEAN, CANNES, ALPES MARITIMES,
"March 8, 1886.

"MY DEAR GENERAL:—I hasten to thank you for your letter
of the 23d ultimo, and it is with the greatest pleasure that I
send, through you, a greeting of sympathy to all my old
comrades of the Irish Brigade, with whom I fought nearly a
quarter of a century ago, on the banks of the Chickahominy.

"I have been, during the years of exile, the guest of the
British people, and I made it a rule never to meddle in
the political questions which might divide the inhabitants of
the British Islands; but I never forget the cordial sympathy
which, as a Frenchman and a Catholic, I met whenever I
landed on the soil of Erin.

"It was therefore with pleasure that I met the Green Flag
with the Golden Harp, waving at the head of Meagher's

brigade, in the Army of the Potomac. Strange to say, the first time I met the brigade under arms was on the occasion of Gen. Prim's visit to our camp. I was in attendance upon the Spanish general, and introduced to him Gen. Meagher. I always remembered this little fact as illustrating the curious way in which Providence seems, at certain times, to put strange people together. A month later we were sorely pressed, our losses were large. We were collected, all mixed together, on a small eminence which commanded Alexandria Bridge. The sun, like a piece of red hot iron, was, too slowly for us, sinking behind a dark curtain of smoke, when suddenly we heard a hearty cheer. It was Richardson, who, at the head of Meagher and French's brigades, had come to our rescue on the left bank of the Chickahominy. The Irish Brigade (I find it noted in my diary) came in shirt sleeves, yelling at the top of their voices. The assailants were tired, and when they saw the strong line of Meagher's brigade, they delivered a strong volley and stopped. The day was saved, as far as could be, by those two brigades.

"This is one of the facts that I remember most distinctly, after the lapse of years. Believe me, my dear general,

"Yours truly,

"PHILIP, COMTE DE PARIS."

SAVAGE STATION.

At Savage Station, where the *Vieux Sabeur* Sumner stood at bay on Sunday evening, June 29, and threw back from our lines, in bloody repulse, every assault of Magruder's men, the Irish Brigade did noble work. But let others tell the story. Dr. Ellis, who witnessed the last charge of our troops, says: "The rebels came determinedly across the fields, firing as they advanced, until Sumner ordered our troops up at double-quick. About four thousand of them went up at once, with a roar that might have drowned the musketry. The rebels kept their position for a moment, and then fell back to the rear of their batteries. Meagher's brigade, however, succeeded in charging right up to the guns of a Virginia battery, two guns of which they hauled off, spiked, and chopped the carriage to pieces."

And here is a letter from Gen. W. W. Burns, on the same subject.

"OFFICE DEPOT, COMMISSARY SUBSISTENCE,
"160 W. FORYETTE ST., BALTIMORE, Md., Aug. 1, 1883.

"COL. JAMES QUINLAN:--It gives me pleasure to write your gallant service at Savage's Station, since you were distinguished beyond your fellow officers of the Irish Brigade, on that occasion. Having been sent back to check the enemy, with two of my regiments, under the misapprehension that Gen. Heintzleman still occupied the works at Seven Pines, I found on arrival, that Gen. Heintzleman had withdrawn from the works and crossed White Oak Swamps, and the whole Confederate force, on the right bank of the Chickahominy, was confronting my position.

"I notified Gen. Sumner at once of the new conditions, and demanded re-enforcements. Among others, Gen. Meagher was ordered to my support. The Eighty-eighth New York, with a few others, was all of the brigade that reached the field in time.

"I asked : 'What troops are these?'

"The answer was : 'Eighty-eighth New York !'

"'Who is in command?'

"'Major Quinlan !'

"I directed Major Quinlan to form his men facing toward Richmond, down the Williamsburg road, where a battery had been established, and was sweeping my line from the road as fast as formed across it. When Major Quinlan had formed his troops, I directed him to march toward the battery ; first in quick time, then double quick, and when he reached my line of battle, the order : 'Charge !' was given ; when, with a cheer,

the gallant Irishmen rushed upon the battery, and it was
driven from the road, to molest me no more.

"WM. W. BURNS,
"Late Brig.-Gen. Vols., Lieut.-Col. U. S. Army."

WHITE OAK SWAMP.

At White Oak Swamp Bridge where Franklin,
with the division of Smith and Richardson, held the
ford so well, defeating every effort of Jackson to
force the crossing, the brigade supporting the line
of batteries and exposed during the long, hot afternoon of June 30, suffered quite severely. Calm and
unflinching, it held the ground where the enemy's
shells and round shot fell in showers. At five o'clock
in the evening it was sent on the double-quick to
Glendale, near the New Market road, where Longstreet and A. P. Hill were pushing our troops.

As the brigade went in on a run, Gen. Sumner
gave the men a cordial greeting. "Boys," said he,
"you go in to save another day!" The Lincoln
Cavalry and the whole line of battle gave them a
lusty cheer as they swept past and rushed into the
fight which only closed with the darkness. And here
let me quote a letter of Gen. Wm. B. Franklin:

"HARTFORD, CONN., April 14, 1886.
"MY DEAR GENERAL:—I saw the Irish Brigade in two fights
—that of Savage Station, and that of the next day at White
Oak Swamp Bridge. At Savage Station, I saw the brigade led
into the fight by Gen. Sumner, and no men went in more
gallantly, or in better order. On the next day the brigade was

in position on the left of the White Oak Swamp Bridge, close to the stream. It was subjected to a very severe artillery fire during nearly the whole day, under which it never flinched. Its behavior was admirable, and in spite of its nearness to the enemy, the brigade headquarters were ornamented, during its exposure, with the United States flag and the Green flag, waving together as calmly as if all hands were miles away from the fight; and the officers and men were as calm as the flags. I always thought its behavior that day was in the highest degree suggestive of Irish pluck and endurance.

"Very truly yours,

"WM. B. FRANKLIN."

MALVERN HILL.

The Peninsula campaign was not to close without more glory, more blood, more death for the brigade. On Malvern Hill, the superb fight it made added to its glory whilst depleting its ranks. The day had almost gone, and for hours the roar of artillery had been deafening. All the infantry attacks on Porter's and Couche's lines had been thrown back in a bloody repulse; but the enemy was massing troops in Porter's front, and the brigade was called for. The men, thinking that they would not be wanted, were making coffee and getting ready for a good night's rest.

"Ah," said Capt. Joseph O'Donohue, "some of us who have prepared our supper will never come back to eat it." He was one of the first to fall.

Quickly forming line, the four regiments moved to the front. "I wish there were 20,000 men in

your brigade," said McClellan to Meagher. "I envy
you the command of that brigade," said Fitz John
Porter, as the men swept over the hill under a crushing fire, and threw themselves on the foe. "Here
comes that damned green flag again!" called out a
Confederate officer, as under a fierce fire, the Sixty-
ninth and Eighty-eighth moved on, delivering volley
upon volley, and strewing the hill with dead and
dying.

With wild cheers and enthusiasm they rushed
forward, and as the darkness gathered, reached the
hill on which the enemy stood. A fierce struggle ensued. No time to load now. Bayonets were
brought into play, muskets were reversed, and men
were brained and clubbed to death. The foe made
a gallant stand, but were gradually forced back, firing
a parting volley as they retired; and the battle of
Malvern Hill ended with the rapidly darkening woods
echoing the hurrahs of Meagher's men.

With what ardor Gen. Fitz John Porter speaks of
this eventful day: "On one occasion," writes the
general, " I sent an urgent request for two brigades,
and the immediate result was the sending of Meagher
by Sumner. This was the second time that he had
sent me Meagher's gallant Irish Brigade and each
time it rendered valuable service. Advancing, accompanied by my staff, I soon found that our force
had successfully driven back their assailants. About
fifty yards in front of us, a large force of the enemy
suddenly arose and opened with fearful volleys upon

24

our advancing line. I turned to the brigade, which
thus far had kept pace with my horse and found it
standing ' *like a stone wall*,' and returning a fire
more destructive than it received, and from which the
enemy fled. The brigade was planted. My presence
was no longer needed."

Lieut. John H. Donovan, of the Sixty-ninth, was
left on the field, shot through the eye, supposed to
be mortally wounded. Next morning the Confederate General Magruder, *en passant*, remarked: "I
presume you will not risk the other eye." "I beg
to differ with you," replied Donovan, "I have still
one eye left which I am willing to risk for the
Union." "And if you lose that also?" "Then,"
said the lieutenant, "I shall go it blind!"

During the second day's fight, two or three women,
wives of soldiers, accompanied the Brigade, and one
of them, Mary Gordan, wife of a soldier of Company
H., Eighty-eighth New York, especially distinguished
herself in caring for the wounded, tearing into
strips her very underclothing to bind up the wounds.
With a rugged nature, but a kind, and noble heart,
she remained with the men on parts of the field where
surgeons seldom ventured, and by her prompt action
she often saved the life-blood that was fast ebbing
away; and was the means of saving many a life. Gen.
Sumner saw her thus occupied at Savage Station, and
when our troops reached Harrison's Landing, he had
her made brigade sutler, and gave her permission to
pass free to Washington and back, in all government
boats.

ANTIETAM.

Wednesday, the morning of September 17—the men of the Irish Brigade call it the "glorious 17th"—broke clear and bright, and Hooker promptly reopened the fight which he had left unfinished the night before. This renewed attack was witnessed and enjoyed by the brigade, which had been lying on the east bank of the creek supporting the batteries.

Capt. Jack Gosson, neat and natty as usual, came up to Meagher—who had been sleeping on the ground without even a tent-fly to cover him—and remarked that the general was "all over dirt," and at the same time producing a whisk-broom, he suggested a brush. "Yaas," drawled the general, " a good ideah; we shall all have a brush before long." Ten minutes afterward he slowly rode off, followed by the brigade.

Before fording the creek, Meagher ordered the men to take off their shoes and stockings, and, after crossing, waited until the last man had put them on again; then dry-shod, with the Sixty-ninth in the lead, they made a rush for the line of battle to the left of the Roulette House. As they went on the double-quick over the corn stalks, crash came a volley on the right of the line, and the Twenty-ninth got a dose. Then the Sixty-third caught it; the Eighty-eighth coming up in time to get its share of the first course of the heavy repast that was to ensue. This was followed by a brief rest in the deep furrows of the field with the sharp-shooters busy picking off great numbers of our men. Chas. M. Grainger and W. L. D. O'Grady, of the Eighty-eighth New York, both old British soldiers, volunteered to push out and pick off the riflemen of the enemy, which they did most effectually; while other volunteers tore down the fence that was within 200 yards of the enemy's line.

The command was given: "Attention! Forward! Guide! Center! March!" Then began the advance over the heavy ground toward the sunken road, the men dropping in rapid succession. But on, on, until within fifty yards of the road, which was now a cloud of smoke and flashing fire. The brigade replied in turn with buck and ball, and poured a withering fire into the three Confederate brigades of Colquitt, Ripley, and McRae; and then a bitter stand-up fight, face to face, until the last cartridge was fired. The color-bearers of all the regiments were shot down in rapid succession. The Sixty-third, holding the crown of the hill, suffered most in this respect—losing fifteen. When Capt. Cluney, of Company F., raised the flag from the ground his leg was soon smashed by a ball, and he fell. The gallant fellow raised himself on his remaining limb, and upholding the colors waved them aloft until another ball pierced his head, and he fell never to rise again.

When the last cartridge was fired, the brigade was ordered to give place to Caldwell's, and the lines were passed by, the regiments breaking to the rear in

companies, those of Caldwell to the front, as steady
as when on drill. Filling their cartridge boxes, the
men of the brigade were quickly back in the fight,
and, passing Caldwell's line, they poured a volley into
the Confederates. Then came a wild cheer, rising
in a volume of sound that for a moment drowned the
roar of artillery; a charge, a fierce struggle, and the
sunken road is cleared!

"The Irish Brigade," says McClellan, " sustained
their well-earned reputation, suffering terribly in
officers and men, and strewing the ground with their
enemies, as they drove them back."

Six hundred dead Confederates in the sunken
road attested the desperation of the fighting at this
point. Eleven officers killed, and fourteen wounded,
was the record in the three New York regiments of
the brigade for the two hours at Antietam.

During the fight Meagher was badly crushed, and
Lieut. James Macky of his staff was killed at his
side. The day after the battle, the officers of the
brigade called upon Gen. Richardson, who had been
mortally wounded. In his dying agony, he said to
them: "I placed your brigade on the ground you
occupied because it was necessary to hold it, and I
knew that you would hold it against all odds, and
once you were there, I had no further anxiety in
regard to the position."

When Lieut. Lynch, of the Sixty-third New York,
fell mortally wounded, he quietly handed his sword,
watch and ring to a comrade, to be sent to his family,

facing death with a self-possession and courage that marked the true soldier.

Here again, note the gallantry of John Hartigan, a boy of sixteen, of the same regiment, who, advancing in front of the line, defiantly waved the colors in the face of the enemy. Of such men as these was the brigade composed, and it was with good reason, when Sumner next met it, that he hailed it as "Bravest of the brave!"

FREDERICKSBURG.

It was a cold, clear day when the brigade filed over the bluffs to cross the river and enter the town. The crash of 200 guns filled the valley of the Rappahannock with sound and smoke; while the color-bearers shook to the breeze the remnants of the torn and shattered standards —

> "That old green flag, that Irish flag;
> It is but now a tattered rag;
> But India's store of precious ore,
> Hath not a gem worth that old flag."

The Fourteenth Brooklyn gave the brigade a cheer, and the band of Hawkin's Zouaves struck up "Garry Owen" as it passed. Not so pleasant was the reception by the professional embalmers who, alive to business, thrust their cards into the hands of the men as they went along. The cards were suggestive of an early trip home, nicely boxed up and delivered to loving friends by quick express, sweet as

a nut and in perfect preservation, etc., etc. The
boys, however, did not seem altogether pleased with
the cold-blooded allusion to their latter end, and one
of them called out to a particularly zealous undertaker: "D'ye moind thim blankets? Well, only that
we were in a bit of a hurry we'd be after givin' yez
the natest koind av a jig in the air."

To charge an enemy or enter a battle when one
knows that there is no chance of success, requires
courage of a higher order than when the soldier is
sustained by the enthusiasm born of hope. It is
recorded that a commander once gave to his subordinate the order to "go there and die." The reply
was "Yes, my General." When our troops, debouch-
ing from the town, deployed upon the plain in front
of Mary's Heights, every man in the ranks knew that
it was not to fight they were ordered; it was to die.

During the morning of December 13, the Irish
Brigade stood in line on the main street of the city
amidst bursting shells and falling walls, listening to
the roar of the battle, and calmly awaiting their own
turn. Meagher plucked a sprig of green box-wood
from a garden near by, and placed it in his cap. A
happy thought! Bunches of the fragrant shrub
were quickly gathered and passed along the line
ranks, and soon every man had the green sprig in
his Irish cap. Then Meagher, passing along the line,
addressed each regiment in the most eloquent words
we ever heard him utter.

Shortly after noon the command moved out to the

fields in the rear of the city, filed across the canal —
on what was left of the bridge — and formed line of
battle behind a rise in the ground.

The noon-day sun glittered and shone bright on
the frozen ground over which solid shot, in great
numbers, ricochetted and went plunging through the
ranks.

A few moments to get breath, then "Forward!"
at "Right shoulder," "Shift arms!" in perfect
order; and in silence the line passed to the front.
No cheers or wild hurrahs as of old, as the men
moved toward the foe — they did not go to fight;
they went to die.

Forward, over the crest which had sheltered them
a moment before, now swept by a blizzard of fire.
On, over the awful plain that had no spot free
from the fire, no place of shelter — every man
knowing the desperation of the undertaking, but no
one faltering or looking back. Onward, still onward,
with batteries on every side pouring a rain of shot
and shell upon the devoted band.

On, past the line of French's troops! On, past the
brick house! — the line withering, diminishing, melt-
ing away, but still pressing forward; and the torn
flags often falling, only to be quickly raised again.

On, on, past the farthest points reached by any
other troops; still forward, until within thirty feet of
the Confederate works. Up to the muzzles of Walton's guns the line still presses, but not all those who
marched from the town a short half hour before,

Fifty per cent. of the number was already strewn, dead and bleeding, on the frozen ground over which the brigade had passed. In their front, lines of battle and batteries rose in tiers. On each flank, more batteries and more lines of battle. No hope. No chance to make even a fair show of fighting — the men were only there to die. There was nothing left for the brigade but to fall back, after pouring a few volleys into the foe, and the Irish Brigade, for the first time in its history, recoiled. Falling back, the dead of the brigade were left within thirty paces of the Confederate line.

The bodies of Major Wm. Horgan and Adjutant John R. Young, of the Eighty-eighth New York, lay nearest to the stone wall and, by actual measurement, within twenty-five paces of the guns of the Washington artillery. There are some who would dispute the fact of the Irish Brigade advancing farthest on that awful day. It is absurd to do so. The proofs are too strong to question. The men of this brigade advanced and fell nearest to the enemy; and many of them are there to this day. With a spade you can find them.

Lieut. Wm. E. Owens, of the Washington artillery (Confederate), asserts that: "In front of Mary's Heights, upon the plain over which the Federal column passed, they counted 1,498 bodies. A soldier of Meagher's Irish Brigade was the nearest body to the stone wall, and, by actual measurement, it lay within twenty-five paces of the wall."

"Meagher's Irish Brigade (from "Camps of the Confederate States") attacked Mary's Heights with a gallantry which was the admiration of all who beheld it; but they were literally annihilated by the Washington artillery and the Confederates lining the sunken road, who themselves hardly suffered any loss."

Col. Heros Von Borcke, chief of staff to Gen. J. E. B. Stewart, tells us that "more than twelve hundred bodies were found on the small plain between Mary's Heights and Fredericksburg. The greater part of these belonged to Meagher's brave Irish Brigade which was nearly annihilated during the several attacks."

The correspondent of the *London Times* witnessed the charge. In admiration he offers this splendid tribute: "Never at Fontenoy, Albuera, or at Waterloo was more undaunted courage displayed by the sons of Erin than during the frantic dashes which they directed against the almost impregnable position of their foe. After witnessing the gallantry and devotion exhibited by these troops, and viewing the hillside, for acres, strewn with their corpses thick as autumn leaves, the spectator can remember nothing but their desperate courage. That any mortal man could have carried the position before which they were wantonly sacrificed, defended as it was, seems to me, for a moment, idle to believe. But the bodies which lie in dense masses within forty yards of the muzzles of Col. Walton's guns, are the best evidence

as to what manner of men they were who pressed on
to death with the dauntlessness of a race which has
gained glory on a thousand battlefields, and never
more richly deserved it than at the foot of Mary's
Heights, on December 13, 1863."

As the brigade neared the Confederate line the
men of Cobb's brigade, the larger part of which
were Irishmen also, saw the green in the caps of our
men, and, recognizing the brigade, called out: "Oh
God! what a pity we have to fire on Meagher's men!"

During Sunday—the day after the battle—no
assistance could be given to the wounded, who lay
in great numbers out on the plain; but after dark
on Sunday evening many of the men made heroic
attempts to bring them in, although the enemy was
vigilant and fired at every object seen moving against
the sky. Sergt. Sheridan, of Company G, Eighty-
eighth New York, lay far out on the field with a
fractured leg, and four of his comrades determined
to go to his relief. Working themselves out on their
stomachs, they succeeded in reaching him, but found
him very low. As he had a compound fracture of
the leg, it seemed impossible to move him, his agony
was so great. The men dared not stand up, and were
at their wit's ends to know what to do, when Sergt.
Slattery came to the rescue. Said he: "Begob, boys,
did yez ever see rats trying to get away wid a goose
egg? One rat lies down, the others roll the egg on
top av him; he holds it in place wid his four paws,
and then they pull him off by the tail. Now I'll lay

down on my back, you lift Sheridan on top of me, and I'll do my best to keep his leg even." The suggestion was adopted. The men would push themselves on a couple of feet, then pull Slattery, with his precious load, up to them, and so on until, before daylight, they reached the city, and had Sheridan attended to and his leg amputated; but too late to save the poor fellow. He died from exhaustion. The clothes were literally ground off Sergt. Slattery's back, and his cuticle was so sore that he was unable to do duty for a week afterward.

CHANCELLORSVILLE.

There is a charm and a dreamy balminess in the Virginia spring atmosphere. On one of these, the sweetest of mornings imaginable, the army withdrew from the camp at Falmouth, and moved for the fords that cross the Rappahannock, to strike the enemy once again.

The paths of the columns lay through virgin, blossoming forests, and the perfumed air of the woods seemed laden with hope and promise. Many of the wounded of Fredericksburg had returned to the ranks. The men had, in a measure, forgotten that mournful field. The morale of the army was excellent; and the change of commanders had a salutary effect upon all. A new life had taken possession of the Army of the Potomac, that army which, though often defeated, was never dismayed, destroyed, or conquered.

On the first and second day of the battle, the brigade held the extreme right of our army, at Scott's Mills, and did excellent service in checking the disaster of the Eleventh corps. On the morning of Sund⸱y, May 3, the brigade was marched to the Chancellorsville House to support the Fifth Maine battery.

During a moment's halt, as the column moved up the road, with the shells exploding and falling around them, a sergeant, looking back, waved his hand to the air and earth, and, in the most ludicrous manner, exclaimed: "Good boi, wurreld!"

As the brigade went into position with the left resting near the Chancellorsville House, Lepine's battery (5th Maine) dashed up the road, unlimbered, took position in the orchard, and opened fire. An appalling scene of destruction immediately followed. The Confederate batteries were almost within a stone's throw of Lepine's, and opened with a concentrated fire of more than twenty guns to his six. Never, during the war, was a battery knocked to pieces so rapidly as the Fifth Maine on this occasion. The enemy's shells burst among the men in rapid succession. The ground seemed as though torn up by an earthquake; and in a few moments every horse was killed, and the men went down in squads. The caissons were blown up, one after another, until all had disappeared; and, in one instance, several of the men were blown up with the ammunition, and their torn limbs, pieces of debris, and apple-blossoms came down in a shower together.

Lepine fell, mortally wounded, and was carried to the rear dying. In the midst of the storm, flames were seen issuing from the Chancellorsville House. It was filled with wounded, and a platoon from the Second Delaware volunteered to save them. Rushing into the burning building, they dragged and carried all out, and laid them on the ground. Capt. John P. Wilson, of Hancock's staff, and Col. Joseph Dickenson, of Hooker's staff, assisted in the work, and, when the wounded were safe, gallantly offered their arms to three ladies who were in the mansion, to conduct them to a place of safety. One of them refused to come into our lines, and ran toward the Confederate position; but she fell, struck by a bullet, as she crossed the field. The other two, however, got away safely.

The scene at this time was one of wild desolation. The large house in flames, the orchard and plains swept by the fire of the Confederate batteries, and all of Lepine's men, except two, had been shot or driven away. Corporal Lebroke and a private stood alone among the abandoned guns, endeavoring to fire an occasional shot. Suddenly, the enemy's fire ceased, and a line of their infantry was seen advancing to seize the abandoned guns. Once more the Irish Brigade goes to the rescue. The One Hundred and Sixteenth Pennsylvania Volunteers happened to be on the left of the brigade and nearest to the battery. Rushing into the orchard, they faced the advancing lines and held them back, while 100 men of the regiment dragged the pieces off the field. Then the whole force fell back, and Chancellorsville fell into the enemy's hands.

During the fight one of Lepine's guns, a brass Napoleon, was struck fair in the muzzle, and the brass was turned and twisted as though it were pasteboard. As the men gathered around one of the pieces, tugging at the wheels and trying to pull it away, a shell burst right over the gun, knocking them in all directions, killing a couple and wounding several. The boys who were not injured promptly jumped to their feet and went at it again, and succeeded in saving the guns.

As the saved battery was passing the Third corps, Gen. Sickles gave the men a cheer which was echoed along the entire line.

One of the saddest incidents of the fight was the peculiar death of Major Lynch, a noble gentleman of the Sixty-third New York. A bursting shell drove his own sword through his body, killing him instantly.

This was the last battle in which Gen. Meagher commanded the Irish Brigade. He resigned shortly after the fight, was re-commissioned again and transferred to the West; but the fighting qualities of the organization remained, even when the general had gone; it never missed a battle, and was present until the end.

Gen. Meagher's departure was greatly regretted. A most brilliant leader he was, who seemed at his best in the midst of a combat. He had great faith in "buck and ball and the bayonet," and frequently urged on the men the use of the latter weapon. "Take everything with the bayonet," was the standing command when about to close with the foe; and that well-known and oft-repeated order was the occasion of a most amusing incident. One evening the brigade commissary had received new supplies; and among other things, some barrels of molasses beside which a young Irishman was placed on guard to prevent the men from getting at it until the proper time. Seeing no one around as he walked up and down, he thought he would enjoy the sweets of life, and succeeded in picking a hole in one of the barrels with his bayonet. Then dipping the weapon into the molasses, he would draw it out and transfer it to his mouth. Meagher happened to catch the boy in the act, and reproached him in rather strong terms for stealing the molasses over which he was placed to guard. The young man was astounded and overcome with terror for a moment at seeing the general, but quickly recovering himself, he quietly pushed the blade into the syrup, pulled it out dripping with the sweet liquid, took a big lick of it and reminded the General: "Sure, don't ye be always telling us to take everything wid the bayonet?"

GETTYSBURG.

At Gettysburg the brigade was led by a new commander, the aimable, noble Patrick Kelly, colonel Eighty-eighth New York, who, like Elias of old, was destined to ascend to heaven in a chariot of fire. The brilliant Meagher was gone, but his mantle had fallen on one who was well worthy to wear it.

Before advancing upon the enemy, on the afternoon of July 2, a religious ceremony was performed that, in the sublime magnificence and grandeur of its surroundings, was never equalled on this continent. As the men stood ready to move, their chaplain, Father William Corby, proposed to give them general absolution before going into the fight. Standing in front of the brigade, which was drawn up in a column of regiments, he made a fervent and passionate appeal to the men to remember in the hour of battle the great Captain of all, Jesus Christ, and to have contrition for their sins, that they might be prepared to die for the cause for which they fought.

Every man fell upon his knees, the flags were dropped, and Father Corby, looking up to heaven, called down the blessing of the Almighty upon the men. Stretching out his right hand (as the lips of the soldiers moved in silent prayer) he pronounced the words of absolution:

"*Dominus noster Jesus Christus vos absolvat, et ego auctoritate ipsius, vos absolvo ab omni vinculo excommunicationis et interdicti, in quantum possum et vos indigetis, deinde, ego absolvo vos a peccatis vestris in nomine Patris, et Filii, et Spiritus Sancti, Amen!*"

There was silence and peace in the ranks; but to the left, Little Round Top was wreathed in flame and smoke. The troops of the Third Corps were falling back from the peach orchard and Devil's Den, under Longstreet's crushing blows.

Out by the valley of death the hills and dark woods were re-echoing the roar and crash of the batteries. Amen! Load! Fix bayonets! And on the right of the division (Caldwell's) the brigade swept toward the fire, and, entering the timber to the left of the peach orchard, at the spot now called the "Loup," they met the enemy. The lines were very close before seeing each other.

The deployment and advance were made on the double-quick, and as the lines rushed forward through the trees and bowlders that were scattered over the ground, the Confederates were discovered.

They, too, were advancing; and when within thirty yards of each other the lines halted, and a sheet of flame burst out. A few short moments of serious work. Face to face the men stood pouring in their deadly volley of fire, the officers emptying their revolvers in the melee, then snatching up the muskets of the dead and fighting in the ranks with the men. A loud shout of "Forward! Charge!"—a dash to the front, and in a moment the men of both armies were mingled together. The firing suddenly ceased and an officer called out; "The Confederate troops will lay down their arms and go to the rear." They quickly did so, and the brigade sent as many prisoners to the rear as there were men in the ranks. The position gained, however, was not tenable.

The right regiment of the brigade (One Hundred and Sixteenth Pennsylvania Volunteers) was also the right of the division, and rested close to the peach orchard. In a short time after the victory, Caldwell withdrew the division, the brigade passing toward Little Round Top, and losing heavily in the wheat field, where it received a cross-fire without having a chance to reply. Many of the men who fell wounded at that point were killed in the evening during the charges and counter-charges that passed over the whirlpool; and many who were captured, afterward died in Southern prisons.

On the afternoon of July 3, and the third day after the battle, the brigade occupied a position on the main line, and during the great charge of Pickett's division and Hill's corps, was in front of Wilcox and Perry's brigade, as they moved forward on Pickett's right. The losses on this afternoon were light; except in the brigade battery, which was almost annihilated; and its gallant commander, Capt. James Rorty, killed.

Gettysburg had proved that, although its old commander was gone, the brigade had lost none of its old-time heroism.

THE WILDERNESS.

The brigade went into action to the left of the Brock road, in the dense woods near the gold mines. On that bright May day, ten field officers were mounted and in line with the five regiments. Within six weeks every saddle was empty. Six of these officers, Cols. Kelly, Byrnes, and Dale, and Majors Touhy, Lawyer, and Ryder, were sleeping in soldiers' graves; and the other four were torn and lacerated in the hospitals.

The brigade was commanded in the early days of the Wilderness campaign by the beloved Col. Tom Smyth, of Delaware—making a glorious fight on May 5 and 6, meeting every charge of Longstreet's veterans, and throwing them back in bloody repulse.

On the afternoon of the 6th, during one of the many fierce onslaughts of the enemy, the rails and logs, of which we had built our field works, caught fire and quickly reached to the timber. Amidst clouds of smoke and crackling flames the fight went on, the musketry rattled and roared, and many a noble soul fell, while the fire still leaping and sweeping through the trees, burned up both the dead and wounded of both armies. Among others who were killed at this time were Major Ryder and Capt. Jas. B. Turner, A. A. G. Turner was an excellent soldier, an accomplished gentleman, and a graceful writer. During a lull in the firing, I remember seeing two men carrying a dead officer to the rear. I raised the handkerchief from the face and looked upon the

calm and noble features of my good friend Ryder.
But every day now, brought death to the brigade.
The tremendous battles that drenched the Wilderness in blood became an every-day affair.   Fight all
day, move a few miles to the left, and charge again
next morning, seemed to be the standing rule.   May
the 5th and 6th on the Brock road; the 8th at Todd's
Tavern; the 10th at Po's River; the 12th and 13th
at Spottsylvania; the 18th near the same place; the
23d at the North Anna; the 29th at the Pamunky
River; the 30th and 31st at Tolopotomy; the 2d and
3d of June at Cold Harbor; and so on to Petersburg.
Col. Smyth commanded the brigade until May 20,
when he was assigned to a brigade in the second
division of the Second Corps, and Col. Byrnes
assumed command.   He fell dead at Cold Harbor,
and Col. Patrick Kelly succeeded him; and here at
Cold Harbor, Capt. Frank Lieb made a noble charge
with the One Hundred and Sixteenth Pennsylvania
Volunteers, capturing works, colors, and prisoners
from the enemy.

At Spottsylvania, where the superb Hancock made
the great success of the campaign, the flags of the
brigade were among the first to pierce the lines of
the enemy: and again more prisoners were sent to
the rear than there were men in the ranks.

On the evening of June 16, the brigade swept
across the plain in front of Petersburg and pushed
upon the Confederate works; and here Col. Kelly,
the last of the field officers who had started with it

in the spring campaign, fell, pierced through the head. The carnage up to this time had been terrible. Not only were the field officers gone, but nearly all the line officers had been killed or wounded, and more than one thousand of the men had fallen.

And now the long, ten months' work in the trenches in front of Petersburg began, to be interrupted at intervals when battles were to be fought at other points—twice to Deep Bottom, where, on the 2d of August, the brigade, with a rush like a cyclone, sprang on the Confederate line and captured the works without firing a shot.

At Reams' Station, August 25, the brigade added another laurel to its crown of glory, receiving the thanks and congratulations of Gen. Miles and others. In this fight the loss was heavy, and among the dead were Capts. Nowlen and Taggart, One Hundred and Sixteenth Pennsylvania Volunteers, each of whom was shot through the heart. Nowlen was in command of the regiment when struck, and turned quickly to look up and down for his own company. Waving his hand to the men he had led so well, he called out, "Good-bye, boys," and fell dead.

Shortly after the Reams' Station fight, the One Hundred and Sixteenth Pennsylvania Volunteers was transferred to the Fourth brigade, and the Seventh New York heavy artillery assigned to the Irish Brigade, Col. Nugent assuming command. Then, with replenished ranks, the brigade fought in the trenches at Petersburg until the end of the siege, every day gathering fresh honors and achieving new triumphs.

Then on to Hatchers' Run—to Five Forks, Amelia Court House, High Bridge, Farmville, Sailor Creek and Appomattox, where the brigade closed its noble and honorable career, only when the last shot of the war was fired, and the last enemy of the Republic had laid down his arms

Of the men who, at different times, had led the command, three were killed in battle—Smyth, Kelly, and Byrnes; and Meagher—the brilliant citizen and gallant soldier—found a grave in the turbulent waters of the upper Missouri.

Few of those brave souls who, under the Green Flag of their own native land, fought so well to defend the Stars and Stripes of the land of their adoption, are now with us. Those who lived through the storm of the battles are rapidly passing to the other side, to join the heroes who fell in the fight. The few survivors assembled at Gettysburg a year or two ago, there to erect and dedicate to their memory, monuments in granite and bronze, and stand once more on the spot that had been crimsoned by their blood; and like Melchisedech, on Bilboa's field, to pray for their comrades slain, that the God of Moses and Joshua, He who loves the brave and good, may grant sweet rest to the souls of those who died in defense of their adopted country

Appendix 1

Paul Henry Wood and his Painting
Absolution Under Fire

For generations Catholic schoolchildren have been reminded of Father Corby's service at Gettysburg by the inclusion of Paul Henry Wood's painting *Absolution Under Fire* among the illustrations in their American history textbooks. It has also appeared as an illustration in numerous other works over the past century, from Corby's own memoirs to the Gettysburg volume in the recent Time-Life series on the Civil War.[1] Few who see the painting, however, know anything about the origins of the work or the tragic story of the youthful artist who painted it.

Paul Wood was born in Elgin, Illinois in 1872. From a very early age he displayed an unusual facility for drawing, but it was not until after his parents moved to Chicago in 1883 that his artistic talent caught the attention of the Sisters of Mercy at St. James' Parochial School there. Realizing that the boy needed instruction that they could not provide, they introduced Paul to Sister Pius, the director of the Art Department at St. Xavier's Academy. Sister Pius was herself an artist of some distinction, and for the next two years she instructed him in the principles of drawing and portrait painting. His progress under her guidance was remarkable. In early 1887, when Paul was still only fourteen years old, Sister Pius concluded that his gifts were of such an order that he had already outgrown her ability to provide adequate instruction. She was able, however, to gain him an audience with the great Italian painter Luigi Gregori, Director of the Art Department at the University of Notre Dame.[2]

---

[1] The painting appears opposite p. 183 in Corby's *Memoirs*. It can also be found on p. 278 of *Brother Against Brother: Time-Life Books History of the Civil War* (New York: Prentice Hall, 1990).

[2] Manuscript outlines of the life of Paul Henry Wood (written by his father, Samuel F. Wood), Paul Wood Collection, UNDA; "A Youthful Genius," *Notre Dame Scholastic* 25 (January 9, 1892): 503–5.

Gregori had been brought to Notre Dame from Italy in 1874 by Father Edward Sorin, the founder and first president of Notre Dame, to decorate the interior of Sacred Heart Church, which was being built on the campus of the university. Pope Pius IX had personally recommended Gregori to Father Sorin. The much celebrated Italian artist had just completed the official portrait of the Pope before coming to America. After examining Paul Wood's work and watching him sketch from life, Gregori declared that "never have I seen in Europe or America a child with such extraordinary talent."[3]

In the spring of 1887 Paul entered Notre Dame to study under Gregori. Over the next few years he progressed from drawing to the use of oils. Gregori was particularly known for his genius with color, and he imparted to his young student the knowledge he had gained from many years of fresco and portrait painting in Italy. The instruction was difficult, since Gregori spoke no English and Paul spoke no Italian, but Professor James Edwards of Notre Dame became the medium through which teacher and student understood each other.[4]

While Gregori had him working on portraits and religious scenes, Paul longed to satisfy his youthful desire to paint grand panoramas of war and carnage. His best boyhood sketches had always been battle scenes, probably stimulated by war stories related by his father, a veteran of the Army of the Potomac. This interest was heightened by his viewing of the mammoth cyclorama "The Battle of Gettysburg" by Paul Philippoteaux when he was twelve years old. So when on September 30, 1890, Professor Edwards came to him with the news that a gentleman had offered to give him one hundred dollars to paint Father Corby giving absolution to the soldiers at the Battle of Gettysburg, Paul was ecstatic. He confided to his diary that this was "just the kind of work which I love to paint: scenes of blood, carnage, death, sudden and fearful, mangled corpses, fire, smoke and battle in its most horrible aspect." He knew that as the soldiers would be "in the attitude of prayer" he could not

[3]Raymond M. Murch, "Luigi Gregori—Notre Dame's Artist," *Notre Dame Scholastic* 54 (November 13, 1920): 113–15; "A Youthful Genius," p. 504.
[4]"A Youthful Genius," pp. 504–5.

incorporate all of these picturesque horrors into his painting but he could give the men "the appearance of having passed through the great part [of them]."[5] Excited as he was about the commission, he wasted no time in getting started. That very day he announced that he had "the picture all mapped out, both drawing and colouring, and . . . a good general idea of the way it will appear when finished." Thereafter he continued to work rapidly, but with some attention to detail. He had Professor Edwards consult with Father Corby himself to determine how he was dressed on the occasion. Corby told Edwards that he customarily wore a light cassock under his uniform which was "drawn up around the upper part of his body so that it could be easily lowered when on active duty as a priest." After nearly thirty years, however, he could not recall whether on that particular occasion he had had time to pull it out. He *was* certain that he had put around his neck a purple stole that he always carried in his pocket. As to the cassock, since he could not be sure one way or the other, he said that he preferred to be represented in the garb of a priest rather than an army officer. Father Corby observed the work in progress and Paul reported that he was "well pleased."[6]

Within a few weeks the painting was complete. The canvas measured 72 inches by 102 inches, the largest work Paul had ever done. He was understandably proud of it, and may be forgiven his slight gesture of vanity: he painted himself into the scene, as the bespectacled Zouave drummer boy standing nearest Father Corby. On November 14, 1891, the *Notre Dame Scholastic* declared that the painting satisfied "all who have seen it." "The kneeling figures of the soldiers and the worthy chaplain are well portrayed, and the atmospheric effect good." It congratulated "the artist on his work and the University on this valuable addition to its historical treasures."[7]

[5]Manuscript outlines of the life of Paul Henry Wood; Paul Wood Diary, entry for September 30, 1892 [Actually 1891], Wood Collection, UNDA.

[6]Paul Wood Diary, entry for September 30, 1891; manuscript notes on "Absolution Under Fire," [probably by Prof. James Edwards]; Paul Wood Diary, entry for October 13, 1891, Wood Collection, UNDA.

[7]Size of finished work from Snite Museum of Art, University of Notre Dame, Notre Dame, Indiana; Manuscript notes on "Absolution Under Fire,"

Meanwhile, even greater things were in the works. When Professor Gregori decided to return to Italy after nearly seventeen years in America, Professor Edwards began immediately to make arrangements for his student to follow him. As a result of his efforts, commissions poured in from American art patrons for Paul to copy famous European art works. These commissions would finance his studies with Gregori in Florence. Paul went home to Chicago for Christmas break rejoicing at his good fortune and eagerly anticipating his next giant step in his artistic career.[8]

But it was not to be. The vacation raced by with books, art, and happy family moments filling the days. Then, about two o'clock in the morning on January 4th, a fire alarm went off in the hotel where Paul's family had their fifth-floor apartment. As Paul quickly dressed and found his parents the halls rapidly filled with smoke. They all entered an elevator crowded with panicky residents trying to make their way down from the fifth floor. Evidently overloaded, the elevator's gearing gave way and the car fell. Paul Wood was crushed to death, caught between the car itself and the first floor of the building. He was only nineteen years old.[9]

There was a cruel irony in the nature of Paul's end, coming as it did in the midst of a scene like those battlefield landscapes that so fascinated him: filled with fire, smoke, blood, and death—sudden and fearful death. The terrible fact was that the only mangled corpse in this scene was his. The campus at Notre Dame went into mourning as the students returned from Christmas break to hear the news. Father Corby himself traveled to Chicago to sing a Solemn Requiem High Mass at the funeral in St. Mary's Church. Paul Wood was buried in Mt. Olivet cemetery. *Absolution Under Fire* was the grandest work of his tragically short life. Today it is part of the permanent art collection at the University of Notre Dame, where it hangs inside the entrance to Corby Hall.[10]

Wood Collection, UNDA; "A Notable Picture," *Notre Dame Scholastic* 25 (November 14, 1981): 175–76.

[8]"A Youthful Genius," p. 505.

[9]"Paul H. Wood," *Notre Dame Scholastic* 25 (January 9, 1892): 318; South Bend *Weekly Times*, January 8, 1892.

[10]"A Youthful Genius," p. 505.

Appendix 2

St. Clair Mulholland
and the Statues of Father Corby

WERE IT NOT for General St. Clair Mulholland, there would probably be no statues of Father Corby. Both of the existing statues, on the Gettysburg battlefield and on the campus of the University of Notre Dame, owe their existence to Mulholland's persistent efforts over many years to preserve the memory of his good friend's special moment in Civil War history. As the commanding officer of the 116th Pennsylvania, one of the regiments of the Irish Brigade, Mulholland was among the battle-hardened soldiers who knelt before Father Corby on that memorable day in 1863 when he intoned the Latin words of the absolution. Years after the war, he was primarily responsible for keeping this memory green through countless speaking engagements before the meetings and encampments of numerous veteran's organizations.[1]

It is unclear when General Mulholland first conceived the idea of having a statue of Father Corby placed at Gettysburg to commemorate the event, but it took many years before the task was accomplished. He believed that such a statue would not just be a fitting memorial to his old friend Father Corby, but it would also "be of great benefit to the Catholic Church, identifying the church with patriotism on the battlefields of our country." He first took up the matter with the pastor of the Catholic church in Gettysburg, probably sometime in the 1890s. He thought the church could be turned "into a memorial of the battle and the Catholic soldiers who died in the wars of the Republic." As part of this memorial, he proposed that a statue of Father Corby be placed either in front of the church or on the battlefield itself.[2]

[1] *Gettysburg Compiler*, November 2, 1910.
[2] St. Clair Mulholland to Brother Leander, C.S.C., December 23, 1907, Papers of GAR Post #569, UNDA.

This early effort foundered for lack of funds. Many of the old veterans were too poor to contribute and the few wealthy American Catholics were already overwhelmed by fund-raising requests from churches, convents, schools, asylums, and other Catholic charities. Mulholland did not give up, however. His efforts finally began to bear fruit after he delivered his now-famous account of Father Corby at Gettysburg to a meeting of the Federation of Catholic Societies in Philadelphia on December 13, 1908. His masterful retelling of the story aroused great enthusiasm among those assembled, an enthusiasm that finally led to a sustained effort to realize his dream.[3]

A few weeks later, on January 17, 1909, the Catholic Alumni Sodality of Philadelphia created a committee, to be headed by Mulholland, to raise the funds to place a statue of Father Corby at Gettysburg. This time Mulholland's pleas met with a good response from both the church and the laity. The archbishops of New York, Philadelphia, and Baltimore and the bishop of Pittsburgh all endorsed the plan. The president and alumni of the University of Notre Dame offered their support, and they eventually developed their own plans for a replica of the Gettysburg statue to be placed at Notre Dame.[4]

Samuel Aloysius Murray, a Roman Catholic son of Irish immigrants, was commissioned to create the statue. Murray was a Philadelphian who had studied with Thomas Eakins and was one of the most promising sculptors of the decades around the turn of the century. His works won recognition at Chicago's Columbian Exposition in 1893, the Paris Salon of 1900, the Pan American Exposition in Buffalo in 1901, and at the Louisiana Purchase Exposition at St. Louis in 1904. Philadelphia and Harrisburg, Pennsylvania are still dotted with his statues and busts of famous Americans. His works also grace the Pennsylvania state monument at Gettysburg.[5]

Sadly, General Mulholland did not live to see the project he

---

[3]Ibid.; *Gettysburg Compiler*, November 2, 1910.

[4]Ibid.; Wayne Craven, *The Sculpture at Gettysburg* (n.p.: Eastern Acorn Press, 1982, p. 71; See also Frederick W. Hawthorne, *Gettysburg: Stories of Men and Monuments* (Hanover, Pa.: Sheridan Press, 1988).

[5]Craven, *Sculpture at Gettysburg*, p. 71; *National Cyclopaedia of American Biography*, (New York: James T. White, 1951), Vol. 37, pp. 186–87.

had begun successfully completed. He died on February 17, 1910, still working on its behalf. On the very day of his death he wrote a letter to the University of Notre Dame about the Corby statue. Then he spoke with Henry A. Daily, the president of the Catholic Alumni Sodality of Philadelphia, and begged him to carry on his efforts. Mr. Daily gave his pledge to Mulholland that he would see the statue completed, and a few hours later the old general breathed his last.[6]

By March 3rd, Murray had finished a model for the proposed statue, but problems with Corby's dress caused his original design to be disapproved. Murray had depicted Corby in the uniform of an army captain rather than in the attire of a chaplain in accordance with the army's regulations of 1863. One this mistake was rectified work went forward quickly.[7]

The official unveiling took place along Hancock Avenue on October 29, 1910, close to the spot where Father Corby had raised his right hand in the rite of absolution nearly a half century earlier. Hundreds witnessed the event. Interested townspeople mixed with aged veterans and distinguished Catholic officials who had traveled to Gettysburg to attend the ceremonies. Band music, orations, and both high and low masses marked the occasion. When the Stars and Stripes covering the statue was pulled away by Henry Daily's young daughter, the crowd stood for a moment in silence "in token of their regard, esteem and respect" for the man whose memory was being honored.[8]

A similar ceremony took place on Decoration Day, 1911, when a replica of the Gettysburg statue was unveiled in front of Corby Hall at Notre Dame. Once again, music and oratory was the order of the day, with the Very Rev. John P. Chidwick,

[6]*Memorial of the Monument Erected on the Battlefield of Gettysburg to Very Rev. William Corby, C.S.C.* (Philadelphia: Catholic Alumni Sodality of Philadelphia, 1911), pp. 18, 34; *Notre Dame Scholastic* 18 (February 19, 1910).

[7]National Park Service Classified Structure Field Inventory Report, Father William Corby Statue, Gettysburg National Military Park, Gettysburg, Pennsylvania. On the confusion about chaplains' attire, see Sabine, "The Fifth Wheel," p. 18.

[8]*Gettysburg Compiler*, November 2, 1910; clipping from unidentified Gettysburg newspaper dated October 29, 1910, St. Clair Mulholland Papers, Civil War Library and Museum, Philadelphia, Pa.

the famous chaplain of the ill-fated battleship Maine, delivering the address. On this occasion the unveiling brought "the official college cheer" and a wave of applause that was taken up by the whole assembly.[9]

Samuel Murray was known for being able to capture not just the physical appearance of his subjects but also "the spiritual being of the person represented." This quality is certainly evident in his statue of Father Corby. The identical statues represent Corby with right hand raised in absolution and his left hand over his heart. His hastily doffed hat and gloves lay at his feet. Though the moment was dramatic, Murray does not emphasize the heroic aspects of it or idealize his subject. Murray's Corby is a figure of quiet strength and simplicity, whose natural dignity alone gives force to the work. The statues are mounted on natural boulders, as was Corby on July 2, 1863, rather than on formal pedestals whose ornamentation would be out of place in such a scene.[10]

On the 100th anniversary of the battle of Gettysburg, thousands of Notre Dame alumni and friends dedicated a new identifying plaque for the battlefield statue; otherwise both monuments remain as they were when dedicated so many years ago.[11] Each year thousands of visitors to Gettysburg view the statue there. As to the version on Notre Dame's campus, football-crazed students affectionately refer to it as "fair-catch Corby," a nickname based on an anachronistic but witty gridiron interpretation of the meaning of Father Corby's upraised arm. No doubt Father Corby himself would not object to the joke; he was always known for his genial good-humor.

[9]*Notre Dame Scholastic*, 44 (June 3, 1911): 548.
[10]Craven, *Sculptures at Gettysburg*, pp. 71, 73.
[11]"Gettysburg—Yesterday and Today," *Notre Dame* 16 (1963): 3–7.

Appendix 3

I

All day, up Round Top's crested crown,
　Two armor'd hosts are led;
Two banners wave, as night goes down,
　Each over its soldier dead.
For far away, o'er ridge and slope,
　The lone Palmetto tree
Still cheers those rebel lines to hope,
　Their leader, gallant Lee.

Old Gettysburg to-day must stand,
　Or with the flag go down!
Thus vow'd our boys of Northern land,
　To save that loyal town.
Our fathers' flag—to heroes given—
　To-day shall wave *their* deed;
Shall wave each fold in sight of heaven!
　Thus spoke our dauntless Mead.

Fall in! the thundering guns sing loud,
　Thro' morning's peaceful air;
Fall in! a soldier needs no shroud.
　No time for soldier pray'r.
A moment Nugent's men may rest,
　To jest or laugh the while,
Each folds upon a loyal breast
　The Green of his loved Isle.

A moment—'neath yon shelving stone—
　Within that awful field—
Those heroes bend in deep atone,
　While Death's dark shadows yield;

A soldier-priest, with hands extend
    Absolves their sins! Forgiven—
Short shrift was theirs, Faith makes amend
    Beneath approving heaven.

Forward! Thro' bristling lines of steel
    Their gory work soon done,
The shattered columns backward reel
    Our field to-day is won:
To-night the moon's pale rays shall rest—
    Each in his narrow bed—
To-morrow flowers with perfume prest
    We garland round our dead!

Old Gettysburg yet lives to tell
    When night each star bends down,
How rebel hail of shot and shell,
    Plow'd thro' that loyal town.
And well hath Gettysburg relied
    On soldier boys' brave deed
While little Round Top points with pride
    To Corby's loyal creed.

                ——James J. Creswell[1]

II

Two armies stood in stern array
    On Gettysburg's historic field—
This side the blue, on that the gray—
Each side resolved to win the day,
    Or life to home and country yield.

"Take arms!" "Fall in!" rang o'er the line
    Of Hancock's ever-valiant corps—
For to the left the cannons chime
With music terribly sublime,
    With death's unceasing, solemn roar.

[1]*Notre Dame Scholastic* 27 (January 20, 1894): 279.

With spirits ardent, undismayed,
  With flags uplifted toward the sky
There stands brave Meagher's old brigade
Whose noble laurels ne'er will fade
  Upon the page of history.

"All forward men!" No, pause awhile—
  Dead silence follows like parade
At "order arms," for 'long the file
There moves a priest with holy smile—
  The priest of Meagher's old brigade.

All eyes were toward him reverent turned,
  For he was known and loved by all,
And every face with fervor burned,
And with a glance his mission learned—
  A mission of high Heaven's call.

Then spoke the priest: "My comrades, friends,
  Ere long the battle fierce will surge,
Ere long the curse of war descends—
At such a moment God commends
  You from the soul all sin to purge.

"Kneel, soldiers; lift your hearts to God,
  In sweet contrition crush the pride
Of human minds; kneel on the sod
That soon will welter in your blood—
  Look up to Christ, Who for you died."

And every man, what'er his creed,
  Kneels down, and whispers pass along
The ranks, and murmuring voices plead
To be from sin's contagion freed
  And turned from path of mortal wrong.

Across the vale the gray lines view
  The priest and those who, kneeling now,

For absolution humbly sue,
And joining hearts, the gray and blue,
Together make the holy vow.

The smoke of battle lifts apace,
And o'er the field lie forms of men,
With glazen eyes and pallid face—
Dead—yet alive, for God's sweet grace
Has saved them from the death of sin.

——Smith Johnson[2]

[2]Undated clipping from *The Monitor*, William Corby Collection, UNDA

INDEX